BORDER TERRIERS
TODAY

Anne Roslin-Williams

HOWELL
BOOK HOUSE

NEW YORK

HOWELL BOOK HOUSE
A Simon & Schuster / Macmillan Company
1633 Broadway
New York, NY 10019

MACMILLAN is a registered trademark of Macmillan, Inc.

Library of Congress Cataloging-in-Publication data
available on request.

ISBN 0–87605–054-2

Manufactured in Singapore

10 9 8 7 6 5 4 3 2 1

CONTENTS

**This book is dedicated to the memory of
Smuts and Quill,
the first Mansergh Borders**

Acknowledgements

Many people have helped me with this project by supplying information and photographs. I am extremely grateful to them all, too numerous to mention individually, and to the photographers for permission to reproduce their lovely shots. The photographers are acknowledged under the photographs.

Janet Lee kindly agreed to strip a Border at one session for me to photograph the process. Bob Hand had promised to photograph his bitch whelping and did not let me down despite this event coinciding with a family emergency. My thanks to Janet and to Bob and the Hand family.

To Steve Dean, Lesley Gosling and Marie Sharp, who read the book and advised me on certain sections, I offer my thanks for the benefit of their wisdom and for their time.

I am indebted to the following who collected the overseas information for me: Pat Quinn, USA; Pam Dyer, Bill Walkley, Canada; Robert Bartram, Australia; Mary Whittington, New Zealand; Elsbeth Clerc, Switzerland; Betty Dickinson, Ireland; Diana Tillner, Germany; Ted Hunt, Holland; Hanne Sonne, Denmark; Margareta Carlson, Sweden; Kim Fangen, Norway and Tuija Saari, Finland. Without their help I could not have managed.

My special thanks to Marie Sharp for her patience and uncomplaining dedication to the task of converting my garbled and illegible manuscript into a presentable form and for keeping a watchful eye on the content.

Anne Roslin-Williams

Note on titles: since many overseas dogs carry a number of titles and qualifications these have, of necessity, been simplified to that of the highest order for each dog, omitting all titles won at one show on one day. A. R-W

Title page photograph: Ch. Froswick Button of Mansergh, Ch. Mansergh Toggle and Ch. Mansergh Denim.

Chapter One

INTRODUCING THE BORDER TERRIER

A small dog with a large dog's attitude to life is an apt description of the Border Terrier. The breed has risen in popularity dramatically in the last decade and is now listed among the twenty most numerous breeds in the British Kennel Club's registration statistics. There has also been a marked escalation in numbers in Holland, where the Royal Family own Borders, while the breed enjoys a steady following in America, Sweden and Denmark, and it is in the ascendant in Finland.

This is amazing to those who remember the time when the breed was known chiefly by hunting folk, and only recognised by the general public in certain areas of the British Isles. Now Border Terriers are known throughout Britain in both the country and the city. They appear in films and on the television, are used in advertising, and appear as companions to celebrities.

Border Terriers appeal because they are a handy size, yet not a toy dog, they have the natural appearance of a normal, unexaggerated dog, their tails are not docked, they have attractive heads and, above all, they have equable temperaments, not being so hot-headed as some other terriers. They make great companions, being very adaptable. They will work to hounds, go ratting, follow a horse at exercise, walk for miles with energetic owners, or be equally content pottering around at home with their owner. They enjoy car rides, are not usually car sick after the first two or three journeys, and think that the parcel shelf was specially designed for their comfort. As a family dog they are ideal and make a wonderful first dog for a boy, being game for anything. They adapt to living in the house or in a kennel equally well.

Some Borders work as therapy dogs, visiting hospitals and old people's homes. Others compete in Obedience and Agility. In Sweden they have proved to be one of the best breeds for tracking a blood scent. Some people use them as gundogs, although this is not really their metier because they can be gun-shy, and their colour is not ideal for a gundog. They have good game-finding and flushing ability but some tend to kill the game, if possible, rather than making a tender-mouthed retrieve.

THE TERRIER INSTINCT

"The Border Terrier is essentially a working terrier" used to be the opening words of the Breed Standard. This is the most important thing to know about the breed. Never believe anyone who claims to have bred the working instinct out. It is latent, even though, in some cases, the dog's ancestors may not have been used for work for generations.

Sadly, some Borders get into trouble because people take them on thinking they are an attractive little dog without realising that they are a terrier – no more, no less. Their well-developed sense of smell, plus a keen interest in all living creatures, and the instinct to go to ground, can be most inconvenient and difficult at times. It is anti-social to own a terrier which kills pet rabbits, chickens or cats. This must be discouraged, but it is not easy to stop a determined Border who will patiently await the right opportunity.

If brought up young enough with cats, a Border will learn not to chase the family cat. Some have been taught this at an older age by a street-wise cat swiping at the Border before the dog has had a chance to make the first move. The temptation to try putting a Border down a hole should be resisted. Never show the Border a hole, or earth, unless you mean business. Otherwise the dog will return to investigate the hole at any opportunity and could become lost underground. This has been the sad fate of several Borders.

THE WORKING ORIGINS OF THE BORDER

The breed evolved in the Border districts around the Northumberland and Scottish Borders to work fox, but they are adept at working other quarry. Their character, activity and shape evolved from their use with Foxhounds. In temperament, the Border was bred to get on well with other terriers and hounds but with the courage to deal with their quarry and the sense to keep out of trouble. From the breed's long association with hounds and horses come two interesting traits. One is singing in the kennel, which stops as suddenly as it starts, so there is no point in trying to check this – and they can't hear anyway when singing. The other is an inherent lack of fear of a horse's hooves. Borders will walk under a horse with complete disregard for their own safety.

Anyone who uses the term "wimp" in connection with a Border should be barred from owning one. It means that person just does not understand the dog's character. I have yet to meet a wimpish Border. By nature they are well-behaved and like to do the right thing. If someone tells me that their Border is disobedient, I know at once that this means that the dog has not understood the instruction which has been given. A Border who has not understood an order becomes rattled and will either try to oblige by doing something else, or will go away and sit elsewhere to keep out of trouble.

Borders do not have the instant response to a command of a gundog or one of the pastoral breeds and reserve a certain degree of independence while complying with the order – for example, a Border may stand stock still on the command Sit, instead of sitting, or may finish the task in hand first. When called, or told to go in, the dog may lie down as a surrender to your wishes. A bored Border may well seek some mischief for amusement, just as any other bored dog would, so it is advisable to keep the dog's mind and body exercised in some way or other.

As workers they are often slower to enter, that is to take to working underground a quarry such as a fox, than some of the more fiery terrier breeds, being comparatively slow-maturing by nature; yet once entered they make brave and reliable workers. Being terriers, Borders are equipped with a good mouthful of large teeth with which to defend themselves if necessary. Though not generally aggressive towards other dogs, Borders will look after themselves if set upon. Once in a fight they are difficult to separate because their method is to lock on to the adversary's throat.

THE COMPANIONABLE BORDER

The breed is sensitive, despite the apparent self-assurance. A young male, in particular, can become unsure of himself when between twelve to eighteen months or so. It is important not to squash him while he is growing up. Puppies need socialising early, meeting lots of people and dogs. A scolding is sufficient reprimand for a Border. Harsher treatment would break the dog's spirit. After a scolding, with dignity upset, a Border can sulk for days, by which time the owner feels more guilty than the dog!

Borders are companionable by nature, but not effusively demonstrative. They will keep near you and even, when apparently oblivious of what is going on, will be keeping an watchful eye on you.

ABOVE: Border Terriers adapt to living in the house or in a kennel.
                Photo courtesy: Sylvia Clarkson.

RIGHT: A small dog with a large dog's attitude to life.
                Photo courtesy: Kate Seemann.

They can become totally deaf to calls, though, if pursuing an animal or scent. They like a little chat and a pat or tickle on the chest from time to time, though it is unlikely that a Border will gaze lovingly into your eyes, preferring probably to lean against you and stare straight ahead. Their very presence indicates their deep affection.

Most Borders are excellent with children, loving them and being very patient with them. A child must not be allowed to torment any dog, neither should a child interfere with a dog who is either eating or sleeping. The breed has one habit which could be misconstrued and which must be understood. They have a form of greeting or communicating pleasure by brushing their teeth against the wrist. There is no malice in this and it is not a bite, but a child could be frightened by feeling the teeth on the skin. A tug on the clothing is another form of greeting which has to be understood.

THE VERSATILE BORDER

As a breed they are not yappy, although some strains are more excitable and noisier than others. Borders tend to bark if they can see or hear something unusual, or at birds, cattle and the like. They bark when playing together and also at the approach of a mealtime. In a pack they can develop a naughty habit of rushing up and down a fence or behind a shut gate, barking at passers-by, which is difficult to stop. As house-dogs they have acute hearing and will bark at the doorbell, or the sound of the gate opening, but they are not really good guards, being too friendly.

ABOVE: Sw. Ch. Qusins Balissa Girl: A Border will live in peace with the family cat, as long as they are brought up together.
Photo courtesy Margareta Carlson

LEFT: The Border takes a keen interest in everything that is going on.
Photo courtesy: Sylvia Clarkson.

They take readily to, and enjoy, Agility. When being trained for this, they do not need any psyching up, as do some of the larger breeds; indeed such treatment results in over-enthusiasm. In obedience, and also in the agility ring, their independence and consequent lack of concentration, can lose them points on occasion, but on their best days they are very good workers.

As a show-dog they are not the most extrovert breed. They are not clowns and certainly not fools and are really too sensible to dance about showing off for no reason. Some of the truest Border characters can become very dour and mulish if the handler tries to put pressure on the dog to win the class. They must be humoured along in the ring, as they can become bored by showing, if this ceases to be fun. Presentation of the coat is not difficult to learn, but a Border can test the skills of a handler in the ring.

PHYSICAL ASPECTS OF THE BORDER
The coat needs stripping twice a year – pets, workers and show dogs alike. It is unkind not to strip them. It keeps them reasonably tidy and hygienic to live with, as well as being more comfortable for the dog. They shed hairs constantly, which may worry a house-proud owner. My house dogs leave a halo of hair where they have been lying, even though I keep their coats tidy. On the credit side, Borders have neat feet, are easily house-trained, take up little space, and the adults are not usually destructive in the house. A well-bred and well-reared Border is usually physically robust. A properly regulated and supervised endurance test was run for them in Holland at which they

acquitted themselves very well indeed. In a numerically large population of any race, physical defects are bound to occur from time to time. The odd incidence of technical unsoundness has turned up in the breed, but it would be fair to say that Borders are not alleged to have any specific hereditary problem. Indeed, many veterinary surgeons recommend the breed to their clients. Borders often live well into their teens. The breed heals remarkably well from wounds. They are brave about pain to a degree which is not always in the dog's best interest. It is difficult to find the spot when trying to locate an injury on a Border, who will stare stoically ahead rather than wincing when the tender spot is touched.

THE HUMOUR OF THE BORDER

Coupled with their dignity, their slightly reserved but nonetheless affectionate nature, their determination and dourness on occasion, the Border also has a sense of humour. Some yodel when amused, or indicate this by a facial expression, or by leaping up and down at you so that you will share the situation. I have seen Borders who are "smilers", baring their teeth with embarrassment or pleasure, often in greeting, although this is not a common trait in the breed.

Puppies are interesting to watch at play, particularly in traditional terrier games such as worrying things, or going to ground under something and baying and baiting, or being baited by another pup. They do not like to be treated as puppies for long, and Border puppies will make it quite plain that they want to be proper dogs, not puppies, long before the time is right for them to take on the adult routine.

The true Border character is admirable but not understood by everyone, because these are not dogs wearing their heart on their sleeves, so to speak. The deep character is somewhat opaque and needs understanding. It is to be hoped that the breed character will remain unaltered in the future, not moulded for convenience to suit a way of life far removed from that for which the breed was originally developed.

THE ORIGINS OF THE BREED

Whatever their more recent background, be it from Sweden, Holland, Finland, America or wherever, all Border Terriers share the same origins, descending from those early Borders called Flint, Rock, Venom, Gyp and Piper, which are so difficult to sort out because early breeders used the same names – and over and over again! The breed was known, for many years before acquiring the name of Border Terrier, in the district where Northumberland (England) and Roxburghshire (Scotland) meet. Previously known as Coquetdale Terriers, the name they now carry stems from the time the Foxhound packs, owned by John Robson of Kielder and John Dodd of Catcleugh, amalgamated and become known as the Border Foxhounds, in 1857.

Breed history is tied up with that of the Robson and Dodd families, several members of which were Masters of Foxhounds and Otterhounds in the area. The Robsons are known to have hunted the North Tyne country early in the eighteenth century. At about that time, two characters called William and James Allen, father and son, surface in the history of the Dandie Dinmont and Bedlington Terriers. Both breeds originated from roughly the same area as the Border and there is something of an egg and chicken quandary as to which breed begat the others. The Bedlington was known as the Rothbury Terrier, Rothbury being a town lower down Coquetdale than the area from which the Border is reputed to have come. The earliest terriers we know about in the district were bred by the tinkers, gypsies or muggers who frequented both sides of the Scottish-English Border. The Allens came of such stock. Ned Dunn of Whitelea and James Davidson, who was an early Dandie breeder, had terriers from the Allens, whose terriers were known to be very game.

A letter from John Carruthers, a well-known Border breeder whose family had bred them before

Douglas and Henrietta, 1887. The Border Terrier is unmistakable in this portrait of Earl Haig.

him, tells us: "The Border Terrier of today owes his origin to what was known as the Whitlee breed. These terriers, my father's uncle, William Carruthers, in 1837, described as belonging to the workmen who worked at the Carter Fell lime-kilns, also the Rooken Edge in Redesdale. This breed originally came from Holystone in Coquetdale, a place renowned for its terriers. These lime kilns have long ago been laid in and it was left to the followers of what is known as the 'Border Foxhounds' to carry on the breed. I have heard that they were crossed with the Dandie, which may account for the silky hair on the crown which every 'Border' used to have, as far back as I can remember."

Jim Dodd, of the famous Dodd and Carruthers partnership which produced many good specimens of the breed, believed that Borders descended from the old-fashioned type of Bedlington, and the old crossed-type of Dandie. He claimed to be able to trace the breed back to 1817 and commented that the old-time breeders were not interested in shape or colour so long as the terrier could go to ground and tackle and bolt the fox. Borders were bred on farms in the Border district and were owned by yeoman farmers and shepherds. Their function was entirely to work fox, so the breed evolved to suit this end. There were slight regional differences in type.

Obviously, when breeding specifically for gameness, the opportunity to use a good terrier would not be lost, so other breeds did go into the make-up of the modern Border. Letters from both John and Tom Robson confirmed that Borders, even when crossed with a white terrier, threw true to type and never threw white puppies.

Only Borders were worked with the Border hunt during the long period of Masterships (almost a century) of the Robson family. They were used with other Foxhound packs in the Border district and with Otterhounds, where they proved proficient, although fox was their prime raison d'être. One of the first Otterhound packs to use them was the Northern Counties, of which Tom Robson was Master. The Dumfries Otterhounds worked them for about sixty years.

Borders working with the Percy Hunt in about 1912. William Weddell, the hunt's earthstopper is pictured with Rap and Nailer. Many Borders trace back to Weddell's Rap.

RIGHT: The first CC winner: Miss Bell Irving's Tinker, a well-known worker.

LEFT: Wattie Irving with Ch. Station Masher (second from left) and Ch. Joyden (third from left) photographed in the early 1930s.

THE FIRST SHOW DOGS

A natural progression was for sheep breeders and farmers to want to show their terriers at the local agricultural shows. Classes were scheduled for the breed for the first time at Bellingham Show in 1881. This show was to become an important Border Terrier show, a win here being highly prized. The first record of a Border being shown, a dog called Bacchus, was at Newcastle eleven years earlier. In tracing back the ancestry of the modern Border, the earliest Border in line is Jacob Robson's Flint, born 1878. His line descends to Miss Bell Irving's Tinker and then on, via Wattie Irving's Arnton Billy and Mr T. Adamson's Ch. Ben of Tweeden, down to the present day. The first of the breed to be registered at the Kennel Club (KC) was Mary Rew's blue and tan dog, Moss Trooper (The), born 1912, registered 1913.

An attempt to gain KC recognition of the breed with its own breed register was turned down in 1914. World War One intervened. In September 1920 recognition was granted, along with the application to register The Border Terrier Club. The first secretary of this club reported that, although there had been one hundred and fifty registrations up to that time, he estimated that there were between eleven and twelve hundred Borders in the Border regions. John and Jacob Robson and J. Dodd, Riccarton, drew up the first Breed Standard, that of the Border Terrier Club.

The first Championship show of the Border Terrier Club was held later in the same month, judged by Simon Dodd, Joint-Master of the Border Foxhounds, and held at Carlisle. His report was as follows: "It was disappointing that there was not a larger entry. The first time the Border has been shown at a Ch. show, although some very good specimens of the breed were forward. Miss Bell Irving's Tinker, by North Tyne Gyp, probably one of the most successful sires at the moment, who won the Dog Challenge Certificate, is a hard-looking little red dog, a little weak in his coat, but otherwise a typical Border. From his markings he evidently is a workman too. Mr (W.) Forster's Dan who won the novice class, was also a little weak in coat but is a working-looking terrier. Mr Wm. Barton's Liddesdale Bess, the winner of the Bitch Challenge Certificate, is quite one of the best of the breed shown; she is a nice size with a splendid coat but could have done with a little stronger head. Mr T. Hamilton Adams' Ivo Roisterer, Mr Barton's Red Gauntlet, and Mr Lawrence's Teri, were all nice terriers – the latter two rather too big."

We know the weights of some of these competitors but it is not known at what stage of their lives they were weighed. Tinker and Dan weighed 15 lbs; Ch. Ivo Roisterer 14.5 lbs, 12.5 ins. tall; Ch. Liddesdale Bess 15 lbs and Ch. Teri 17 lbs. Right from the time of KC recognition, letters appeared in the dog press expressing concern about the divergence of types within the breed and the size – topics which are still aired regularly.

A second breed club had been formed prior to KC recognition of the breed but did not appear on the KC lists until 1923, and proved to be short-lived: the Northumberland Border Terrier Club, whose aim was to keep the working attributes of the breed. This club had its own Standard, not much different from that of the Border Terrier Club, except preferring a smaller terrier. Within a short time, both Standards were altered to take a middle-of-the-road position on size, with only half-a-pound difference, for a male, between the two Standards. There are now seven breed clubs covering most of the United Kingdom. Some of these honour the working tradition of the breed by scheduling classes for Working Certificate holders at their shows.

The first breed Champions were made at Ayr on the same day in 1921 – Tommy Lawrence's Ch. Teri and William Barton's Ch. Liddesdale Bess. Many modern Borders descend from Willie Barton's bitch line through Adam Forster's Finery, the paternal granddam of Ch. Future Fame, who is in most pedigrees. Tinker also came from Willie Barton's bitch line. The winner of three Challenge Certificates (CCs), he was not a Champion because two of these came from the same judge.

THE BREED MOVES SOUTH

The breed gradually became known in the South. Mrs Woods had them in Norfolk from 1910. The first Secretary of the Border Terrier Club, Mr Hamilton Adams, lived in the South. Later the Pawson brothers, Kineton and Dipley, who had Northumberland family connections, helped to establish the breed in the South. The Southern Counties Border Terrier Club, now the Southern Border Terrier Club, was founded in 1930. Masters of Foxhounds in the South were at first suspicious of the colour of the breed, maintaining that they would be too easily mistaken for a fox by hounds. However, the breed gradually became accepted as good workers, up and down the country.

THE FAMOUS TRIUMVIRATE

Breed history would be incomplete without mention of the famous triumvirate, Adam Forster, Wattie Irving and John Renton, each a pillar of the breed for many years, holding positions of importance in the Border Terrier Club, and each producing Champion after Champion. None of them had an affix. Adam Forster and his family had such famous dogs as Coquetdale Vic, the well-known sires Rival and Revenge, Ch. Ranter and the 'FF' line including Ch. Future Fame. Wattie Irving's kennel included Ch. Station Masher and Ch. Joyden, the sires Arnton Billy and Rab O'Lammermoor, Ch. Rising Light, Ch. and Am. Ch. Brieryhill Gertrude and Ch. Bright Light. Wattie's grandson, Ronnie Irving, is another without an affix. John Renton's kennel housed the litter sisters Ch. Tod Hunter and Ch. Happy Mood, Ch. Rona Rye and Ch. Happy Day among others.

   The bloodlines of David Black's Tweedsides, Kathleen Twist's Hallbournes, Marjorie Russell's Swallowfields, Hester Garnett-Orme's Raisgills, Phyllis Mulcaster's Portholmes, Sir John Renwick's Newminsters, Dr Wm. Lilico's Bladnochs and John Pawson's Dipleys, along with those of the trio of great breeders already mentioned, played an integral part in bringing the breed through the difficult World War Two years. Sir John died shortly after the War and Helen Vaux, a pre-war exhibitor, incorporated the Newminster line into her Dryburns.

A group of legendary Border breeders pictured at Dandyhow, 1962. Left to right: Mrs Forster, John Renton, Mrs Renton, Miss I.D.R. Hall, Bertha Sullivan and Adam Forster.

Photo courtesy: Mrs Sullivan.

History in the making: Ch. Brannigan of Brumberhill winning Best in Show at Driffield Ch. Show 1986. Handled by Ted Hutchinson with co-owner Stewart McPherson (left).

Photo courtesy: Dog World.

POST-WAR ACTIVITY

The first Championship Show after the War was the Border Terrier Club, held in conjunction with the Lakeland Terrier Club, in 1946 at Workington, where John Renton judged in place of Mr Bonsor. Mr and Mrs Adam Forster's Fire Fighter won the dog CC, with Dr Lilico's Ch. Bladnoch Spaewife winning the bitch CC and Best in Show. The entry averaged eleven per class. Fire Fighter won BOB at Bellingham the same year, judge Wattie Irving.

After World War Two, kennels coming to the fore, as well as those already mentioned, were Robert Hall's Deerstones, Arthur Duxbury's Ribblesides, Phyllis Leatt's Leattys, Walter Gardner's Maxtons, Barbara Holmes' Wharfholms, Bertha Sullivan's Dandyhows, Bobby and Edna Benson's Daletynes – all to be found somewhere in modern pedigrees, all part of the Border today.

Unfortunately for the Border, the political climate has changed the working scene and it has now become difficult to work them with Foxhound packs, although some owners still manage this. Otterhunting has finished in the UK but it is still legal to work with Minkhounds, which is a different type of work to that with Otterhounds. The day could well come when all hunting is history. This will be a sad day for the Border because it will follow that the time will come when there is no-one alive who knows first-hand about working a Border to fox with Foxhounds – who knows what the breed is all about.

Chapter Two

CHOOSING A BORDER TERRIER

Ownership of any dog can, at times, be somewhat of a nuisance and a tie so, before taking on a dog, the full responsibilities of ownership must be realised. Keeping even a small dog the size of a Border is an expense. Along life's way there will probably be some veterinary expenses too. However, any inconvenience is more than compensated for by the addition of a well-behaved dog into the family.

Having established that a Border Terrier is the dog for you, decide your exact requirements. Do you want a male or a female, an adult or a puppy? Have you any colour preference, and do you know what purpose your Border is expected to fulfil? For show or work there are specific requirements as to size and shape which are not so important in the companion dog. It is not a good idea to buy two litter-mates at the same time. If you want more than one Border, buy them with some time between the purchases, so that each develops individually.

CHOICE OF BREEDER

Before rushing into ownership of a Border, it is sensible to look around first at as many as possible. There are slight variations of type which are all acceptable within the breed Standard. Look at every Border you see and, if you like one particularly, find out the origins, the breeder, and the bloodlines or family. Try to attend several dog shows, or hunt terrier shows, and study the appearance and character of all the Borders. Remember that temperament is all-important, as you will have to live with the dog. While it may be entertaining to watch a terrier which spars up to other dogs, it will not be so funny to try and take such a character for daily walks. Make enquiries from the breeders of those dogs which you like about the possibility of obtaining one. Be prepared to wait for the right one. Borders are not mass-produced and one of the right type, sex, age and colour cannot be taken off the shelf to meet your order just when you fancy having one.

DOG OR BITCH?

When choosing a companion, some people prefer dogs, some bitches. It is wrong to generalise, as every Border is an individual character, and much about how the dog turns out depends on the owner. If the intention is to found a line and to breed Borders the choice must be a bitch. *Beginning with a dog is an absolute non-starter as, unless he happens to be truly outstanding, no-one will be interested in using him at stud.* Buying in a bride for him is only of use in the first generation. Then both parents occupy valuable kennel space for the rest of their lives, causing a log-jam in the kennel.

A bitch will come into season twice a year from the age of between six and twelve months right through until the end of her life. During that time she must be kept secure, for about three weeks.

A male may become very interested in bitches and, if allowed to roam, become a perfect pest, following scents of bitches in season – although many males behave perfectly.

NEUTERING

Before having a bitch spayed, or neutered, the owner should find out exactly what is involved. This is a major operation, which is best performed when the bitch is sexually mature and has had one season. The operation should be done when the bitch is between seasons. She will need careful post-operative nursing for a few days after the operation. Many owners like the convenience of their bitch having been spayed – no need to bother with "all that". They should be aware that the weight of their Border will need careful watching afterwards, as they are a breed which tend to put on weight easily. The coat texture may become woolly and difficult to strip. There is a possibility that the bitch may become slightly incontinent in later life. Sometimes the bitch remains sexually interesting to males, although of course she cannot conceive.

The neutering or castrating of males is less common. This has been known to calm some difficult dogs but will not cure established fighters. It is possible to show neutered dogs of either sex under Kennel Club rules in Britain. The Kennel Club must be informed before so doing, although it is not necessary to ask their permission before performing the operation. In the United States such dogs may only compete as the parents in a progeny class. If you are thinking of purchasing a bitch puppy and having it spayed at the first opportunity, why not get a dog instead?

SELECTING THE PUPPY

Unless one is extremely fortunate, the pick of the litter will not be available, since most reputable breeders breed primarily for the purpose of keeping a puppy, or maybe two, for themselves. The breeder may have allocated puppies to people who have made a specific booking for colour, size or sex, so do not be surprised if you are not given a free choice. But on no account buy a puppy which, for some reason, you are not happy with. Some breeders discourage visitors to the litter

Allow plenty of time to study the litter at play before making your choice.

before the puppies have had their first parvovirus inoculation. There is nothing sinister in this. They are merely concerned for the health of their precious puppies at a particularly vulnerable stage of their lives.

When looking at the puppies, ask to meet the dam. Her character will have been passed to the litter, both through her genes and by her example. Unless the breeder has a large kennel, it is unlikely that the sire will be there, as he will probably be owned by another breeder. Allow plenty of time to study the litter, their character, style and deportment as they play. Choose a friendly puppy of steady demeanour, neither the extrovert mad fool, nor the shrinking violet skulking at the back of the kennel. Avoid one that shows any signs of aggression either towards its siblings or people.

Between six and eight weeks is the best time to pick, as conformation can be seen and felt then and the puppy is roughly the shape of the finished adult. After eight week puppies start to grow unevenly, a bit at a time, and can look pretty strange. It goes without saying that it would be inadvisable to take a puppy from a litter in which any member looked off-colour, with running nose or eyes, staring coat or signs of sickness or diarrhoea in the kennel.

SELECTING A COMPANION

Choose one that appeals in character. Some technical defect such as large ears, a wide front, a poor head, a single coat or a thin pelt, might eliminate a Border as a show prospect, but would not matter in a companion. A male may not be entire, which means that one, or both, testicles are not fully descended into the scrotum. This is reputed to be a possible source of cancer in later life but I have never actually known, or heard, of this at first hand.

SELECTING FOR WORK

For work it is essential that the Border be freely constructed, of narrow build and, above all, of a size to be able to get to ground in a small place. It is no use whatsoever having a large terrier who cannot get to ground. Large teeth, strong jaws, a good weatherproof jacket, a thick, loose skin, firm but not over-strong bone and good feet are also important. Temperament should be equable, able to get on with people not known to the terrier, who may be passed around between unknown persons when working, and able to get on with other terriers and hounds with whom the terrier may have to work. There is no time for fights at the earth. A gassy and hot-headed terrier will receive unnecessary punishment from its quarry. The sensible and courageous dog who can, by baying and baiting, cause the quarry to leave, and who has the sense to keep out of trouble, is the right sort.

SELECTING FOR SHOW

It is impossible to guarantee that any promising puppy will make a show dog. Picking a show puppy is always a gamble as it takes so little wrong to wreck a show-dog. Apart from the physical aspects of correct conformation and breed detail, the puppy must be correctly reared, and the character developed through education and socialisation, so that a show is not a trauma.

At between six and eight weeks of age, the outline of the puppy can be ascertained with some accuracy. Although the puppy is rounded by comparison to the finished product, the neckline, proportions, tail-set and carriage are already evident. When the puppy is set up on a table, in show pose, the basic construction can be felt – narrowness at the shoulders with long, well-laid blades, rib-cage carried back with ribs not over-sprung, correct length of back, straight front with elbows well-held, correctly angulated forehand and rear, low-set hocks which turn neither in nor out.

The skull should be broad with small V-shaped ears set on the side of it, never breaking higher

RIGHT: Hobhill Burnt Toast: When a puppy is eight weeks old the conformation and outline will be similar to that of an adult.

BELOW: Hobhill Burnt Toast, aged three years, owned and bred by Sue Pickerin.

Photos: S. Pickerin.

than the level of the skull. The eyes must be dark, not too round nor prominent nor set too close together. The muzzle should be short and strong, well-filled under the eyes and about one-third to two-thirds the ratio of the skull. The stop should be very slight. No-one can guarantee that a Border puppy whose first teeth are correct will change them and still have a perfect bite. The lower jaw must be strong and fairly broad but, if it is too prominent on a small puppy, there is a strong possibility that the second teeth will be undershot. Feet must be small and tight, with thick pads, but they will never be as neat on a puppy as on an adult. Large feet, thin feet and flat feet are easy to see.

Am. Ch. Traveler of Foxley, owned by Barbara Kemp, bred by Pat Quinn. Photographed at eight years of age, this dog still retains his correct build and workmanlike lines – obviously a wise choice of puppy by his owner.

CHANGES WHICH OCCUR WITH MATURITY

Certain things about a small puppy may change with maturity. It is helpful to know the bloodlines well, as points in certain families improve, whereas they may not on a puppy from another family. Heads are difficult to weigh up without knowledge of the bloodlines. In some lines the head will carry on improving up until two years of age, whereas in others, if the head pattern is not there at eight weeks, there is no hope of improvement. Ear-carriage may drop in certain families with maturity. Some puppies may grow into what may appear over-large ears when they are babies. However, round ears can never become the correct V-shaped ear. The front legs on a small puppy, even on a superbly fronted one, will never be dead straight but it is easy to see whether they are just babyish or actually bowed.

Colour changes considerably. Reds and grizzle-and-tans tend to finish somewhat similar in hue to the top of the skull when they are small puppies. A blue and tan will be born black and tan, but from five weeks onwards there should be silver showing in the coat when it is pushed back. The correct light-coloured tan on the legs of a blue and tan puppy usually indicates that the blue will be correctly coloured. The incorrect black and tan colour is usually accompanied by rich tan legs. Provided that there are plenty of silver hairs evident, the colour should change correctly. Some change quickly, others take up to a year. The attractive sooty mask of a Border puppy will fade with maturity, so do not choose a puppy for this point or you will be disappointed in a couple of years' time.

It is permissible to show a monorchid in the UK and some other countries but this is a pretty pointless proposition – as is showing a Border with a less than perfect mouth: competition is such that there is no need for a judge to place a dog with such faults. The Breed Standard does permit a level mouth in Britain, but not in America. This is where the teeth meet edge-to-edge, like a pincer, instead of the top ones overlapping the bottom ones in a scissor-bite. Choosing a puppy with a level bite for showing, would be a short-term proposition, as this could well become undershot when the teeth wear down with age.

FINDING AN OLDER DOG

It is sometimes more convenient to take on an older Border rather than a puppy. The best way to find one is through a breeder or breed club. Sometimes a breeder may part with one of two puppies which have been run on to the teenage stage, to see which turns out the better. Provided that there is no serious fault, this second choice from a good breeder can make a very good foundation.

Several breeders part with an older bitch, or dog, once they have finished their showing and breeding days. These old friends are not usually advertised but kept until a suitable retirement home presents itself. Usually such dogs settle very happily into the comforts of the best armchair. Having been taken to shows they are civilised, friendly with people and other dogs, and used to travelling, and are probably naturally house-trained, having spent days in halls and leisure centres. I have placed several bitches very successfully in carefully chosen pet homes where they are a special dog, not one of a crowd. Provided they change to this new life by about four years old, they seem to take to it very easily.

There is a welfare system which rehouses Borders who have fallen on hard times through their homes having broken up, or their owners dying or being unable to keep them. Some very nice dogs have been successfully rehomed. A prospective owner will be carefully vetted as to suitability. I would advise the prospective owner to do likewise regarding the dog they may take on. Find out all there is to know about the dog before committing yourself.

BREEDING TERMS

A breeder may offer a puppy or an adult bitch for sale on breeding terms. This means that, in part payment, the purchaser will be required to breed a litter, by a sire chosen by the vendor, from which litter the vendor will take back a specified number of puppies. While the prospect of not having to part with so much money at the time of purchase may appeal, such an arrangement should be thought over carefully before you agree to anything.

The bitch might not have a big litter and it could be soul-destroying to go through the whole palaver of breeding only to see the breeder of the dam take the puppy which you would have liked to keep. If there is only one bitch puppy and it was agreed that the vendor should take a bitch puppy, there is no argument – she is not your puppy.

The terms of any breeding agreement should be specified quite clearly at the time of the purchase of the bitch. How many puppies, from how many litters, of what sex, and by which dog, and when, should be settled, and the arrangement must be honoured. I have been fortunate in that any friends who have had bitches on such terms from me have always honoured the arrangement without any pressure having to be applied. However, normally I prefer to keep a bitch myself until I have bred the puppy I want from her. Accidents can happen. One lovely bitch which I had let go on terms met an early end before her owner had a chance to breed my puppy.

Chapter Three

CARING FOR YOUR PUPPY

CHANGING HOMES

The puppy who has left the litter to go to a new home, or the one who is left alone after the litter-mates have departed for pastures new, will feel lonely and require much human attention. The owners of a puppy starting life in a new home would be well advised to place the puppy's bed within a playpen or a fenced-off corner of the kitchen. This provides a safe area for the youngster to play in without being under the feet of humans or constantly pestering any resident dog or cat. A small box makes a snug bed; the size can be increased as the puppy grows. The puppy will miss the warmth and companionship of the siblings, so a large toy or lump of vetbed, or even an old brush-head, will be something to snuggle up against. The first night away from the brothers and sisters may cause the puppy to yowl. This is best ignored. The puppy will eventually become exhausted and go to sleep. If you respond to the plaintive cries, the puppy will soon learn that you can be summoned by yelling.

A puppy will play flat out for a short time and will then sleep flat out, to recharge the batteries. After every playtime the puppy should be put back into the area with the bed and be allowed to sleep undisturbed. A young puppy will play using the teeth freely. While this may be amusing when done by a youngster, it must be gently discouraged because an adult mouthing people is not so funny. A quiet but firm "no" when the puppy grabs, plus unhooking the teeth from whatever they have latched on to, will be enough discouragement if this is consistently repeated every time the puppy does it. The breeder who is running on two puppies from a litter would be well advised to split them up once the litter mates have left as, otherwise, they will become a gang of two, dependent on each other for support, rather than developing into separate personalities. They may, of course, be allowed to play together.

It may be deeply traumatic for an older Border to change homes but they are much too stoic to show this. Be prepared to give the new dog lots of attention for the first few days, until the dog appears to be relaxing and getting into a routine. Take every precaution to prevent any attempts to escape and, should a bid for freedom prove successful, contact the previous owner of the dog immediately. Keep a new adult tied to a chair, or table leg, or in a cage, and always on the lead for the first few days. Exercise the dog on a lead in a secure area. Keep calling the dog up for petting. Once there are signs of acceptance, such as tail wagging or a little lick on the hand, drop the lead in a contained area and call the dog up to you. Allow the dog to trail the lead until you are confident that the dog will be caught happily.

Show the Border where to sit and where the bed is. The adult must be able to rest and sleep in peace. Those without a quiet bed to which they can retire during the day for a snooze become mentally exhausted. It is natural for all members of the canine race to sleep a great deal of the

Border Terrier puppies have a natural sense of curiosity and will play with a variety of toys.

The Border Terrier puppy needs to be given something legitimate to chew and play with.

time. If introducing an adult Border to an established resident dog or bitch, make the introductions carefully, outside. A good way is to enlist help and take them for a walk together without having to face up to a proper introduction first. The lead can present problems but cannot be dispensed with on a new dog. Be careful not to make the resident jealous by over-doing the attention to the new Border. The newcomer may be a welcome friend, but Borders are devoted to their owners and can become jealous if not given enough attention.

HOUSE TRAINING

A baby puppy cannot be house trained immediately because nature requires that a youngster urinates frequently. Most Border puppies try to be clean by getting as far away from the bed as possible, so a newspaper placed away from the bed, near the door, will be a start towards house-training. Put the puppy out immediately after waking up and straight after every meal. Praise the pup when a penny is spent in the right place and encourage the idea by the words "hurry up" when the pup is put outside.

There is no point in scolding the puppy for mistakes, which are bound to happen until the puppy gains more bladder control. The call of nature is very sudden and urgent to a puppy. Warning signs are the quickening of steps, the puppy running in circles, maybe whimpering, and the tail raised. If you can catch the puppy in time and rush outside and then praise the puppy, the idea will soon get through. Open doors into the garden help the puppy become clean. Should a puppy, or adult, puddle on the carpet, soda water applied quickly to the spot and then wiped up with a damp cloth and cleaned in the normal way will prevent a stain.

TEETHING

When teething, a process which starts at about sixteen weeks, a puppy needs lots of toys to chew, otherwise the furniture will suffer. Pulling games should not be allowed as these can cause incorrect bites. If any teeth appear to be lodged, that is if there is a milk tooth in the place where the new adult tooth is coming through, try to dislodge the puppy tooth by moving it around. If this is firmly fixed it may need removing by the vet, as this can cause teeth to come in misplaced. While teething, a Border may fly the ears so that they stick out sideways instead of folding over neatly, close to the cheeks. Whenever you talk to the puppy, fold the ears over correctly and massage the folds. This should encourage them to fold correctly. However, if the ears continue to fly, a little help may be needed, or they may fly forever. Usually the application of a few strips of elastoplast on the tips of the ears will be sufficient extra weight to correct the fall. Otherwise, fold the ears correctly and stick the tape around the edges of the folds to hold them together, about one third down the ear.

UPSET STOMACH

The feeding regime to which the puppy is accustomed should be followed until the pup has settled in completely and become accustomed to the change of environment and the change of drinking water. Go easy on the milk to start with, and do not give liver or heart. Should a change of home be followed by an upset stomach, in either a puppy or an adult, it can be settled by feeding a stiffly-made, plain rice-pudding.

INOCULATIONS AND SOCIALISATION

It is a not a good idea for a new owner to take an uninoculated new puppy to visit the vet unless there is a problem. To do so would be misguided, as the puppy must not be taken to places where infection might be picked up until the puppy is fully inoculated. The vet's waiting room may be like the doctor's waiting room, with patients there who are ill. The vet can check the puppy over, if that is the owner's wish, at the time of the next inoculation. Most vets understand that you may not wish to bring a puppy onto their premises until inoculated and will give an injection in your car, if it is reasonably near the surgery. Most vets, for an extra fee, will do house visits to do innoculations. That a youngster or adult should have the correct inoculations is vitally important. Until fully inoculated against distemper, hard pad, leptospirosis, hepatitis and parvovirus, and one week has been allowed to pass for any reaction to have taken place, the dog must not go out onto doggy ground or be allowed to mix with other dogs. Socialisation of the puppy should start as soon as possible after this. It is good for the puppy to meet lots of people, play with children, meet other dogs, hear different noises and go out into the world, both on foot and by car.

FEEDING FROM PUPPY TO ADULT

The eight-week-old puppy will be on four meals a day. My menu for puppies is given in Chapter Twelve. By twelve weeks the lunch-time meal can be reduced and then stopped. The last meal then can be reduced gradually and then stopped. If the weather is cold or nights long, the last meal is continued for longer. As breakfast is reduced in quantity, so the evening meal is increased. A Border should never be blown out with food, because this springs the rib-cage. My adults receive part of their diet in the morning for this reason.

Until the puppy teeth have changed completely, breakfast with milk and calcium should be continued, although less will be required. Once the teeth are all through, the puppy can go onto an adult diet unless looking a shade thin. How much food to give is a problem. A rough guide is to imagine the size of the dog's stomach. A Border puppy should be covered with a layer of flesh through which the ribs can be felt, neither too fat nor too thin. Feeding is an art – knowing just when to add a little and when to knock a little off. One must feel a Border to establish how prosperous, or not, the dog is, as the thick coat and skin can be deceptive. Borders are greedy and also scavengers, so figures must be watched. They put on weight quickly and also lose it as quickly. In hot weather a dog needs less food, whereas in cold weather more is required, with a higher protein ratio. In spring and summer young stinging nettle tops, weedkiller-free of course, lightly boiled, and their juices, serve as a good blood conditioner. Spinach is also good. Until the teeth have changed, keep the puppy on small puppy biscuit or soaked and mashed-up adult biscuit. Chop all meat finely.

Many owners find the modern complete feeds convenient. If this is the chosen method, the recommended regime of feeding should be followed, since these foods are scientifically balanced. If fed dry, water should always be available. My preference is for the old-fashioned type of feeding, which has suited my adults and puppies well for years. By this method I can increase the protein level in the diet when necessary and make other adjustments according to the needs of the individual dog.

My adults are fed on a plain biscuit, which is thoroughly soaked in hot gravy or water, and fed cool. Cooked beef, canned meat, fresh tripe, or fish is fed in the ratio of slightly less than one third of the total meal. Eggs, cheese and cooked vegetables are added and also any household scraps which are suitable – but never any cooked bones. The main meal is in the evening. For breakfast, the Borders have some all-in-one dried food. Everything is gone through carefully for lumps, and the meat is chopped small, because two of my Borders choked.

EXERCISE
Borders love to go out for long walks, being very interested in country pursuits. A regular walk of whatever length is the highlight of the day, and keeps them mentally well-adjusted. Bored dogs become naughty; bored terriers fight if their natural energy is not released somehow.

To condition the Border for show, a combination of road-walking and free galloping is ideal. Regular road-work, with the dog walking correctly with the weight back on to the hindquarters and the head held up rather than poking forward, develops muscle on the rear-end. If the dog leans forward, pulling into the lead, shoulder muscle will become over-developed. Pacing, which means the dog moving both legs on the same side together like a camel, packs muscle onto the wrong parts and must be discouraged. Road-work helps to keep feet tight and pasterns strong but can never correct really bad feet.

A walk is the highlight of the Border Terrier's day. Free galloping develops the loin muscles and strengthens the back.

Photo: S. Pickerin.

Free galloping develops the loin muscles and strengthens the back. The muscle-bound dog packs on muscle through walking but lacks the freedom and suppleness which comes from opening up when galloping. Weak hind-quarters can be improved by walking the dog uphill with the weight on the rear-end. Walking the dog over rough grass, or through tussocks, on a lead, which makes the dog use each hind leg separately, can improve cow-hocks and generally tone up the hindquarters. The dog must not be allowed to bunny-hop through the grass. Pulling the collar up behind the ears, with the lead straight up, will balance the dog back onto the hindquarters.

ROUTINE CARE

Apart from being stripped twice a year and intermittent brushing and combing and the odd bath, when necessary, there are a few small tasks which one must perform to look after the dog properly. Toenails and dewclaws must be kept trimmed, otherwise it becomes difficult for the dog to walk, and they may also scratch human flesh and clothing.

Giving the dog bones or hooves or hard biscuits to chew from time to time helps to prevent tartar accumulating on the teeth. Flat rib bones are the best shape for a show Border to chew, because those nice round marrow bones bring the whiskers off the muzzle when it is poked inside the bone and heavy bones wreck the bite. When a rib bone is eaten down to a stub, it should be removed,

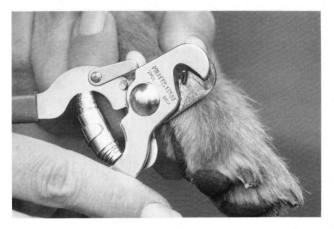

Toenails and dewclaws need to be trimmed on a regular basis.

because it can become lodged across the top of the mouth. To dislodge it, push the bone up and back towards the wider part of the mouth. Some dogs are more prone to tartar than others. If it is not removed, it will build up into a thick crust on the teeth and may cause gum infection and tooth decay and bad breath. It is easily flicked off with a thumb nail or a blunt blade or nail file. Care must be taken not to injure the dog's eyes. My dogs are used to this treatment and lie quietly on my knee while I use a tiny, blunt, fruit knife.

FIGHTS, BITES AND SCRATCHES

When dogs fight there is no point in shouting, it only makes them worse, as does hitting them. Never try to pull them apart but rather push them together so that they do not tear each other. Borders fight by locking on. When changing the grip, or being forced to leave go, they will seize the first thing they see, which is when people get bitten.

The best way to separate fighting dogs is by emptying the pepper-pot around their noses. Eventually this will make them sneeze and then they have to leave go. Grab one of them and put this one away out of reach of the other, over a fence, through a door, into the car. Carry the terrier high, out of reach of the other, who will try to grab the opponent again. Plunging locked combatants into a filled bath or trough will eventually separate them, as will choking them off.

Unfortunately Borders, bitches in particular, who have fought may never be safe together again. The fact may have to be faced that one may have to go. In the forty-plus years during which I have owned Borders I have had three bouts of fights. I have always got rid of the catalyst quickly, the trouble-maker, and the others have settled down again, thankfully and peacefully. One wrong 'un can get the whole kennel on edge. I never knowingly use an aggressive stud dog.

After a fight, each dog should be examined for bites and tears. An arnica tablet administered quickly helps prevent bruising and shock. Any wounds should be disinfected. Borders heal very quickly. If a terrier has tangled with a cat, it will take some time before the full effect of the deep scratches from the claws is manifest. The best treatment is to dunk the whole dog, including the muzzle, in a sink full of disinfectant as soon as possible, before the claw marks seal up. I had one cat-exterminator who missed a great many shows through festering catclaw pin-pricks before I learnt to deal instantly with this.

TRAINING YOUR BORDER

Every puppy should be taught basic manners. This makes the dog a pleasure to live with, rather than a nuisance. Whatever the future lifestyle of the dog, it is useful to have one which will walk on a lead, not jump up when greeting people, who does not push through doors and gates, is reliable on livestock, can be tied up and left to wait, can be left alone in the house or car and who enjoys car travel. Borders are easily trained provided that they understand what is required. Persuasion and bribery with food, coupled with praise, are the best ways to train a Border. Trying to adopt a direct approach to training, with sharp commands given while staring into the dog's face, will be counter-productive with a Border, as will getting cross with one.

An example of what I mean about coercion rather than a direct approach is my method of telling my Borders to go in their kennel. Holding the door open and commanding while looking directly at the dog does not usually achieve anything, except possibly that the dog will go and lie down just out of arm's reach as a surrender. However, if I open the door and turn my back on the dog, looking into the kennel while giving the command, the dog will go in quickly, brushing past my leg with pleasure while doing so. Borders are not naughty by nature. They have a strong working interest which can cause problems but, that apart, they do try to behave well. If there is a behavioural problem, it is because the dog and owner are not understanding each other. Maybe the owner is treating the Border too much as a dog. A Border forms a partnership with an owner, rather than being an obedient slave.

LEAD TRAINING

This can be done at any time from eight weeks onwards. A tight-fitting collar and lead are required, rather than a slip lead which can be dangerous when the puppy suddenly pulls against it. Choose a day when you are feeling happy and relaxed, with plenty of time and patience for the puppy, rather than a stressful day when your temper may fray easily. Put the collar and lead on the puppy and carry the puppy to an open space where no injury will be caused when the youngster flies around. Praise the puppy throughout. The collar may have been rather a surprise – and worse is to follow. Try to persuade the puppy to follow, or come towards you. Food can be a good bribe. The puppy will probably lie like a starfish, pulling back against the lead, but may be persuaded to take a step or two towards you if you crouch down. Praise the puppy for every step taken.

At some stage the puppy will fly around like a fish on a line to try to escape from the collar or pull the lead from your hands. Both must be avoided. Play the puppy like a fish, and praise the youngster when this stage is abandoned and the puppy comes to you. Always finish on a positive note, with the puppy doing right and having been praised. Resist the temptation to do too much at one session. A puppy likes to show off to other dogs, so should be allowed to swagger on the lead past their run or kennel. Keep up the praise.

Do not attempt to take the dog out in traffic until properly lead trained and able to walk to heel on the lead without jerking or pulling. Walking beside an older dog on a lead can be a steadying influence, but practise this within the confines of the home. A pulling dog is a nightmare to take out. Should a Border become an incurable puller, there are effective devices to prevent this. The Halti is one which makes it impossible, without involving any cruelty, for a dog to pull. Somewhat like a halter in design, it is worn on the dog's head with the lead attached to it. When the dog pulls forward, the Halti tightens around the dog's muzzle, pulling the head round to the side and making it impossible for the dog to continue pulling. This device may rub whiskers off the Border's face. There is another form of anti-pulling harness which is worn around the dog's chest and shoulders.

BASIC TRAINING

To teach a puppy to walk to heel when on the lead, walk close to a wall or bank, with the puppy on your left, close against it. Every time the puppy gets ahead, give the lead a gentle tug back and say "Heel". If the puppy persists, use a twig to gently tap the nose or the chest when the dog is in front. Using the twig like a windscreen wiper in front of the walking puppy will deter further pulling. Once the dog is walking steadily to heel on the lead, the exercise can be repeated off the lead to teach the dog to walk to heel without it. Never take a dog into traffic without a lead, however well trained.

A gently administered nudge with the knee against the chest will knock a jumping dog off balance. This, coupled with "Down", will teach a dog not to jump up. "Wait" is a useful command to stop a dog pushing through a door or gateway – a maddening and potentially dangerous habit – and also to stop a greedy dog falling upon the food bowl before it hits the ground, spilling the contents. To teach this, hold the dog back with your hand while saying "wait", and then gradually remove your hand.

If the Border is to be shown, do not teach "Sit", because the dog must stand in the ring. To teach a dog to sit on command, press the rear-end down and push back against the chest with the other hand while saying "Sit". Barking without a good reason should be curbed right from the start. A well-rinsed out washing liquid bottle filled with water will act as a water-pistol. A squirt into the face of a barking dog, with the command "No", soon gets results.

Train the puppy to be left alone, without yelling, from an early age. A dog cannot always be in close attendance and must be able to be left quietly alone. A bone or a hoof to chew will serve as a comforter. The puppy can be left in a cage to start with, then progressing to being left with the cage door propped open, and finally being left with a bed to go in and out of at will. Accustom the youngster to being tied up near you when you are working in the house or garden. In an emergency a dog may have to be tied up somewhere out of harm's way. If the dog may have to go to boarding kennels from time to time, it is a good idea to start this when the dog is young and not too set in routine. A few days is enough for a start.

LIVESTOCK

It must be instilled into country-living Borders not to chase livestock. At some time every Border worthy of the breed name will try to chase poultry, sheep or other animals. A thorough scolding should be given if the Border looks interested in forbidden animals. If caught red-handed, in hot pursuit, a good scolding while being held to the ground or being taken back towards whatever was being chased, should register. If that fails, try taking the culprit out on a collar and lead and also on a long cord, and then remove the former. The dog may think that this is freedom and set off chasing, in which case a sharp tug will pull the dog up smartly. Rather than have a terrier getting into mischief, it is better to use a long lead for exercise. Retractable leads are ideal for this, allowing enough freedom to gallop; but they must not be used extended when the dog is walking on roads.

CAR TRAINING

Start taking the puppy out in the car from an early age. Until fully inoculated, the dog should not get out of the car, nor be exposed to strange dogs, but a few rides will do no harm and will accustom the youngster to travelling. A cage is ideal in a car, because the dog will relax in it instead of standing or sitting up throughout the journey. Decide where in the car the dog will travel and put the puppy firmly there, once car-sickness has been overcome. Borders are usually car-sick for the first few journeys. It is not kind to feed a puppy a large meal just before a car journey – just a 'token' will suffice. Should the dog continue to be car-sick after a few outings, a mild car-sickness tablet specifically for a puppy will cure the habit after a few journeys with this administered.

It is highly dangerous to have a loose Border in the car, tearing up and down, looking out and maybe barking, when the car is in motion. If this bad habit starts, take a friend out armed with the 'water-pistol' to squirt the dog while saying firmly "no" every time this is attempted. If this fails, buy a cage. Beware of leaving any dog loose in a car, unattended, wearing a collar. There have been tragedies, with dogs being hung on levers.

THE CANINE GOOD CITIZEN TEST

To encourage responsible dog ownership, the KC and the AKC have introduced the Canine Good Citizen Test, details of which can be obtained from local canine societies or dog training clubs. The aim is to produce a well-mannered, socialised dog who can fit in well with the community. Attending a training class for the scheme is good socialisation for the young dog, and fun for the owner, not being too ambitious for a beginner trainer.

Whether the dog and owner go to classes to learn these rudiments of good behaviour, or spend time together learning them privately, it is worth the effort to establish the pattern of civilised behaviour early as this makes for happy dog ownership.

Chapter Four

HOUSING AND HEALTH CARE

HOUSING

Few people set out to start a kennel of Borders. Most people start with one or two as working dogs or companions. Numbers creep up gradually and it is only then that the necessity to make specific housing arrangements for the dogs becomes apparent. Whereas a kennel dog will nearly always take readily to the "promotion" of living in the house, it would be unkind to relegate a house dog to life in a kennel. However, it is useful for every dog to be accustomed to spending some time in the kennel, happily. This should not be used as a punishment or the dog will be miserable in it.

LAYING OUT A KENNEL

The main requirements are that it should be easy to see the dogs from the house. The kennel should be near enough to the house to be able to hear what is going on, placed so that it will not annoy the neighbours and set so that the dogs receive full benefit of sunlight yet with shelter from the elements. The ideal arrangement would be to have indoor kennels and runs within a room attached to the house for use in inclement weather, and a range of outside kennels and runs for good weather – but this is a pipe-dream.

Borders are sociable towards each other but it must be remembered that they are terriers. The great thing when keeping terriers is to avoid any situation arising which may cause a fight. For this reason, it is better not to house bitches together, although a dog and a bitch may live together except when she is on heat. My tried and tested method is to have a row of individual kennels: each has a small house which contains a bed, and a run which contains a small, low table to sit on. Thus my dogs enjoy the companionship of a neighbour without any possible jealousy arising over who has which bed, and so on.

While a very small hut is all that a Border needs, the owner will find a larger kennel, with room to stand up straight in it, much easier to clean. All parts of the kennel should be easily accessible in case of an emergency. The entrance to the hut should be sheltered to keep out wind and rain. Some sort of snug, draught-proof bed in it will be somewhere for the dog to sleep when the weather is not conducive to sitting out in the run. Bedding, which should be changed regularly, will help prevent pressure points being rubbed on the legs and elbows.

The surface of the run should be hard, with a slight incline for drainage. Concrete is easily cleaned. Gravel or chippings help to keep feet tight but are not so easy to clean. Partitions between the runs must be high enough to prevent the dog hurdling in to visit a neighbour. The back and sides of a low hut should be fenced to a height to prevent the dog from using the hut to jump out.

The choice of mesh is important. This should be tough and of a small gauge to prevent the dog either getting a grip on it with its teeth, which can damage the mouth, or a foothold to climb out.

Borders are good climbers and it may be necessary to invert the mesh slightly over the top if one persists in climbing out. All wire ties should be made with no ends sticking out on which an eye could be injured, or feet, should the dog stand up against the wire. There are some good custom-built kennels on the market. Those with large mesh netting or kennel railing may need a strip of fine-gauge mesh adding to prevent whiskers being rubbed off when muzzles are poked through. Several have a board around the bottom. This is not ideal for Borders who will stand with their front feet on this, possibly spoiling their fronts by so doing.

EXERCISE RUNS

To be Border-proof, a run must be fenced with high wire-netting, buried to the depth of about six inches all round, and taut so that there is no foothold or mouth hold. A path will be worn around the inside of the wire. To avoid this becoming a mud track, it is good to pave it or make a gravel

ABOVE: Border Terriers will spend hours playing together.

RIGHT: A characteristic of the breed is a love of sunbathing. Borders will seek the sun whether they are indoors or outside.

Photo: S. Pickerin.

path. Borders will exercise more freely if the grass is kept short. The run should contain a weatherproof shelter for the dogs and a few boards for sun-bathing, plus a water bowl of course. My Borders spend hours playing together and sun-bathing in exercise runs. However, I never leave them out together when I cannot hear them, so that I know what is happening. Nor do I leave them together with bones or other objects of possible contention.

SECURITY

Traffic and Borders do not mix, so great care should be taken to prevent accidents. If the front door opens onto the road, always make sure that all the dogs are behind a shut door before opening the front door. If possible, fence the garden securely with buried wire. Remember to block off the place where the dog might be able to squeeze under the front gate. Check the fence regularly for weaknesses. Keep the gate shut at all times and, if possible, fix a spring which automatically shuts it. Before opening any dog-run or kennel door, check that all garden gates are shut. If possible, plan the lay-out so that the kennel runs open into exercise runs which, in turn, open into a fenced garden, thereby having double security.

The other aspect of security is to make it difficult for a dog to be stolen. Sad to say, several Borders have been stolen in recent years. Each dog can either be tattooed with a number in the ear or have a microchip with a number implanted at the withers. This is the dog's individual identity which, theoretically, makes it easy to trace the owner should the dog be found. Locking kennels securely is not easy, by the nature of their construction. One has to weigh up the probability of someone trying to steal the dogs against that of the owner having difficulty getting into the dogs quickly in case of emergency such as a fire or hearing one of the dogs in distress.

THE HOUSE DOG

Although the house dog may have the run of the house, every dog should have their own personal, individual place to which they can retire in undisturbed peace. A basket, box, cage or arm-chair will do equally well. However, it is useful to be able to shut the dog in, should the need arise. Not all visitors like dogs. Borders love cages or crates. However, they should not live in these. They must be able to stand up and walk about freely and should only be put in the cage to sleep or to be out of the way for a while. It is not fair to confine an active dog to a boring, sedentary life. Cages are not draught-proof and heat is lost through the top. Therefore a cage should be carefully positioned, remembering that there are usually floor draughts in any house. If necessary cover the sides and the top. A thick blanket should keep the dog warm from below.

WATER

The housedog needs access to water at all times, as do those fed on dry food. In hot weather, kennel dogs should have water at all times, but otherwise this is not necessary – they are likely to tip it out anyway. However, water should be offered first thing in the morning, always on return from exercise, and before going to bed. In summer many Borders will enjoy a shallow bath in which to wallow and cool off. I have never found this detrimental to a well-textured coat.

HEATING

It is not necessary to keep adult Borders in heated kennels. Provided that the kennel is well-built, free from damp and draughts, and in a sheltered spot, they can tolerate cold, given a snug bed. Older dogs and puppies need more heat. New-born puppies must be kept very warm for a few days, then at a steady background heat, gradually being weaned off this. An elderly dog may feel the cold just as an old person does.

Electric wiring and plugs are of interest to idle dogs so they should be placed carefully out of reach and encased in metal. Chewing wires and plugs can be lethal. A trip-switch which will disconnect the electricity supply to the kennels gives peace of mind as does a switch which will disconnect that supply completely when not required. Sensor lights whose beam covers all pathways and gates are a terrific invention. These enable one to walk out to feed puppies or dogs in the dark with arms full of dishes, without having to struggle to turn on switches with elbows while trying not to spill the food.

ISOLATION KENNEL: It is necessary to have somewhere secure and away from the main kennel to put a bitch in season or an ill dog. An ill dog will probably require heat, so there should be facilities for this. Personally I bring any unwell dog into the house in order to be under my supervision at all times. The isolation kennel should be kept empty – so that, in an emergency, it is empty, not full of junk which has to be removed first before the patient can be accommodated. The kennel should be easy to disinfect afterwards.

DISPOSAL OF WASTE: An unavoidable by-product of dogs is their droppings. The days of leaving these to rot on the ground, or of having an open muck heap at the corner of the garden, have passed. Droppings should be picked up regularly and either burnt or placed in a plastic sack for disposal.

LOCAL REGULATIONS: Different countries and different authorities within these countries have different laws regarding the number of dogs which may be kept in certain areas and where one may breed dogs. These should be researched before setting out to breed dogs, or buying a house with that in mind.

NEIGHBOURS: Neighbours should be respected. Dogs must not be allowed to create a nuisance by barking unnecessarily. If departing early for shows, one must try to do this without disturbing the neighbours' slumbers. Borders like to chase cats but they must not be allowed to molest the neighbourhood cats. If the cats are so stupid as to flaunt themselves in the Borders' garden – then that is different.

INSURANCE: Everyone who owns a dog should be covered for third-party insurance for each dog. Should a dog cause an accident or bite someone, the owner could be liable for enormous damages. Some household policies cover this. Others don't. It is nothing short of crazy not to be covered for this eventuality.

HEALTH CARE
The golden rule of health care is to get veterinary advice sooner rather than later – illness is best treated as quickly as possible. If I am at all worried about a dog I consult my vet, and never grudge the cost of timely reassurance. Better safe than sorry. Symptoms of illness include vomiting, diarrhoea or constipation, running nose and/or eyes, lameness, inflamed skin, itchiness, lack of usual vitality, pain on being touched (difficult to spot in a Border), rubbing the head on the ground, raised or low temperature, panting or shivering for no reason, increased thirst, loss of appetite, dramatic loss of weight, pink whites to the eye, swollen glands in the neck, an arched back or tucked-up stomach, an abnormal smell of either the breath or the dog. Reporting any of these symptoms, or other noticeable abnormalities, will assist the vet in diagnosis.

FIRST AID KIT

A simple first aid kit should cover dealing with minor ailments and administering simple first aid in an emergency until the vet sees the dog. Mine contains:

Animal thermometer; Bandages; Roll of adhesive tape; Lint; Scissors; Tweezers; Disinfectant liquid: TCP or salt and water instead; A skincure ointment (containing sulphur, boric acid, zinc oxide, cade oil, salicylic acid); Tube of antiseptic ointment; Tube of eye ointment; Liquid paraffin; Glucose; Bitter Apple spray; Small lumps of washing soda; Antiseptic powder containing zinc oxide and boric acid; Thermal type vet bed; Hot-water bottle; Honey; Apis Mel homoeopathic tablets; Arnica homoeopathic tablets.

TAKING A DOG'S TEMPERATURE

It is helpful to know the temperature of an unwell dog before telephoning the vet. The normal temperature is 101.5 degrees F or 38.5 degrees C. A puppy up to six months of age may have a slightly higher temperature. The animal thermometer should have a round-ended bulb. Always disinfect the thermometer before and after use. Having shaken the mercury down, insert the bulb into the dog's rectum, making sure that the dog remains standing throughout, while holding the thermometer with the other hand. Leave the thermometer in for at least one minute to obtain the correct reading.

SHOCK

Following an operation, an accident, a mauling at work or a fight, a dog may suffer from shock. Keep the patient warm by lying the dog on a thermal-type vet bed or blanket and cover the dog with a towel or coat. Place a warm, not hot, hot-water bottle wrapped in a towel against the dog's back. Give a sip of glucose and water, if the dog can take this, or wipe a little on the tongue and gums at intervals, if not. Give one arnica tablet as soon as possible, followed by another two hours later.

INFECTIOUS DISEASES FOR WHICH VACCINES ARE AVAILABLE

CANINE DISTEMPER – HARD PAD: Because there is a large reservoir of dogs who have not been inoculated in certain communities where distemper is rife, it is important to inoculate puppies and to keep up boosters throughout adulthood. Symptoms include: raised temperature, runny eyes and nose, loss of appetite, vomiting, coughing, diarrhoea, depression. Veterinary treatment is essential and a long period of quiet convalescence if the dog survives, otherwise the after-effects may be severe and permanent.

CANINE VIRAL HEPATITIS: This is a disease of the liver. Symptoms include a raised temperature, a cough, increased thirst, lack of appetite, being generally "down'. Veterinary treatment is essential.

LEPTOSPIROSIS: There are two types of this disease, one passed from rats to dogs through drinking from puddles and water bowls in which rats have urinated; the other is passed from dog to dog. It can be passed to people. The symptoms include the temperature raised to start with, then becoming subnormal as the disease progresses, vomiting, diarrhoea, dehydration, dullness and depression, loss of appetite, possibly with increased thirst. Jaundice may occur. Again, veterinary treatment is essential.

KENNEL COUGH: While this is not normally more than a mild illness in otherwise physically robust adults, it can seriously affect young puppies and old dogs. An intra-nasal vaccination may be effective but as there are many strains of kennel cough, as with flu or the common cold in humans, it is impossible to cover them all. The symptoms include the dog appearing to clear the throat, maybe bringing up a little frothy mucus, which may develop into a more chesty cough; sneezing or snuffling; there may be a drop of discharge from the eyes, and the whites of the eyes may become shell-pink. The dog will not otherwise appear to be ill, normally, and will remain bright and cheerful, with a good appetite.

The condition usually clears after several weeks. Cough medicine or honey may relieve the symptoms. The dog should be kept quiet, dry and at a constant air temperature because excitement and changes in air temperature irritate the cough. Should the animal appear to be really unwell, and in the case of puppies or old dogs, veterinary advice should be sought. The coughing will gradually decrease but will be noticeable first thing in the morning and when the dog is excited, or pulling on a lead, for some weeks. This inconvenient illness is highly infectious, so dogs should be kept away from other dogs and gatherings for several weeks. Dogs do not have to have been in kennels to contract kennel cough – the single pet may also get it.

PARVOVIRUS: This is a potentially deadly disease, now mostly confined to young puppies, but any dog who has not been inoculated is at risk. The onset of the symptoms is acute, with violent and persistent vomiting together with profuse watery diarrhoea. Both are particularly foul-smelling and may contain blood. Urgent veterinary treatment is essential. Time is of the essence because this disease can kill within twenty-four hours.

An alternative manifestation may occur in young puppies who drop dead in the nest, without other symptoms, or a puppy which has had the disease, without showing symptoms, may drop dead later in life. It is important to inoculate early against this disease. Follow veterinary advice, keep up boosters. Should the disease strike, the premises must be thoroughly disinfected afterwards using a specific disinfectant. The virus is resilient and can live on the premises for months.

RABIES: This disease is not present in the British Isles but is endemic in many countries, where inoculation is routine. Dogs exported to such countries must be inoculated, as must those being imported into the British Isles. The symptoms are that either a normally placid dog becomes ferocious or a normally aloof dog becomes dependent and affectionate. A dog hangs the head over water; there is salivation. The disease is passed through saliva entering a bite or wound. It is a fatal disease, transmissible from dog to human.

A-Z OF COMMON AILMENTS

ANAL GLANDS: These refer to two sacs set at the base of the anus, inside the dog. In the normal course of events the dog will empty these when defaecating, but on some dogs these must be cleared manually, regularly. Signs that this needs doing are the dog tobogganing along on the rear-end – often mistaken as a sign that the dog needs worming – biting pink holes around the root of the tail or on the flanks, plus a rather strong aroma sometimes. Evacuating these glands is a rather unpleasant task but not difficult to learn from your vet or dog expert. If it seems too much to face, take the dog to the vet.

Standing to the side of the dog so that you do not get sprayed, with the dog in a standing position, lift the tail and, with the other hand, place the finger and thumb at approximately "eight o'clock" and "four o'clock" at the base of the anus. Push back and squeeze the finger and thumb together in an upward direction. You may feel the resistance of the sacs full of liquid which will be evacuated in a squirt as you squeeze. Once the knack has been mastered, squeezing can be done through a cotton wool pad into which the unpleasant-smelling ooze can be caught. Since this substance is used by dogs as a territorial marker, the smell of it has aggressive associations for other dogs, so be careful that other terriers are not hovering to pick a fight with a dog who has just been dealt with.

ARTHRITIS: This condition affects old dogs. It is inflammation of the joints, which is a painful condition which restricts activity. A warm bed helps, so an electrically heated cat pad may be beneficial. Analgesic tablets from the vet, or an aspirin, will relieve the pain.

BAD BREATH: This is a symptom of some diseases so, if it is coupled with other symptoms, a vet should be consulted. It may indicate the presence of worms, or be caused by bad teeth, gum disease or a heavy encrustation of tartar.

BITES AND CUTS: Any open wounds should be washed with tepid diluted disinfectant, or salt and water, then dried and dressed with either antiseptic cream or wound powder. Unless the bleeding is heavy, or the sides of the wounds need pulling together, they are better not covered. Sometimes it may be necessary to apply a temporary tourniquet using a tight bandage above the injury (but this should not be left on for many minutes) or to apply pressure on a vein. Prompt assistance from the vet is required. Torn ear-flaps bleed profusely – and spray everything when dogs so injured shake their heads! Bandage the ear up over the skull. Puncture marks following a cat or dog fight, or working injuries, are best disinfected by thoroughly dunking the dog in a bath of tepid disinfectant as soon as possible. Afterwards the dog must be carefully dried and kept warm. One arnica tablet administered immediately after an injury, followed by another after two hours, aids healing. A wound which does not heal quickly, or a very deep wound, may need antibiotic treatment from the vet.

CANKER: The inside of the ears should be checked regularly for signs of canker mites. If the ear channel appears inflamed, has little scabs, or anything resembling grey waxy blobs, or if the dog is scratching the ears, or one ear is hanging strangely, the ears need attention. Do not poke about inside the ears with orange-sticks or cotton buds. This is dangerous. There are powders and potions specifically for treating ear-mites which are available from pet shops or the vet.

CONSTIPATION: This is not usually a problem but it may be caused by the dog being fed an incorrect diet, eating bones, or over-indulgence in certain foods, such as cow-cake or too much grass, or through eating something like a bandage or a sock. The symptom is that the dog strains to pass a motion. A desertspoonful of liquid paraffin should ease the situation. This should be administered immediately if the dog has been observed swallowing something likely to be difficult to pass.

DEAFNESS: Ageing dogs may become hard of hearing and this may increase to total deafness if they live long enough. Nothing can be done. Communication may have to be through physical contact, in which case care should be taken when waking up the deaf dog, so as not to give the dog a fright. Never be cross with a deaf dog for disobedience. Should a normally well-behaved dog start to be disobedient, consider the possibility that the hearing may not be as sharp as before.

DEPRAVED APPETITE: The unpleasant habit of eating faeces, or droppings, from dogs is something many Borders do which is quite natural, although offensive to their owners. Puppies learn this by copying their mothers who diligently clean up after the litter. One can try to discourage it by scolding the youngster caught in the act or by putting pepper, or some such, onto the heap before the youngster gets to it. The best method is prevention, by picking up after the dogs. Suggested remedies include feeding the dog charcoal or pineapple – worth a try but I did not have much success with the latter, although maybe I gave up too soon.

DIARRHOEA: This has been dealt with in the relevant chapters when it affects puppies and nursing mothers. In other dogs it may be a symptom of illness or caused by something the dog has eaten. Take the dog's temperature. If is it normal, this would indicate the latter case, so withhold food for at least twelve hours and make sure that the dog has fresh water to drink. Kaolin and morphine mixture, suitable for children, may be administered. If there is a temperature or the diarrhoea persists, contact the vet. If there is blood in diarrhoea, always contact the vet quickly. A stressful situation may cause diarrhoea but, in my experience, Borders are not usually upset in this way. Feed bland foods such as plain boiled rice or rabbit until the dog appears to be recovering.

EATING GRASS AND OTHER PLANTS: This is perfectly normal canine behaviour. It is natural herbal medication. Dogs often eat grass first thing in the morning and relish leaves of certain plants at certain times of the year. This may make them sick, which is nothing to worry about.

ECLAMPSIA: This is dealt with in the chapter on the pregnant bitch.

EYES: A healthy dog does not have running eyes, apart from a slight drop of "sleep" first thing in the morning. The constant presence of a tear-drop means that something is wrong. This could be caused by an infected ear, or by something wrong with the teeth, or through the presence of a foreign body in the eye. Watering eyes or a creamy or green-coloured tear drop are symptomatic of disease, so the vet should be consulted. A foreign body can be washed out of the eye with lukewarm water or with eye ointment. The eyes are very sensitive so they should not be messed about with. If simple treatment does not work at once, see the vet.

FLEAS: Country Borders investigating other animals and their beds can easily pick up fleas. Signs, black specks of flea dirt, are usually easier to find than the actual fleas and are to be found on the skin in front of the root of the tail. A dog with fleas scratches in a frantic manner and will also bite the fur. Treat the dog with either flea powder or spray, following the instructions, because some are powerful and unsuitable for small puppies or nursing bitches and others must be brushed out after a certain time. Treat the bedding also. Flea collars are a deterrent but any collar worn constantly will create a line in the hair which is difficult to deal with on a show dog.

FITS: These can be caused by a multitude of reasons. When having a fit the dog may froth at the mouth, the body may stiffen and the legs extend stiffly. After a few minutes the legs may start to move, as if running, and the dog may lose control of bladder and bowels. The dog returning to consciousness may be unsteady and bewildered, or may be apparently normal quite quickly. While the dog is in the fit do not interfere, but remove any objects nearby which could cause injury. The dog, once out of the fit, should be kept quiet in a darkened place to recover. Puppies when teething may have a fit. Other causes include past injuries, eclampsia, diet, poison, lead paint, fumes from chemicals – to name but a few. Try to eliminate the possibilities. If the dog has more fits, consult the vet because epilepsy can be controlled by drugs.

GRASS SEEDS: These can work their way into and through a dog's tissue. Those with a hook are difficult to remove. It may be necessary for the vet to do this, particularly if seeds are hooked into the third eyelid. Prevention is the best cure. I ruthlessly pull up every growth of wild oats which appears in the garden.

INTERDIGITAL CYSTS: These are small abscesses between the toes, causing lameness. Soak the foot several times daily in hot water with a teaspoon of salt in it, until the abscess bursts, or apply friar's balsam to the area. Once the abscess or cyst has burst, it will heal quickly.

LAMENESS: This requires you to study the dog when walking, to identify which limb is being favoured. Examine that foot for an oncoming interdigital cyst, a cut, a splinter, sting, thorn or grass seed in the pad, or between the pads or toes; check for balls of dried mud between the toes or caking around the toe-nails; look for a pulled toe-nail or dewclaw. Remove any foreign body if possible and clean and disinfect any wound. A cut pad is a slow healer.

A torn toe-nail should be trimmed back, if possible. If the bed of the nail appears sore or inflamed, apply antiseptic ointment. If the nail falls off, a new rough nail may grow back which may need trimming as it grows. This will probably not be as strong as the original nail. Sore pink areas between the pads can be treated with friar's balsam which is allowed to dry on the affected area – a messy treatment. If the cause of lameness cannot be found in the foot, examine the leg, feeling for swelling or heat and comparing the feel of the leg with that of its matching partner. Try bending the joints and moving the leg. A Border will be loath to indicate the source of pain but, if you know your dog well, you may just be able to spot a stiffening when a certain spot is touched. Temporary lameness passes quickly, cured with rest and sleep, but if it persists, or if the dog still cannot put the leg to the ground after a few hours, consult the vet.

LICE: These are more usually found on puppies than adults and are tiny, light-coloured insects which may be found at the top and back of the ears and in cracks and folds of skin. Treat in a similar manner to fleas.

LYME DISEASE: This is passed by ticks from deer. The symptoms include lameness and general debility. Veterinary treatment is essential.

MANGE: The various types of mange are identified through skin-scrapes. Apart from ear-mites, already mentioned, a potential source of great nuisance is the rabbit mite, the cheyletiella mange mite. This is a microscopic mite which looks like scurf and can cause great irritation on the skin of some dogs. It is treatable with a wash, available from the vet, but all other dogs and the bedding must also be treated at the same time and the treatment of all repeated as specified.

Most dogs harbour the demodex mite throughout their lives, this being passed from their mother, without any ill effects. Stress may set off a population explosion of these mites, resulting in loss of hair, skin-scaling and rednesses and soreness of the skin – demodectic mange. This can be treated successfully by following the vet's instructions. The course prescribed may take several months to be effective. Sarcoptic mange, or scabies, is contagious from other infected animals and bedding. Terriers can catch this off foxes and their bedding. The musty smell of this type of mange is instantly recognisable, one never forgets it. Other symptoms are fur-loss, scratching and inflamed skin. This is treatable, over several weeks of treatment, and all bedding and also the kennels must be treated or re-infestation will occur.

MASTITIS and METRITIS: These conditions are dealt with in Chapter Twelve.

POISON: If you suspect poison, make the dog sick as quickly as possible. Washing soda lumps put down the throat, or a mouthful of salt, should do this. Try to identify the poison, ring the vet, and get there as quickly as possible, taking the poison container with you, if this is feasible.

PYOMETRA: This is a life-threatening condition in which the uterus fills with pus. It can occur in a bitch of any age, whether or not she has had a litter. Symptoms include a heavy thirst, lack of appetite and a slightly enlarged stomach. There may be a smelly discharge, combined with a general dullness which may not be realised until the bitch has recovered and is back to normal. It requires urgent veterinary treatment.

PHANTOM (FALSE) PREGNANCY: This occurs at about the time when a bitch, had she been mated, would be preparing to have a litter and she may start nesting, collecting toys, have milk and become generally broody. Some bitches do this every time, whereas others may never show any signs. Make her bed cooler by removing warm blankets from underneath her. Remove the toys and try to involve her in active life, such as walks, to take her mind off the nest. This condition should pass in a week or so. If the milk becomes a problem, the vet will be able to help.

SKIN PROBLEMS: The cause can be greasy coats, anal glands, fleas, lice, ticks, and mange-mites. Skin can also be irritated by allergies to such things as household cleaners or treated carpets, or by diet. Dogs can also chew their feet or legs through boredom. Wet eczema patches can be caused through too rich a diet or through the dog chewing a patch because the anal glands are full and uncomfortable. After the cause has been dealt with, the skin can be helped by the application of either boric acid-based antiseptic powder or a skin cure. Prompt treatment of itchy of inflamed skin with one of these items usually prevents this becoming a major problem. Boredom chewing must be stopped. Spray the paws and legs with bitter-apple spray and give the dog something to occupy the mind and teeth – a bone, hoof or toy.

SNAKE BITES: Just get to the vet, quick! Try to keep the dog still.

STINGS: A bee leaves the sting behind so the little sac with the sting, if still in the dog, must be pulled out between your finger nails or with tweezers. Bathe with vinegar and water for wasps, bicarbonate of soda for bees. An apis mel tablet administered at once, followed by another after two hours, seems to prevent swelling. If the sting is inside the mouth, veterinary attention is required. If the mouth or throat appears to be swelling, apply an ice pack (a packet of frozen peas) while getting the dog to the vet.

SUNSTROKE: Some dogs will sunbathe until they have sunstroke! The same treatment applies for heat exhaustion in cars. Apply ice-packs, packets of frozen peas or cold water to the dog's skull and back of the neck to bring the temperature down quickly. Do not submerge the whole dog in very cold water as this may cause further complications. Offer sips of cold water afterwards. Keep the dog quiet and in a dark place and seek veterinary advice.

TICKS: These are picked up when exercising through long grass, particularly in sheep or deer country. Ticks vary in size and colour. They dig their heads into the flesh and inflate with blood. Pulling them off leaves the head embedded in the flesh, which may lead to trouble. A dab of spirit or covering them with Vaseline will usually remove them completely. Ticks in deer country may carry Lyme disease, debilitating to both dogs and humans, but treatable by antibiotics. In tropical countries ticks carry potentially lethal diseases and dogs are washed regularly to prevent ticks.

VOMITING: This can be caused by travelling in cars, eating grass and herbs and eating unsuitable objects. A dam will vomit for her puppies. Vomiting for no apparent reason could be symptomatic of disease. If vomit contains blood, contact the vet. Also, if the dog shows any others symptoms, such as a raised or lowered temperature, take action. To make a dog vomit, see Poison.

ROUNDWORMS: A dog of any age may have roundworms, Toxocara canis, the worm associated with hysterical reportings of a transmitted disease to humans. It is extremely rare for a human to become infected. Normal kennel hygiene such as picking up and burning all droppings, and washing hands after handling dogs, and not allowing dogs to lick one's face, should reduce any risk.

TAPEWORMS: Part of the complicated life-cycle of Dipylidium caninum, the tapeworm most commonly found in dogs, involves the flea. A dog that looks out of condition, thin and with a poor coat despite eating well, may have a tapeworm. Light-coloured segments may be seen in the faeces or on the trousers of an infected dog. Tapeworm treatment must come from the vet, as it must be specific. Other types of tapeworm may be picked up by dogs scavenging on farmland, particularly where sheep are kept in large numbers.

HOOKWORM AND WHIPWORM: These are less common than roundworms or tapeworms but, if a dog is not thriving despite having been treated against both the former types, it is worth considering the possibility of the presence of some other type of worm. There are effective preparations which can be given against several types of worm which cost rather more than the single-type wormer, but are well worth the extra money if there is a suspicion that a dog is not prospering as well as expected.

HEREDITARY DISEASES
The Border is not universally known to suffer from any specific inherited disease. However, there have been the occasional incidences of Hip Dysplasia, Cataract, Legg Perthes Disease, Epilepsy, Patella Luxation and Heart Murmurs, while PRA has been reported in the US. At the moment it would appear that none of these conditions is a major problem in the breed. Several breeders are keeping a watching brief by having their Borders' eyes checked – a good thing, because this could show up any problem in the breed, since few Borders are bred within the confines of a closely bred line.

In the US many breeders are having their Borders' hips X-rayed. Hip Dysplasia is found in most breeds. Small terriers are likely to have a score as a normal anatomical feature. HD would be unlikely to cause problems in later life with a small, lightweight breed such as a Border. The inheritance of Perthes is still not clear. Some families seem more susceptible than others; some cases may be the result of genuine injury. Inherited Epilepsy is difficult to diagnose. There are many causes of fits; the pattern of occurrence is a clue, since inherited Epilepsy follows a predictable pattern.

Kinked tails are an abnormality which occur in the breed. Some would appear to be of an hereditary nature, others might be caused in the development of the embryo. There does not appear to be any clear information on the subject. Since deformed tails appear to be linked to spinal defects in some breeds, there is the possibility that heavily kinked tails may be an indication of potential spinal deformity. As with any abnormality, they should be treated with suspicion.

It goes without saying that a reputable breeder, concerned for the future of the breed, would not lay down potential trouble by breeding from either a male or a female, should there be any shadow of doubt about the possibility of inherited disease or abnormality.

ALTERNATIVE MEDICINE

People are becoming increasingly aware that alternative medicines can be useful in the treatment of humans and animals. Some veterinary surgeons are using homoeopathic and herbal remedies in their own practice, or will refer patients to specialists in these fields, or to a chiropractor or osteopath. Undoubtedly there is a place for natural remedies and cures but these should not be dabbled in by amateurs. Fiddling about with home cures could waste vital time; meanwhile the condition deteriorates, and when the vet is finally called in, the case is more complicated than if caught early. A qualified animal chiropractor can resolve some problems which do not respond to drugs.

THE AGEING BORDER

As the Border becomes middle-aged it may become an effort for the dog to take as much exercise as before and to keep up. Dogs slow down and become rheumatic, just as humans do. Middle age for a Border is about seven years onwards. Reduce the amount of exercise and the pace to suit the dog. A dog who enjoys and waits for a walk will be very disappointed if left behind. Dry the ageing Border after a wet walk. The diet may have to be adjusted: an elderly dog, being more sedentary, needs less food with less protein. Watch the waist-line. It is unfair to allow a Border to become square in old age. An elderly dog may start to feel the cold. The outdoor dog may have to come into the house or be given additional heat in the kennel. A heated underpad of the type used for cats can help old bones. If the old dog approaches the feeding bowl with enthusiasm and then turns away, toothache may be the problem.

An absolute responsibility of dog ownership is to know when the time has come to say goodbye to an old friend. It is selfish and unkind to allow a dog who is miserable through an incurable illness or senile decay to linger on, suffering. Making the decision to have a dog put down is worse than the actual deed. Most vets will visit the home to give the final injection gently. Vets are used to tears, so do not feel worried about this. Believe me, this does not get any easier, no matter how many dogs one has owned. When people say to me "It's all right for you breeders, you have lots of dogs", I think "If only they knew." Once everything is over, despite the tears, there will be a sense of relief that the dog is no longer suffering. This is the one final good thing we can do for our dogs. Remember that the decision is better made one day too early than one day too late, from the dog's point of view.

When the time comes to replace an old friend with another dog it is sometimes better to have one of a different colour. Every dog is a different character and it is hard on the new dog to be expected to be the same as the dear departed.

Chapter Five

THE BREED STANDARDS

The current British Breed Standard is based on that of the Border Terrier Club at the time of KC recognition, 1920, with a few adjustments made over the years. A table of points was introduced at some stage and since dropped. Countries coming under the jurisdiction of the Fédération Cynologique Internationale (FCI) use the British Standard, i.e. that of the country of origin.

In North America the first Breed Standard was submitted to the American Kennel Club (AKC) by the embryo Border Terrier Club of America in 1948 and was accepted in March 1950, the year after the Club was officially founded. Basically this follows the ideals of the British Standard but with greater detail on some points. This was slightly altered in format in 1990 and some additions made.

THE BRITISH BREED STANDARD (1986)

GENERAL APPEARANCE Essentially a working terrier.

CHARACTERISTICS Capable of following a horse, combining activity with gameness.

TEMPERAMENT Active and game as previously stated.

HEAD AND SKULL Head like that of an otter but moderately broad in skull, with short strong muzzle. Black nose preferable, but liver- or flesh-coloured one not a serious fault.

EYES Dark, with a keen expression.

EARS Small, V-shaped; of moderate thickness, and dropping forward close to the cheek.

MOUTH Scissor bite, i.e. upper teeth closely overlapping lower teeth and set square to the jaws. Level bite acceptable. Undershot or overshot a major fault and highly undesirable.

NECK Of moderate length.

FOREQUARTERS Forelegs straight, not too heavy in bone.

BODY Deep, narrow, fairly long. Ribs carried well back, but not oversprung, as a terrier should be capable of being spanned by both hands behind the shoulder. Loins strong.

HINDQUARTERS Racy.

FEET Small with thick pads.

TAIL Moderately short; fairly thick at base, then tapering. Set high, carried gaily, but not curled over back.

GAIT/MOVEMENT Has the soundness to follow a horse.

COAT Harsh and dense; with close undercoat. Skin must be thick.

COLOUR Red, wheaten, grizzle and tan or blue and tan.

SIZE, WEIGHT Dogs: 5.9 – 7.1 Kgs (13 – 15.5 lbs); bitches 5.1 - 6.4 Kgs (11.5 – 14 lbs).

FAULTS Any departure from the foregoing points should be considered a fault and the seriousness with which the fault should be regarded should be in exact proportion to its degree and its effect on the terrier's ability to work.

NOTE Male animals should have two apparently normal testicles fully descended into the scrotum.

Reproduced by kind permission of the Kennel Club.

THE AMERICAN BREED STANDARD (1990)

GENERAL APPEARANCE He is an active terrier of medium bone, strongly put together, suggesting endurance and agility, but rather narrow in shoulder, body and quarter. The body is covered with a somewhat broken though close-fitting and intensely wiry jacket. The characteristic 'otter' head with its keen eye, combined with a body poise which is 'at the alert', gives a look of fearless and implacable determination characteristic of the breed.

Since the Border Terrier is a working terrier of a size to go to ground and able, within reason, to follow a horse, his conformation should be such that he be ideally built to do his job. No deviations from this ideal combination should be permitted, which would impair his usefulness in running his quarry to earth and in bolting it therefrom. For this work he must be alert, active and agile, and capable of squeezing through narrow apertures and rapidly transversing any kind of terrain. His head, 'like that of an otter', is distinctive, and his temperament ideally exemplifies that of a terrier. By nature he is good tempered, affectionate, obedient and easily trained. In the field he is hard as nails, 'game as they come' and driving in attack. It should be the aim of Border Terrier breeders to avoid such over-emphasis on any point in the Standard as might lead to unbalanced exaggeration.

SIZE, PROPORTION AND SUBSTANCE *Weight.* Dogs 13 – 15.5 pounds, bitches, 11.5 – 14 pounds, are appropriate weights for Border Terriers in hardworking condition. The *proportions* should be that the height at the withers is slightly greater than the distance from the withers to the tail, i.e. by possibly 1 – 1.5 inches in a 14 lb dog. Of medium bone, strongly put together, suggesting endurance and agility, but rather narrow in shoulder, body and quarter.

HEAD Similar to that of an otter. *Eyes* dark hazel and full of fire and intelligence. Moderate in size, neither prominent nor small and beady. *Ears* small, V-shaped and of moderate thickness, dark preferred. Not set high on the head but somewhat on the side, and dropping forward close to the cheeks. They should not break above the level of the skull. Moderately broad and flat in *skull* with plenty of width between the eyes and between the ears. A slight, moderately broad curve at the *stop* rather than a pronounced indentation. Cheeks slightly full. *Muzzle* short and 'well-filled'. A dark muzzle is characteristic and desirable. A few short whiskers are natural to the breed. *Nose* black, and of good size. *Teeth* strong, with a scissors bite, large in proportion to the size of dog.

NECK, TOPLINE, BODY *Neck* clean, muscular and only long enough to give a well-balanced appearance. It should gradually widen into the shoulder. *Back* strong but laterally supple, with no suspicion of a dip behind the shoulder. *Loin* strong. *Body* deep, fairly narrow and of sufficient length to avoid any suggestions of lack of range and agility. The body should be capable of being spanned by a man's hands behind the shoulders. Brisket not excessively deep or narrow. Deep ribs carried well back and not oversprung in view of the desired depth and narrowness of the body. The *underline* fairly straight. *Tail* moderately short, thick at the base, then tapering. Not set on too high. Carried gaily when at the alert, but not over the back. When at ease, a Border may drop his stern.

FOREQUARTERS *Shoulders* well laid back and of good length, the blades converging to the withers gradually from a brisket not excessively deep or narrow. *Forelegs* straight and not too heavy in bone and placed slightly wider than in a Fox Terrier. *Feet* small and compact. Toes should point forward and be moderately arched with thick pads.

HINDQUARTERS Muscular and racy, with *thighs* long and nicely moulded. *Stifles* well bent and *hocks* well let down. *Feet* as in front.

COAT A short and dense undercoat covered with a very wiry and somewhat broken topcoat which should lie closely, but it must not show any tendency to curl or wave. With such a coat a Border should be able to be exhibited almost in his natural state, nothing more in the way of trimming being needed than a tidying up of the head, neck and feet. *Hide* very thick and loose fitting.

COLOR Red, grizzle and tan, blue and tan, or wheaten. A small amount of white may be allowed on the chest but white on the feet should be penalized. A dark muzzle is characteristic and desirable.

GAIT Straight and rhythmical before and behind, with good length of stride and flexing of stifle and hock. The dog should respond to his handler with a gait which is free, agile and quick.

TEMPERAMENT His temperament ideally exemplifies that of a terrier. By nature he is good-tempered, affectionate, obedient, and easily trained. In the field he is hard as nails, 'game as they come' and driving in attack.

SCALE OF POINTS

Head, ears, neck and teeth	20
Legs and feet	15
Coat and skin	10
Shoulders and chest	10
Eyes and expression	10
Back and loin	10
Hindquarters	10
Tail	5
General Appearance	10
TOTAL	100

Approved March 14, 1950
Reformatted July 13, 1990

Reproduced by kind permission of the American Kennel Club.

INTERPRETATION OF THE STANDARD

The most important words in the British Standard are "essentially a working terrier", and the second most important is the clause which the Breed Clubs insisted on being added when the Standard was re-arranged: "and the seriousness with which the fault should be regarded should be in exact proportion to its degree and its effect on the terrier's ability to work."

GENERAL APPEARANCE AND CHARACTERISTICS

Since every point mentioned in the Standard is relevant to work, it is helpful to know what the work of the breed is and over what type of terrain. The country hunted by the Border Foxhounds has been described as probably one of the wildest and most remote hunting countries in England. To follow a horse across the hills of Northumberland and the adjacent countries the terrier must have sufficient length of leg and a free and active construction. Lithe is a word which comes to mind as the terrier must be able to turn in a tight spot.

Size is all-important. The Border was bred to go to ground after fox for which a narrow dog is needed, as narrow as the fox. A handsome-looking terrier is no use whatsoever if too big to get where a fox can, however willing the dog is in spirit. Gameness is impossible to assess in the ring. Some of the gamest terriers show no spark in the ring. The terrier dancing about on tiptoes, sparring up to other terriers, is not necessarily game, just hot-headed. Aggression towards other dogs is a fault, a nuisance when working.

Scars do not always depict gameness. Some of the best workers bear no scars. Stupid terriers, or good terriers with stupid owners, may be covered with them. Conversely, some very good terriers are marked up through misfortune. Scars should not be penalised. The defunct Northumberland Border Terrier Club had a rule that, if any part of a terrier's face was missing through legitimate work, that part was deemed perfect. Even in my time, a Border with one eye could win a CC. But I have witnessed a judge penalising a missing tooth and another penalising scars, which is just what early opponents of Kennel Club recognition feared – that the Border would become another 'show dog' rather than a worker.

The American Standard lays emphasis on the fact that the Border is a working terrier. However, there appears to be a misunderstanding of the Border's job, which is not to run his quarry to earth. That is the hounds' job. The Border follows the horse, not the hounds. The rider takes a line of

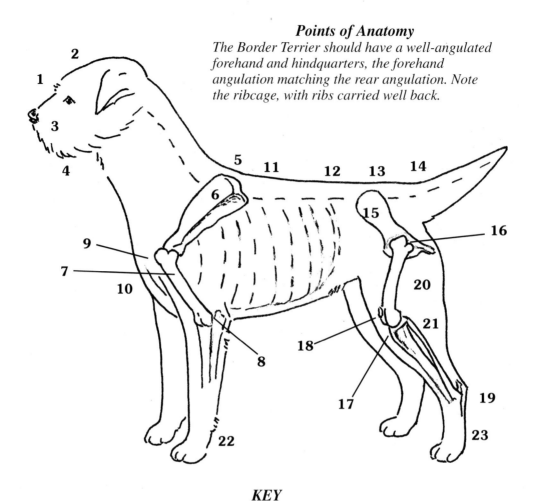

Points of Anatomy
The Border Terrier should have a well-angulated forehand and hindquarters, the forehand angulation matching the rear angulation. Note the ribcage, with ribs carried well back.

KEY

1. Stop
2. Skull
3. Foreface
4. Underjaw
5. Withers
6. Scapula
7. Humerus
8. Elbow Joint
9. Point of Shoulder
10. Chest
11. Back
12. Loin

13. Croup
14. Tailset
15. Pelvis
16. Hip joint
17. Stifle joint
18. Patella
19. Hock
20. Thigh
21. Second thigh
22. Front pastern
23. Rear pastern

country, cutting off the corners of the run rather than following every turn of the hunt. I am not sure that 'body poise at the alert' describes true Border character in the show-ring but it is an apt description of a Border when running free in the countryside.

The American Standard describes the Border as being rather narrow in the shoulder, body and quarter. The first two points I would agree with, but I query whether narrowness in hindquarters is an attribute of a dog who should be able to follow a horse. Narrowness of hindquarters indicates weak hindquarters stemming either from a narrow pelvis or lack of muscular development. Maybe 'narrowness' was used in trying to describe the lightness of the hindquarters, the raciness.

Proportion is mentioned in the American Standard but not the British one. The requirement of the height at the withers being slightly greater than the distance from the withers to tail describes a Border somewhat taller than its length, which is incorrect – surely the measurement should be the other way round, to give the fairly long back, rather than the short back which would fit the former outline? A good maxim to remember when looking at a Border is that the space beneath the dog between fore and hind legs should be oblong rather than square. If it is square, the dog is not correctly proportioned. Within the correct outline of a Border could be contained either a well-ribbed back rib-cage with a loin of ideal length, or a short rib-cage with a long weak loin.

TEMPERAMENT

The phrase 'must combine activity with gameness' was cannibalised from the clause on characteristics to fit the space labelled 'temperament' when the Standard was re-arranged. What is an active temperament, and would we want it in the Border? When going about its daily business, the Border is calm, steady and unremarkable until confronted with some live creature which needs dealing with, whereupon the terrier comes to the fore and the dog is keen and active. A good Border is not 'hard' when working but rather firm and unyielding, capable of holding a fox at bay, or more if necessary.

The American Standard depicts this rather Jekyll and Hyde breed character well, though it describes a terrier somewhat harder than that required for bolting foxes rather than killing them underground.

HEAD

The otter head is unique to the breed. Without this a Border is just another terrier. Since the original Standard was written by people resident in Britain, we can assume that the otter they had in mind was the native British otter, Lutra Lutra, not the Short-Clawed Asian Otter which is the one usually seen in zoos, which has a differently proportioned head.

The otter has an almost flat skull, fairly wide between the ears but not square. The length of the skull is about twice its width. The occiput is flat, not raised, but the back of the skull, when viewed from above, is slightly rounded. A domed, apple-skull is incorrect, as is a square skull, something which is becoming common.

The muzzle is short, in proportion approximately one-third to two-thirds of the length of the skull, and is slightly rounded at the end, never pointed nor square. It should be well-filled below the eyes with no tapering-in. If the muzzle is too short the jaws lose power and the head appears out of balance. Although the American Standard calls for the cheeks to be slightly full, they should not be prominent. An otter-head shows no sign of 'bulliness'. Strength in the muzzle lies in both the top and lower jaws.

Many Borders who appear to have good heads lack underjaw. On handling the underjaw from underneath one should feel plenty of power. The entire head is not particularly deep through. Remember that an otter's head lies on the water like a water-lily leaf and you will have the picture.

*Head like an otter –
Lutra Lutra.*

*Photo: Rob
Williams.*

*Note the similarity in
proportion, the
flatness and width of
the skull, the width
between the eyes,
and the almost
imperceptible stop.
Mansergh Jesse is
pictured.*

An otter head has little stop, just a slight indentation. If the head is on two distinct planes with a sharp drop between the eyes, there is too much stop – also if there is a deep indentation between the eyes. Some Borders are too long in muzzle and narrow in skull, giving a 'terrier head' rather than a Border head. This often goes with eyes or ears that are placed too close together. Incorrect eye placement always indicates that the head is wrong. A dark muzzle and dark ears are desirable according to the American Standard. Both are purely cosmetic requirements, not mentioned in the British Standard. I wonder what happens when the dark mask fades with maturity?

NOSE

A liver or flesh-coloured nose is not considered a serious fault in the British Standard. The nose must be black in America. There, a good-sized nose is required, which is an important breed point, in danger of being lost. The terrier needs a large nose with good nostrils when working, both to breathe through and to use as a scent detector. Some tiny button-noses are appearing in the breed, with small nostrils which are not much use in an emergency. Small noses appear on those 'pretty' cat-like heads which lack strength. Liver noses are still seen occasionally. It was reputed that some of the best workers of yore had liver noses, which is why this was not considered a serious fault.

EYE

The Border eye is dark brown, generous in shape, being slightly on the round side of oval rather than a round full eye, or a tiny beady eye. The eyes are set wide apart, neither to the side nor to the front of the head. Some are set incorrectly to the front, like car headlamps, others incorrectly slanting to the side, like a snake. The American Standard differs from the British one by asking for a dark hazel eye. In Britain the eye must be dark. A hazel eye would be considered untypical, showing too much contrast between pupil and iris. The typical expression is pleasantly interested when relaxed, and keen when alert. The use of the word 'fire' in the American Standard is worrying. 'Fiery' is a denigrating word when applied to a Border in the UK.

EARS

The correct ear set is admirably described in detail in the American Standard.

MOUTH

An important difference between the two Standards lies in the teeth. In Britain a level bite is acceptable, but not in America. This means that a judge in Britain must not penalise a dog for having a level bite, even if not agreeing personally with the Standard. The reason that this is retained is that a Border must have a strong muzzle; some strong muzzles result in a level (pincer) bite. Some judges find it hard to accept a level bite, knowing that with time this may become undershot, as Border mouths do alter through teeth wearing down. Jaws can alter, even on Borders with a scissor bite to start with.

Occasionally an overshot bite is seen, where the top teeth overlap the bottom ones with a considerable gap between the rows of teeth. This is not to be confused with a puppy's mouth, which may have a small gap which will close as the teeth grow through. An overshot bite lacks power. Undershot means a reverse scissor bite, usually with the lower jaw prominent.

A wry mouth is one where the incisors on one side are correct and those on the other side are undershot, caused by a crooked lower jaw. This is a bad fault. However, occasionally the sequence

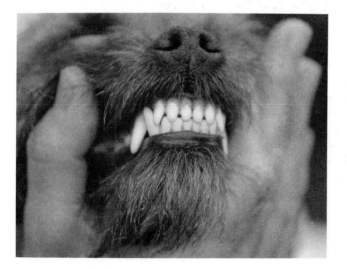

When opening the Border's mouth, the first reaction should be surprise at the size of the teeth. Note the large nostrils.

of teething can cause one tooth to go out of line in an otherwise correct bite in a straight jaw. This is not a major fault, but will be a handicap under most judges. There are enough good Borders in the ring for a judge not to have to place such a fault. This mouth will 'go' with time, as the teeth wear down.

A feature of the breed has always been that their teeth are large in proportion to the size of the dog. When opening a Border's mouth one should get a shock at the size of the teeth. Size of the teeth is mentioned in the American Standard but not the British one. Normal dentition is forty-two teeth: six incisors, two canines, six premolars and six molars in the top jaw and six incisors, two canines, eight premolars and six molars in the bottom.

Judges in Britain do not normally count teeth. In some other countries this is important: a dog with missing teeth would not win in Germany. Missing incisors occur in the breed: this is a sign of a too narrow jaw. Judges should look for this. A straight line of large teeth, which might look correct at a glance, on further examination may contain only five incisors.

NECK

A terrier needs a strong neck to draw a fox. The neck should be of sufficient length to carry the dog's head well away from the chest. Obviously a dog built to follow a horse must be of scopey build which equates with a reasonably long neck. If the shoulder is correctly laid, the neck will be fairly long, running smoothly into the withers. An upright shoulder produces a short neck which runs in at an abrupt angle. The neck should be clean, devoid of folds of hanging skin or dewlap, but the pelt on the back of the neck should be pliable.

FOREQUARTERS

No mention is made of the shoulders in the British Standard, but these are admirably described in the American one – a similar description to the old Northumberland Border Terrier Club's Standard, with the interesting addition that the brisket should not be excessively deep or narrow. When viewed from above the dog should be narrow at the withers. Many Borders with incorrect shoulders are wider at the withers than in the rib or across the hindquarters. The withers must not be the widest point on a working terrier.

The forelegs are straight and not too heavy in bone. Bone should be neither too heavy nor cumbersome nor flimsy. Ideal Border bone is strong but not overdone. Bone is felt below the hock and in the pastern and should be good all the way down the leg, not tapering. The American requisite that the forelegs are placed slightly wider than a Fox Terrier always makes me smile – which particular Fox Terrier, a good-fronted one, or one of those with barn-door fronts? The front should not be wide, neither should it be too narrow with both forelegs appearing to come from one hole. A commonly seen wrong front is the Bedlington front, where the front legs are straight but are not parallel, the front being wider across the top than at the feet, both standing and moving.

Incorrect: Upright shoulder, straight upper-arm, over at the knees.

Elbows are mentioned in neither Standard. They must be well-angulated. It is as important to have the correct angulation from the elbow to the point of the shoulder as from point of shoulder to withers. Pinching-in at the elbow results in a tied-in front, where the dog appears to be wearing an elastic band around the elbows, restricting movement and causing the forelegs to flick or paddle. Loose elbows may accompany wide fronts and heavy shoulders. They can turn out when the dog is either standing or moving. This is less restrictive than being tied-in, but both are unsound.

BODY

The depth of the Border's body allows room for heart and lung expansion while retaining the narrowness to enable the dog to go to ground. A dog with the correctly carried back rib-cage will have the correct under-line described in the American Standard as fairly straight, i.e. not cutting up. This Standard describes the brisket as not excessively deep or narrow. Neither should it be too wide. The Border chest is somewhat V-shaped, not U-shaped.

Mention is sometimes made of forechest or pro-sternum in show reports. These are terms not normally used in association with this breed, but the Border should have a slight, almost imperceptible, degree of chest showing in front of the front legs, if the shoulder and elbow are correctly laid. Exaggerated forechests are not desirable in the breed, neither is a total lack of this, which would denote a 'terrier front' caused by a steeply angled elbow.

The ribs should not be oversprung but neither should the dog be slab-sided, absolutely flat. Spanning we take as being done by an average-sized man's hands. Common sense must be used, as people's spans vary considerably. My span is large and I know that if I am struggling to span a Border, that dog is too big. The fox is not heavily constructed in body, a point to remember since the Border must be able to squeeze in after a fox.

The 'fairly long' body is open to wide interpretation. How long is fairly long? A short-backed

LEFT:
Correct: A well-shaped ribcage – not slab-sided or oversprung – with the ribs carried well back.

Incorrect: The ribcage is oversprung.

Border is anathema to a breed expert – the back being the part of the spine running from behind the withers to the start of the loin. In an effort to avoid a short back, some Border breeders have produced Borders too long in back, weak. The medium length seems about ideal.

BACK AND LOIN

Incidentally, the old myth that a working terrier must be able to touch the root of its tail means little. Yes, they can do so, but so can my ultra-short-backed Elkhound and so could my mother's shortest-backed Labrador. The back is described as strong in the American Standard, whereas the British one asks for a strong loin. The whole back should be strong, with no weakness behind the withers or over the loin. It is important that the loin be strong. The loin couples the front of the dog to the back of the dog and should not be too short, which restricts flexibility, nor so long as to be weak. Some Borders with strong loins show a slight rise over the loin caused by muscular development. This is not to be confused with a roached back, where the spine is curved. The Border should have a level spine.

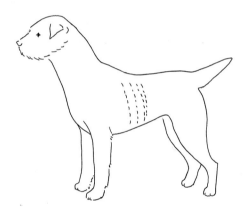

Incorrect: Roach-backed, low-set tail, cut-up underline.

Incorrect: Weak-backed, ribs not carried far enough back .

HINDQUARTERS

The term racy, applied to the hindquarters, sometimes causes problems. In early Standards the word used was 'racing', describing galloping hindquarters, which are not too heavy, and are well-angulated with long thigh muscles. The American description of hindquarters is excellent. Hocks well let down means that the right-angled hock joint is set low down the hindquarters. The leg from hock to foot should be perpendicular to the ground. The hock is a joint. The terms 'long in hock' or 'short hocks' are wrong – a joint cannot be short or long. Sickle-hocks, caused by too much angulation in the stifle and hock, cause the leg from hock to foot to stand forward under the dog, instead of being perpendicular. A sickle-hocked dog lacks second thigh development.

    Straight hocks often go together with straight stifles, both a common failing in the breed. Straight stifles are so much the norm that onlookers from other breeds ask whether Borders have to have these. No, is the answer. Straight stifles, with a lack of second thigh muscle, and straight hocks, are frequently seen on Borders with short bones. The Border should have long bones. There should also be some length in the pelvis from the haunch bones to the tail root to give the required

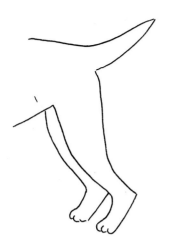

LEFT: Incorrect: Sickle-hocks.

RIGHT: Incorrect: Straight stifle and hocks.

scope in the hindquarters. Stilted action which does not cover the ground results from lack of angulation in either the forehand and rear, or both.

FEET
Feet are most important on a working dog, not just a fancy show point. They are the equivalent of tyres on a car, useless if flat and threadbare. A lame dog at home nursing sore feet is no good whatsoever when the fox is to ground. Early Standards called for cat-like feet – not really workmanlike on a terrier galloping over rough terrain and clambering about in rocky places. A slightly more oval foot with moderately arched toes is a better description. The feet must be small and not spreading. Thick pads are essential. All toes should reach the ground. Short toes on which the terrier does not stand are a fault, the dog needs all the toes to be functional.

The work of the Border never involved digging. A digging foot is a larger, more open-toed foot. A Border which digs when put to ground is a perfect nuisance, wasting time digging itself in and, more often than not, having to be rescued. Those who talk about a Border digging, like those who talk about big dogs to work big foxes, are expressing their ignorance.

TAIL
The correct Border tail is as much a breed feature as the otter head. Please note this is not an otter-tail, a favourite misquote from the Standard! The tail has been likened to a carrot and should be moderately short. Too short is as bad as too long. The tail is used as a handle to pull the terrier out of the hole when working. There must be good thickness at the root and sufficient length to get hold of and enough strength to withstand the counter-forces of the terrier trying to get in and the handler trying to pull the dog out. A long whippy tail is untypical.

The Breed Standards either side of the Atlantic are directly opposite in their description of tail set. The British one states 'set high', the American one says 'not set on too high'. Low set tails have always been around in Borders. One has only to look at photos of some of the early Champions to see this. Maybe it is more natural to breed a low set tail on a long cast dog with racy hindquarters, than a high set tail on such a dog. However, it is not correct. We have reached the point in Britain where a dog with the correct tail, as per the Standard, 'set high, carried gaily, but not curled over the back', is penalised for being different.

The tail must be straight when felt from root to tip, free from kinks. The dog may carry the tail slightly bent, indeed many do, but this is not a kinked tail. It must not curl over the back, a fault usually coupled with a short back. A good point in the American Standard is that the dog may drop the tail when at ease. This is absolutely typical of the breed character.

An interesting point, not mentioned in the Standards but nonetheless typical of the breed, is the band of silver hair which all Borders have about one third up their tail. When artists produce models or paintings and have failed to notice this, their work never looks true to the breed.

GAIT

Putting together both descriptions of gait, i.e. movement, would result in an ideal description. The British Standard, economical with words, indicates a sound and free-moving animal. The American one describes correct movement of a dog whose hind movement matches the front – a balanced dog. If studied from the side, the foot on the hindleg should reach forward under the dog to the spot where the foot on the opposite front leg reached; there is no ground beneath the dog that is not covered by the stride.

Seen from front and rear, the legs should move straight. The front legs should move parallel to each other, neither wider at the top nor at the bottom, and the feet should neither swing out nor pin in. The hocks and stifles should turn neither in nor out. Hind movement should be neither too wide nor too narrow. A good mover will show only either the two front legs or the two hindlegs when coming or going, not four legs in a row.

The stifle and hock should flex, but never in an exaggerated manner. The dog should not be able to kick up behind when moving. Front legs should move with a straight-through, daisy-cutting action, not bending the knees nor lifting the leg up high. A low, ground-covering action is correct whereby the dog progresses smoothly forward, rather than marching up and down on the spot in an uneconomical type of action.

Ground covering movement, illustrated by Ch. Brannigan of Brumberhill.

COAT

Since foxhunting takes place in the winter months and the country in which the Border was evolved is high and bleak, it is essential that the breed should have a weatherproof jacket. Terriers sometimes have long periods of waiting around after a long gallop, tied to a spade handle, with no shelter from wind or driving rain, sleet or snow. Soft coats are not just a cosmetic fault. Like the single coat, they offer little protection to the terrier. A good depth of jacket of the correct texture is vital to the dog.

Correct: Plenty of thick, loose pelt is required.

The recommendation that the Border 'should be able to be exhibited almost in his natural state, nothing more in the way of trimming being needed than a tidying up of head, neck and feet' in the American Standard seems an ideal rather than a reality. Unfortunately the breed is being over-trimmed in many countries. Fashion has changed dramatically in the forty-plus years since I started showing. Then Borders were shown in a good depth of tweedy-looking jacket, tidied by judicious use of finger and thumb in some instances. Then one person started to show them looking smoother, others followed, and now we have reached the depressing state when a Border shown in correct depth of jacket is penalised because the coat needs stripping. Scissor marks, even clippers, are in evidence.

The thick skin, the pelt, is very important. This should be very loose and really thick, offering protection to the terrier against bites or rips. When in a tight spot underground, the terrier will wriggle along inside its own skin.

COLOUR

There are only four colours listed. All are equally acceptable. Borders come in variations of these colours so that it is sometimes difficult to decide just what category the colour of the dog falls into. Even the same animal may vary in colour from coat to coat, also in stages of coat growth. My Ch. Linne of Duthil was a rich red grizzle and tan, yet one summer her adult coat was pure red. I had fun with another of mine who was an unusual colour, somewhere between blue and tan and dark grizzle and tan. I used to progress around the ring while the class was being judged asking the ringsiders what colour she was. It was strange that the long-time breed experts were puzzled by her colour, yet all the novices knew with certainty what colour she was!

Red consists of pure red hairs, no black tips, except maybe the ring on the tail, and often a black mask when young. Rich reds tend to go white at an early age. Wheaten is a pure colour, something like the colour of wheat straw, with a blue muzzle, blue ears and a blue ring on the tail. This colour has almost been lost to the breed. It is not to be confused with a washy red or washy grizzle and tan. Grizzle and tan is the heather-mixture of colour made up of hairs that are banded with dark tips. They range from a washy light red grizzle through to almost blue and tan.

The blue of the blue and tan consists of a mixture of black hairs, silver hairs and silver hairs with black tips, laid against each other, which is what gives the blue impression. This should not be black with a sparse mingling of silver hairs. Black and tan is incorrect and rarely has any undercoat. The tan colour of a blue and tan is light straw-coloured. Rich red is incorrect and usually goes with a too-black back and body. Blue and tans have a blue undercoat and blue skin. A blue skin is not a safe identification of this colour, as some grizzle and tans have it too.

The saddleback is an old colour which we no longer see. A saddleback had a definite saddle, silver blue in colour, often with a light stripe up the back, and the rest of the dog, including the neck, was wheaten. The undercoat was wheaten.

The actual distribution of colour varies greatly on blue and tans and does not follow the normal distribution pattern of a black and tan dog. Walking with a winning team of three blue and tans I realised that they were all slightly different in markings, yet made a matched team. The neck on a blue and tan is blue. Contrary to legend, blue and tans usually have splendid undercoats but because this is the same colour as the dog, people do not notice it. No mention of white is made in the British Standard. A small amount of white on the chest or brisket is not considered a fault. White toes on adults are frowned on.

SIZE

No height is given. It is generally accepted in terrier breeds requiring a good length of leg and medium bone that the 14 lb terrier is approximately 14 inches at the withers. The weights in the Standards should be for a terrier in working condition, which does not mean emaciated. They may be on the light side nowadays, when dogs are possibly better nourished than when the first Standard was drawn up. The elders of the breed, who soon altered the weight in the original Border Terrier Club Standard to cut out the larger dogs, were anxious that the breed should not be too big. There are many over-sized dogs winning. The sad thing is that correctly-sized Borders are penalised for being too small. Credit should be given for their correctness, instead of penalising them.

Dogs of the same weight can be radically different in size and shape within that weight. A small cobby dog with heavy bone could weigh the same as a dog of medium-sized bone built on a much rangier pattern. Some judges assess the weight of a terrier when spanning it, and also the balance, which is not mentioned in any Standard but is important. The terrier should come up in one hand perfectly balanced, not top heavy in front, to enable the dog to be passed around when working. The Border may have to be handed up a steep bank, in one hand, by someone who is hanging on to a tree for anchorage with the other. A top-heavy terrier with the weight in the forehand is awkward under such circumstances.

TESTICLES

A monorchid or unilateral cryptorchid has only one testicle descended into the scrotum. A cryptorchid has two testicles both undescended into the scrotum. The latter is infertile. A grey area appears concerning monorchids in Britain. The current Standard states that a male should be entire. Yet the KC rules permit neutered dogs to be shown; indeed a judge may not penalise a dog for this. Unentire males are ineligible for competition under AKC and FCI rules.

TYPE

Type is not mentioned in the Standards, yet this is really of prime importance when assessing any dog, this being what distinguishes one breed from another. Without type, a Border is just a terrier, not a Border Terrier. Type lies in every part of the dog, not just the head, although it is fair to say that a Border without an otter head is not really typical. When looking at any part of a Border – the head, the legs and feet, the tail, the hindquarters – that part should look only like a Border. If one is reminded of any other breed such as an Irish Terrier, a Griffon Bruxellois, a Whippet or a Collie, then the dog lacks type.

Kennel type is when specimens of the breed can be easily identified as to the kennel from which they were bred, or from which kennel the sire or dam came. Kennel type is not necessarily the same as breed type, as one kennel could produce dogs like peas out of a pod – yet all untypical of the breed. Sometimes those closely involved within a breed can lose sight of breed type because they see kennel type clearly. They can spot which dogs come from which lines with ease, but cease to notice when the dogs no longer look like Border Terriers. Funnily enough, it is often an all-round judge who can see when a breed is losing type and no longer looks like itself.

Within acceptable breed type there may be several variations, all answering the Standard and looking like the breed, yet slightly different. Ideally there should be just one breed type, but breed history tells us that there were differing types from the different areas, right from the start.

FAULTS

Neither the British nor the American Standard contain any disqualifying faults. When comparing any dog against a Standard, it must be remembered that the perfect dog has yet to be born, and that the seriousness with which a fault should be regarded should be in exact proportion to its degree and its effect on the terrier's ability to work.

Chapter Six

WORKING YOUR BORDER TERRIER

Not every Border Terrier owner will be interested in the working aspect of the breed – indeed there will be some who are dead against using a terrier in connection with hunting. However, this is first and foremost a working terrier breed, therefore anyone owning one should at least know what the breed is for, as this is relevant to every Border. This instinct is latent in any Border so that, even if the owner is not interested in pursuing animals underground, the terrier will be, given half a chance!

Any aspirant judge of the breed should be acquainted with the work of the breed, understanding that form follows function, and should realise the type of steep, wild and rugged terrain that the breed was bred to work in. Times have changed greatly since the golden era of the breed, at the time leading up to and following recognition, when the sporting families hunting the Foxhound packs in the Border district bred and used Border Terriers.

Although Borders are still used up and down Britain with various packs and are being worked privately by enthusiasts, their position has been somewhat usurped with the Border packs by the 'in' breeds of working terriers, the Jack Russells, crossbreds and Fell Terriers. The work of the terrier remains unchanged – to go to ground either singly or with another terrier, to bolt the fox if possible, or to hold it to bay by barking and darting at it until dug down to. The Border was not required to kill the fox, as were Lakeland Terriers working with the Fell packs, but occasionally this is necessary, so the Border should have the strength do this and to draw a fox, dead or alive.

The term work, as applied to a terrier, means working fox to Foxhounds, otter to Otterhounds or mink to Minkhounds, or to badger. Although the breed is used for ratting and rabbiting, following blood trails, in obedience, agility and as gundogs, none of these are technically described as work. Since the demise of otterhunting in Britain, athe only terrier work left with hounds is with Foxhounds or Minkhounds. It is now illegal to work badger.

Borders were bred of a build to enable them to follow a horse across the rough and steep country in the Border district. They were not carried on the saddle. Nowadays they are often transported in a four-wheeled-drive vehicle which can get near, or within quick walking distance of, most places where a fox goes to ground. Terrier-men nearly all use locator collars, 'bleepers', when putting a terrier to ground these days. The advantages outweigh the slight risk that a terrier might get hung up by the collar on a tree root. This device enables the terrier to be located underground easily. Working a terrier without this means that the terrier can only be located by listening with an ear to the ground – not easy above wind and rain – and by driving spikes into the ground to try to find the hole and to make an air vent through which to listen, or through banging a spade on the ground, or jumping up and down on the ground, to try to make either the fox or the terrier move.

A terrier should have voice and use it. This tells the owner what is going on down there and the

Ready for work: Three likely looking workers. The central dog is wearing a locator collar.

Photo: I. Farrow.

A fox to ground in the hill country of the Border district.

whereabouts of the terrier. Just because bleepers are now used, there is no need to ignore the attribute of voice. A mute terrier is still a nuisance, because this relays none of the action, even though the location of the dog may be electronically pinpointed. The locator makes terrier work quicker, which suits the hunt, and safer, because digging takes less time and consequently the terrier can be got out quicker, with less damage if in a tight spot.

Another aspect of Foxhunting which has changed is the presence of two-wheel 'scrambling' bikes, or four-wheeled bikes, so handy for hill farmers looking after their sheep and also for getting about hunting – a motorised horse, except they don't jump! While these may be fun to hunt on, enabling one to cross country quickly, the exhaust fumes foul up the scent and the noise of the engines destroys the peace and makes listening difficult. When travelling across country, terriers are often carried in panniers or stuffed inside jackets, for the ride on these machines.

What with all this, plus radio communication enabling people to keep in contact across wide distances, anywhere, one wonders what the early breed pioneers would think of a modern day's hunting in the Borders. Good sport is still enjoyed, so I reckon that they would approve of that, but they might want a few more Border Terriers to be involved.

Working to Minkhounds is quite different to working fox. A mink is a tiny slip of an animal which follows river banks and streams and is fierce towards any adversary. It can get where no terrier could possibly follow but, at other times, may take refuge up inside a hollow tree or in a drain or root, from which it may be possible to bolt the mink with a terrier. In Eire, terriers are still worked with Otterhounds; there are several packs there. A small terrier is essential, one which can run field drains and get into tight places between tree roots.

WORKING TO HOUNDS

When working to any hounds, a terrier is best led until required. The terrier arriving with the hounds and going straight in can hinder rather than help the proceedings by driving the quarry further in. Once hounds have been removed, the hole is inspected and the situation weighed up as to where the terrier would best be put in.

A terrier must be picked up immediately once the fox, otter or mink has bolted. An otter-headed terrier swimming when hounds are looking for an otter is at obvious risk. The terrier who has been to ground will take on the colour of the ground or mud in which the dog has been and will also

A meet of the Wensleydale Foxhounds, a foot pack. Bill Shorthose with Ch. Cuillean Dodger and Ch. John Boy of Todgrove. Ron Hillcoat with Glenlea Sunburst and Madonna Marj.

Photo: P. Cheeseman.

Ian Farrow and Paul Cheeseman with Borders and Foxhounds of the Enfield Chace pack. Borders must be able to get on with hounds.

Photo courtesy: I. Farrow.

smell strongly of fox, otter or mink. Masters of Hounds in the South of England who were used to white terriers, were at first suspicious that the Border's colour would endanger the terrier, through hounds mistaking the dog for the fox. It soon became apparent that even a white terrier could look earth-coloured, so Borders were at no greater risk and became accepted as good workers in the South as well as in the North.

OPPORTUNITIES FOR WORKING TERRIERS

It is becoming increasingly difficult for the lay person who is not a recognised hunt-terrier-man to work terriers. The Master of Foxhounds Association's policy now requires terrier work to be done only by the officially appointed terrier-man to the hunt. This means that anyone wanting a Border worked must be prepared to hand the dog over for some time to this person. The casual working of

Minkhunting:
Hounds marking
at a root.

The hounds have
been taken away
and the Borders
are at work.

Photos courtesy:
F. Wildman.

terriers around the countryside is out, too. Land-owners and the local hunt do not like people interfering with wild-life on their patch. The penalties for disturbing a badger sett are severe – a heavy fine plus the possibility that the terriers will be confiscated. However, there are still those who manage, against the odds, to work their terriers legitimately.

ENTERING THE YOUNGSTER

Borders are not usually ready to enter until they are well over twelve months. An entered terrier means one that goes to ground and is proficient to fox or other quarry. A terrier is said to be entered to fox, entered to otter or entered to badger. A Border that is entered too young may be "overfaced" and put off, or could become too hard. Those which are slower to enter tend to think more and have the Border's sensible approach to work – very game, but not blinding headlong into trouble. The initial introduction to work may be made once a puppy has changed teeth and they are firmly set. A rag moving about on a string will teach the pup to worry. Once this instinct is aroused, the rag can be put under things where the pup will have to crawl a little further each time to get it out. Ratting with other terriers is a natural progression. Rabbiting is inadvisable, because a terrier working rabbits who should be working fox, is a nuisance.

A short drain under a track with daylight at the end is ideal for a youngster to learn to go to ground by following another terrier through it. An older, experienced terrier is useful in teaching a puppy or youngster what to do by example. It is extremely difficult to enter a terrier without the presence of an entered terrier.

It is no good trying to force a young terrier to go to ground. Taking the youngster along with an experienced terrier to watch what is going on, and to have a look, is a good method. If interested, one day the penny will drop and the youngster will cautiously follow the other terrier to ground, a short way at first and then becoming bolder.

Encourage the youngster at any signs of interest; quietly, so as not to distract the dog. Once the dog is to ground, continue this quiet encouragement, especially if there are sounds that the terrier has 'connected'. A working partnership builds up between dog and owner, who learn to trust each other, so that the owner believes the dog who is indicating that a hole needs investigation because it is particularly interesting, and the terrier will come out instantly when called, leaving other holes, and go into the one the owner indicates. Gradually the owner will learn to 'read' the terrier and know what is in the hole and what is happening, by the dog's reaction and tone of barking.

WORKING TERRIER TRIALS

Having seen and read about Working Terrier Trials, where the dog is slipped at a distance from the hole and enters it without any further guidance or encouragement from the owner, I do feel that much of the vital team-work between dog and owner is being missed completely. Working with hounds also tests an important part of the Border character, which is that the terrier is amenable to other terriers and hounds. A fighter who picks a quarrel with another terrier is a nuisance and a terrier who picks a quarrel with a hound could well be killed or worried. This is another essential part of terrier work which is not tested at Trials – the ability to mix with hounds, with whom the terrier may have to travel in a hound van to the meet, as well as their being colleagues throughout the day's hunting.

Working Terrier Trials to live bait are illegal in the UK, where the law is very strict regarding cruelty. Anyone working a terrier to any quarry must be aware of, and respect, the law and also respect the animals. The Working Terrier Trial tests a certain aspect of a working terrier – that the dog will go to ground in a fairly straightforward place and will bay the quarry. However, when the quarry is protected from the advances of the terrier, the common-sense of the terrier is never

The vital teamwork between dog and owner...

Putting the terrier to ground.

Photos: Scarlett Williams.

Am. Ch. Royal Oaks Rhatt Butler: A satisfactory conclusion to a woodchuck hunt in the USA.

brought to question, nor the cleverness involved in bolting the quarry from a difficult spot. Such things as stamina, working in awful winter weather conditions several times a week, and steadfastness, are not really tested, as these can only be tested in the real world of hunting. However, these Tests do at least encourage people to work their terriers to some degree.

WORKING CERTIFICATES

Working Certificates are issued in the UK by a Master of Foxhounds or of Minkhounds, who will certify that the dog is a game terrier who will go to ground and stay with the quarry and has worked with a specified pack in a specified hunting season. This is not a KC award, but the certificates are accepted by breed clubs scheduling a class for Working Certificate holders. It is becoming increasingly difficult for the layman terrier owner to gain such a certificate, for the reasons already stated. All credit to those who can, and who prove that the Border is still worthy of the name.

THE RISKS TO A WORKING TERRIER

Anyone working a terrier must realise that there is a certain amount of risk involved every time a terrier goes to ground. Even with the aid of locators, a terrier may get into difficulties through a fall of earth, or through getting into a spot from which it is difficult to get out again. Some places which look nothing from the outside can have inner ramifications. Terriers can, and do, become fast underground.

The Fell and Moorland Working Terrier Club was founded some time ago specifically to rescue trapped terriers. The organisation has spread throughout Britain, and the Club has access to earth-moving equipment, heat-seeking devices and a band of willing volunteers who will dig their hearts out for days to try to rescue a terrier. Other similar bodies exist and anyone owning a terrier would be well-advised to become a member of one of the local branches. One never knows when a terrier will vanish underground.

A basic first-aid kit for anyone working a terrier should contain a long-nozzled tube of antiseptic ointment. Owners should inspect their dogs for small, deep puncture wounds and for tears to gums or damage to claws or pads. Any wounds, bites or tears should be washed out as soon as possible and treated. Eyes may be full of soil when a terrier has been underground. They should be washed out with tepid water and then eye ointment applied, which helps to lubricate the eyes and further flush out any particles of soil. Teeth may be caked up with soil or bits of tree-root, which should be removed.

A terrier will be tired and may be sore and stiff after a hard day's work. A warm box in the car on the return journey will help ease the stiffness. A chocolate bar will help restore the blood sugar until such time as the dog has a nourishing and well-deserved dinner before bedding down into a warm bed for the night. A good terrier is worth looking after – a bit of coddling will keep your Border active, however tough the dog may seem when working.

There is nothing quite like the thrill of watching and hearing a terrier at work. Once down there, the dog relies on its own sense and instinct, plus the courage to stand up to the fox, or whatever, however gruelling the situation. The normally placid Border becomes a brave and spirited terrier when confronting the traditional enemy of the breed's forebears.

Chapter Seven

THE SHOW RING

The show ring is a gathering ground for Borders from different areas and of different bloodlines, where one can assess the state of the breed in general and one's own terriers in particular. A great deal of knowledge and information is exchanged in the happy banter which goes on between friends in the breed.

There is a definite pattern to an exhibitor's showing career. Most start by showing the family pet, often a nice dog but not out of the top drawer. It will take a while for the novice exhibitor to realise that this dog is not perfect. The next step will be to purchase a puppy or a youngster specifically for show. This is when a little knowledge proves dangerous. This dog will come from a winning kennel of the moment and may actually be inferior to the first, but it will be years before this is realised, by which time it will be too late to do anything about it.

Many people show dogs for a couple of years with reasonable success and then become disillusioned because they are not rising to the top quickly enough. They realise that dogs from certain kennels win consistently. If your dog does not win as much as you had hoped for, do not blame the judges for being dishonest. Instead, look long and hard at your dog to see why. The answer always lies there, in the dog. Maybe better conditioning is required, maybe you are doing something wrong in the handling, or maybe the dog is just not good enough. It takes little to mar an otherwise nice dog.

Do not be afraid to seek the opinion of one or two well-established exhibitors. People with consistently winning kennels are usually willing to offer help and advice if this is sought. Those who stay the course do so by learning what needs improving. Those who don't learn leave the scene within the first five years. It is not difficult to learn how to prepare a Border's coat for show but it is an art to fettle and condition the dog from the inside, through correct rearing and feeding and exercise.

HANDLING

In Britain the standard of handling in the Border ring is not exceptionally good. There is a handful of really good handlers and others who would probably be best described as adequate. It is unusual, but not unheard of, to see a professional handler with a Border in the UK. However, in the US, many Borders are shown by professionals, who are really good, and this means that the owner-handlers have to be good, too, to compete against them.

Borders easily become bored by the show ring. Handling classes are useful to socialise them and to learn the rudiments of ring training but regular attendance could sicken a Border of the ring. This is a breed which looks better shown naturally, on a loose-lead. If you are fortunate to have one that shows freely, do not set the dog up just because every one else in the class is supporting

The Working Class at the Southern Border Terrier Club's Championship Show: Borders look their best when shown naturally.

Photo: S. Pickerin.

their dog's head and tail. A Border shown freely must not be allowed to spar up to another or interfere with another exhibit. The moment a Border is stacked or set up the dog stiffens, straightening the stifles, and the forelegs may stick forward as the dog leans back. The more the handler fiddles, the worse the dog looks.

Repetitive use of the command Stand will depress a Border. They need encouragement in the ring. Try to keep it fun for the dog, and for yourself too. Some Borders are too dour in character to show on a loose lead. Rather than having the dog look like a wet weekend, it is better to keep the head held up, by the lead behind the ears, and to support the tail with a hand. The correct show stance, when either on the ground or on the table, is for the dog to stand with the front legs perpendicular to the ground, not sticking forward, and for the hindlegs to be just far back enough to show the bend of the stifle and for the leg from hock to foot to be perpendicular to the ground. The back should be level, neither sloping nor roached. Never pick a Border up by the tail to position the hindlegs.

A specialist judge should not mind if a Border drops the tail when standing, as this is typical in character. The tail looks good at any angle between level with the back-line and an angle of about 45 degrees to it. If held upright this tends to make the back appear short, but this is the natural tail carriage of some dogs and is acceptable.

DIFFERENT DAYS, DIFFERENT PLACINGS

Sometimes people new to showing are puzzled as to why exhibits are not always placed in the same order if they are being judged against the same Standard. Every judge has their personal interpretation of the Standard. Some lay more emphasis on certain attributes, such as head, feet, or eye colour, whereas others give priority to movement over type, or vice versa. Some will consider size highly important.

Coupled with that, Borders vary tremendously in themselves depending on hormonal cycles or the stage of coat growth. A bitch who has recently been in season may lack muscle tone and consequently move badly. A male may be fretting after a bitch and have lost condition. Some Borders mature quickly and then coarsen and thicken. Others look adolescent for about two years, then they start to blossom. These will last into old age without losing their shapeliness.

THE BITCH IN SEASON: TO SHOW OR NOT TO SHOW?

It is permissible to show a bitch in season in the UK, the US, and in some other countries. Whether or not to show can be a problem. Personally, I show a bitch at the start or at the end of her season, but never when she is at the 'red-hot' stage. I would never show one in mixed sex classes and I always keep her well away from any dog. Care is taken to wipe all around her cage and bench with a liquid odour-destroyer suitable for animals, also her rear-end and the soles of all her feet. I always warn the judge before she is handled. Owners of some males may gripe about the presence of a bitch in season, whereas the owner of a bored male might welcome one to waken the dog up a little. A bitch in season may move badly or blow out in rib at this time, so in either of these cases she would be better left at home.

TYPES OF SHOWS IN THE UK

Shows for Borders fall into two categories in the UK: those which are held under KC rules, and Working Terrier Shows which are not, but are not deemed 'unrecognised shows' by the KC so registered Borders may be shown there and enthusiasts may both show and judge without fear of retribution. Working Terrier Shows are covered later in the chapter. The classification of shows which follows applies to KC shows.

MATCH MEETINGS These are run by the local canine society or by a breed club – ideal for young dogs and novice exhibitors to gain experience as well as being pleasant social affairs. Dogs are judged in pairs on the basis of a knock-out competition. There is usually a puppy and an adult match. Champions and CC winners are ineligible. Entry is confined to club members and is made at the event.

EXEMPTION SHOWS These are fun events, usually run in aid of charity and held in conjunction with the village fete or a local event and advertised in the local press. Classification for pedigree classes is restricted to four any variety classes, but there are also novelty classes for the dog with the waggiest tail and the like, which are fun and good experience for the dog. These shows sometimes attract enormous entries. Champions, CC, Reserve CC and Junior Warrant winners are ineligible. Exhibits need not be registered at the KC. Entries are made at the event.

SANCTION AND LIMITED SHOWS These used to be the starting ground for new exhibitors and young dogs but the Sanction Show has virtually disappeared and the any variety Limited Show seems to be following. Some breed clubs run a Limited Show. Champions and CC winners are ineligible. Entry is restricted to members and made in advance. Sanction Shows, also restricted to members, schedule usually only variety classes up to Post Graduate, which eliminates top winning dogs from competing.

OPEN SHOWS Breed clubs run an Open Show of about twenty classes. General societies run Open Shows catering for many breeds which may include a handful of Border classes. Champions and CC winners may compete at Open Shows. Indeed, it is a good thing that they do, as this is where aspiring judges gain experience. It is essential that a Championship judge should have judged top class specimens before awarding CCs for the first time. Open Shows are open to all, not dependent on club membership. Entries are made in advance.

CHAMPIONSHIP SHOWS In the UK these attract large entries with strong competition. Borders are always among the highest entries in the terrier group. Breed club Championship Shows may attract around 250 dogs. Entry fees for all-breed Championship Shows are expensive so it is advisable to show a youngster at smaller shows to gain experience before laying out big entry fees. Entry is open to all. Challenge Certificates are on offer only at Championship Shows. Borders do not have CCs at all Championship Shows. Championship Show judges are either breed specialists or all-round judges who have had long experience of judging the breed at Open Shows before being approved by the KC to award CCs.

TYPES OF SHOWS IN THE USA
Although there are many more Championship shows in the US than in the UK, entries are smaller there except at Specialty Shows.

MATCHES These are shows where Champions are ineligible, organised by Specialty clubs or all-breed clubs, which do not carry Championship points.
ALL BREED CHAMPIONSHIP SHOWS Winners Dog and Winners Bitch gain points which count towards the Champion title. Some shows have 'Supported Entries' which means that a breed club is backing the show with special prizes; the judge may be a specialist, and there will usually be a higher entry.
SPECIALTY SHOWS These are run by a Border breed club and attract a big entry. The National Specialty expects about 250 entries and is a Championship Show held over two days. The judge is either a breed specialist, sometimes from overseas, or a respected multi-breed judge. Sweepstakes Classes, for the younger end of the entry, have a separate judge, thus allowing exhibitors two chances. Winning the Specialty is a highlight of a dog's career.

The American show scene: Kris Blake's Am. Ch. Nettleby Nighthawk (full brother to Ch. Nettleby Mullein), pictured wiuth judge Ronald Irving.

Photo: Ashbey.

CHAMPION QUALIFICATIONS
UK
To become a Champion a dog must win three CCs from three different judges, the third of which must be won after the dog is a year old. No working qualification is needed. The CC is awarded to Best of Sex at a Championship Show if the judge considers that the exhibit is 'of such outstanding quality as to be worthy of the title of Champion'. This is a quality award, not an automatic award. It is rare but not unknown for the CC to be withheld in Borders. The Reserve CC, awarded to the second best exhibit in each sex, also carries the quality statement but does not count towards the Champion title.

There is no special class for Champions, so a CC is won in competition against Champions. There is no limit on the number of CCs which a dog may win but it is not done to enter a dog again under a judge who has awarded the dog a CC, Crufts and breed club Championship Shows excepted. The Junior Warrant is *not* a title but owners of a dog winning twenty-five points in breed classes between the age of twelve and eighteen months may apply to the KC for this. A class win at an Open Show carries one point, a Championship Show three.

EIRE
The Irish Kennel Club governs canine activities in Eire, whereas Northern Ireland falls under the jurisdiction of the English Kennel Club. The Irish Champion title is won on a points system which is dependent upon the number of the breed exhibited at a particular show. Green Stars to a value of forty points must be won, of which four wins must be of five points or more, or two wins of ten points, which special shows, such as the St. Patrick's Day Show, carry. Some shows carry a guaranteed 'Major' irrespective of the number of dogs exhibited.

The dog and bitch awards do not always carry the same amount of points but the BOB winner receives the same number as the opposite sex winner in the case of the latter winning the higher number. No working qualification is needed. The dog must be registered with the Irish Kennel Club to be exhibited in Southern Ireland.

USA
The American Champion title is won on a points system, a total of fifteen points being required, of which two blocks are 'Majors' awarded by different judges. A Major is three, four or five points – five being the maximum awarded at any show. Points are evaluated within areas and are dependent on numbers of dogs competing. These are reviewed yearly. Points are evaluated on the number in the regular classes for each sex at a particular show. Dogs and bitches may therefore be allocated different points at the same show but the Best of Winners would take the higher number of points if the other sex Winner had more. Champions do not compete for points but are entered in the Best of Breed Class, and the Winners Dog and Winners Bitch go forward into this automatically. Additional points *may* be earned by defeating the Champions. A Champion made up or finished since entries closed may transfer to the BOB class. No working qualification is needed for the Champion title in the USA.

FIRST SHOWS FOR THE PUPPY
In the UK and the USA a dog may be shown from six months of age. In other countries there may be baby classes for puppies between three and six months. Find a show not too far away for the first event, so that the puppy is not worn out by too much travelling. A lower grade show is best to start a puppy, rather than the rather overwhelming atmosphere of a Championship Show. Resist the temptation to enter too many classes. A couple is quite enough to start with. Overshowing

youngsters is counter-productive, as they become exhausted, physically and mentally. An adult dog needs a day of rest after a show. A puppy needs several.

ENTERING SHOWS

With the exception of Exemption Shows and a newer type of Open Show, where entries are made at the show, entries close several weeks in advance. All-breed UK Championship Shows close about six weeks in advance, which is difficult in a breed where coats blow and have to be stripped off. In the US, entries close nearly three weeks in advance of a Championship Show. Shows are advertised in the dog press. Schedules may have to be sent for so one must watch the advertisements closely. The schedule gives the classification, judge, and rules for that show.

After completing the entry form, make a note on the front of the schedule as to which dog is entered in which class and whether a catalogue or car-park pass has been ordered. Keep two files for schedules: one for shows to be entered, in the order of entries closing and with the closing date written clearly on the front, and the other for shows entered, in the order of the shows. Since wins have to be taken into account up to a week previous to the entry closing date, there is little point in entering too far ahead of this date. On arrival at the show, check your entry in the catalogue before judging. It is possible to transfer a dog to the appropriate class, as stated in KC rules, in the case of a mistake in the entry, but obviously this must be done before judging.

PREPARATION FOR THE SHOW

The dog's coat should have been prepared as described in the chapter on coat. The dog should be in top condition, well-muscled, not too fat nor too thin. It is a common mistake to try to whittle an oversized dog down by keeping the dog lean. This merely looks worse, making the dog look unbalanced as well as large.

Bathing is not necessary but the dog should be clean. A chalk block rubbed through the coat a couple of days before the show will remove grease and grime. All traces of chalk must be brushed out before the show. Toenails should be short, trimmed about a week before the show in case trimming makes the dog move tenderly. The dog will move better if nails are kept neat.

Items needed for the show are: a well-fitting collar with lead; a light chain with two swivels in it for a benched show or a crate if this is preferred; a small blanket or towel for the dog to lie on; a water bowl; a show lead; a safety-pin or ring number clip; a comb; a brush; some favourite tidbit for the dog in the ring; and the all-important plastic bags to pick up after the dog. A small bottle of home-water for the dog and a towel to dry a wet or muddy dog are also useful. Regular show-goers keep these items packed in a show-bag. At unbenched shows a cage is somewhere secure to leave the dog in the hall or venue. The car may become too hot or be parked too far away from the ring for the dog to be left in it. The show lead should be lightweight, strong enough to give complete control of the dog, and of a colour which complements the dog rather than distracting the eye by being conspicuous.

Be prepared for wet weather and mud. Borders are often judged outside in the pouring rain. Think out your attire and choose a colour to enhance the dog. A handler wearing blue will make a blue and tan appear black and tan. The dog's outline will vanish if the handler wears black when showing a blue and tan, or russet when showing a red. Flowing skirts may billow across a moving dog, obscuring the judge's view and putting the dog off its stride too. Avoid clothes or shoes which restrict your own movement in the ring, or which need constant attention. Take the schedule and passes with you – and don't forget the dog in the excitement. It has been known for an exhibitor to turn up with an empty cage, having left home when half asleep in the wee small hours!

ARRIVAL AT THE SHOW

Arrive at the show in plenty of time. Borders need time to become acclimatised and hate being rushed from pillar to post. To get the best out of them, dogs need time to settle and relax on the bench or in the hall. Take the dog to the ringside well before the class to absorb the sights and sounds around the ring. Avoid entering two dogs in consecutive classes if possible, so that each exhibit has time for this. Some active dogs need walking-in before being exhibited to settle into their stride and to take the tickle out of their toes. Do this well before the class. It is not a safe assumption that the dog will be able to limber-up going round the ring at the start of the class. Some judges do not move the dogs around the ring. Also the dog should only be seen moving at its best when in the ring. Find out where the ring is and whether the ring numbers are on the bench, or will be handed out in the ring, or must be collected from the secretary beforehand. It does the exhibit no good if the handler is flustered and dashing around looking for the ring number when the class is in.

EXHIBITING IN THE RING

The ring number must be clearly displayed on the handler when in the ring. In Britain one may stand in any order, not necessarily in numerical order unless the judge requests it. When collecting the ring number from the steward in the ring, be vigilant that other dogs do not interfere with your dog when everyone is crowded around the steward. Wait until the crowd has thinned out if necessary rather than having your exhibit upset. It is up to the exhibitor to make the most of that expensive few minutes in the ring. Selecting which dog to stand next to is intelligent ring thinking. If you are showing a large dog, avoid standing next to one at the other extreme of size. If showing a badly-coloured black and tan, do not stand next to a well-coloured blue and tan.

Try not to stand the dog facing down a hill, with the weight heaped onto the forehand. If the ring slopes, use it to your advantage. A light-eyed exhibit is better faced away from the light. Strong wind may blow a longish coat the wrong way. In which case, turn the dog around – provided that the wind does not then blow the ears akimbo! Resist fiddling with the dog too much in the ring. Constantly altering the position of a faulty part only draws the judge's, and everyone else's, attention to this. Instead, try to emphasise the virtues. For example, if the dog's rear end is better than the front, position the dog so that the judge sees the rear. A beautiful otter-head turned to look at the judge at just the right moment can sometimes clinch a prize.

Try to relax and keep the dog's attention through talking and through food. When baiting an exhibit, do not allow the head to 'star-gaze' but keep the nose pointing forward, which will arch the neck and keep the backline correct. Give yourself plenty of room to show your dog. If other exhibitors crowd you, either politely ask them for more space, or move to a more suitable position. If your exhibit is upset by either the dog or the handler next to you, move away if possible.

The novice exhibitor, or an exhibitor showing an inexperienced dog, would do well not to be first in line. Allow a few exhibitors to take a position and then tag on to the end of the line. A ringful of dogs is always moved in a counter-clockwise circle so it is not difficult to work out which is the first dog in line. Look to see what the judge wants and comply with any instructions. If the judge alters the position of your dog when set-up, take the hint and leave it like that. The judge may ask the age of your dog, so be prepared for this.

The judge will take a quick look around the class, then maybe move the whole class a couple of times around the ring before examining and moving each dog in turn. There is no need to keep your dog at attention throughout the class. While the judge is busy examining other dogs, either pick yours up or put yourself between your dog and the judge and allow your dog to relax. On a hot day shade the dog with your shadow – this is when I am thankful to have a capacious shadow!

As the judge gets to the last one or two dogs for examination, collect your dog together, tidy any coat if necessary with the comb, and have the dog standing smartly for the judge, who will look again at every exhibit as they stand around the ring. Some dogs may be moved again. If you have practised movement beforehand you will know the best pace for your dog. Moving too fast can cause the legs to whirl and emphasises faults in movement. Moving a dog too slowly for the length of stride may cause the dog to pace, crab or move wide in compensation. It may be necessary to move the dog at a different speed in each direction.

The dog must always be visible to the judge, so do not put yourself between them when moving. The dog should be on the inside of the ring when going around the ring. If your exhibit is placed first or second, the judge will want to write a few notes for the report, so stay in line until the judge tells you to leave. Always congratulate the winner if you are standing second. And praise your dog, win or lose. It is not the dog's fault if the judge preferred others.

Unbeaten exhibits, that is class winners who have not been beaten in another class, will be required on completion of the class judging for each sex to compete for Best of Sex. At a Championship Show a second prize winner may be called in for consideration for the Reserve CC, so do not go away until this has been awarded. The Best Puppy award will be made after the BOB award. The winners of BOB and Best Puppy in breed (if there is that ompetition) will be expected to compete in the Group or Best in Show and Best Puppy in Show competition.

Try to study the winners constructively to see what makes them winners. Faults are easy to see but look for the virtues. By looking dispassionately at good stock, one develops the eye and knowledge to see what needs improving on one's own stock. On the other hand, do not be misled by judges. Try to evaluate your own dog so that you know whether a win was lucky or deserved, whether the dog is worth showing and whether the dog meets your own ideals. Win or lose, the dog you take home is the same dog which you left home with that morning. A win does not improve a dog, nor a low placing make a good one into a bad one.

WORKING TERRIER SHOWS

Throughout the summer months a series of Working Terrier Shows, or Hunt Terrier Shows, are held up and down the British Isles. On any given weekend most people will have such a show within reasonable distance. These shows have a good following by Border folk. One of the attractions is that they are much cheaper to enter than shows held under KC rules. Terriers need not be KC registered to compete. Entries are made on the day, often as one goes into the class. Sometimes there is good prize money on offer. A good day out can be enjoyed by all the family as Working Terrier Shows are usually held in conjunction with some event such as an open day at the hunt kennels or a country fair, with plenty of other things to see and do. They are advertised in the sporting press and sometimes, but not always, in the local papers.

No provisions are made for the dogs except a roped-off ring for judging, so owners should take something to contain the terriers or to tether them to, and also make provision for shade for them. There may be one judge or two, people reputed to know a working terrier. While they do not judge to the Breed Standard as such, the end result should be much the same because that was drawn up to describe an ideal working Border. Particular attention will be paid to narrowness, correct size, good depth of coat, neat feet with deep pads and large teeth in a strong jaw. Spannability and coming up balanced in the hand are important to people used to working terriers.

Several classes will be scheduled for Borders which might include 'Border types' as well. Pedigree is not important here. The other types of working terriers will have a similar classification. A 'Champion' will be declared in each breed which will compete in a 'Champions Class' at the end for an overall 'Champion' equivalent to BIS. At the end of the show season,

ABOVE: At a Working Terrier Show the dog is examined on the ground.

RIGHT: Spanning and balancing are very important.

'Champions', from all the fifty shows which qualify, compete in a final for The National Working Terrier Championship, run by the British Field Sports Society. There are also other prestigious finals for which certain shows will have qualified winners throughout the season.

Less emphasis is laid on movement at this type of show than in the KC ring. The class may be moved around the ring a couple of times and each dog given a short walk after individual examination. Each terrier will be stood before the judge or judges, in turn, maybe on a plank board or on concrete slabs. The dog will be expected to stand itself, not be set up or supported, and never on a table. Some judges handle the exhibits very little, apart from checking the mouth and feeling the muscle over the loin. Much of the judging is done by eye. Judging can be confusing to watch as there is sometimes a marked lack of consistency in method, with the winners being placed from left to right in one class and the other way round in the next. Everything about the show is taken at a more relaxed and slower pace than at shows held under KC rules. Even the dogs are moved at a much slower walk.

Following the serious judging, terrier racing often takes place. This is a splendid entertainment, enjoyed by both the dogs and the onlookers – who usually have a pint in hand! The beer tent is always a feature of Working Terrier Shows. Races are run in heats of six. The terriers are started from traps, although sometimes hand-slipped, and pursue a lure of some sort or other, usually a fox's brush. The contestants shriek when this is waved in front of them. So do the terriers awaiting their turn. Once released, the terriers fly up the field at an amazing speed to yells of encouragement both from the human and canine spectators. Whoever is operating the lure has to work flat out to ensure that this disappears behind some straw bales before the tykes catch it and worry it.

In the feverpitch of excitement that this sport stimulates, fights are not unknown, so it is inadvisable to enter your budding Champion if you mind about an unblemished complexion. It would also be inadvisable to enter a known fighter in a terrier race. Terrier racing over hurdles is catching on in some areas and provides good spectator sport.

Terrier racing:
A sport
enjoyed by
dogs and
spectators
alike.

THE AMERICAN WORKING TERRIER ASSOCIATION

The American Working Terrier Association (AWTA) was founded in 1971 by Patricia Lent with a view to encouraging Terriers and Dachshunds of correct size and ability to work, and promoting their use for earthwork, vermin control and upland game shooting. It started Artificial den trials in 1972. At these, a Certificate of Gameness (CG) is offered to terriers who locate and negotiate a thirty foot long tunnel with three turns and attack or mark two laboratory rats in a well-reinforced wire cage (wild quarry is not permissible). Borders are among the top three breeds in success rate here. The AWTA also offers two titles for hunting natural quarry. The Working Certificate (WC) is for a terrier who goes to ground and bolts, bays, or draws the quarry. This has to be witnessed and is the most natural form of terrier work available. The Hunting Certificate (HC) is for a terrier used regularly for hunting above ground, for such things as finding birds for the gun, killing rats in the barn, or hunting rabbits for gun or falcon.

In 1994 the AKC introduced their Earthdog Tests for Terriers and Dachshunds. These are run at four levels – Introduction to Quarry, with no title earned, Junior Earthdog (JE), Senior Earthdog (SE) and Master Earthdog (ME). The artificial earth is similar to that for the AWTA tests, thirty foot long, nine inches square and buried in the ground. For JE, the terrier must get to the rats in a limited time and try to get at them by barking or digging, which is called 'work'. Success at this level on two occasions enables the dog to progress to the next level.

For SE the dog must qualify three times. The tunnel has a scented side chamber and a second, unscented, entrance. The dog finds the main entrance by scent and has ninety seconds to find the quarry. After 'working' the quarry, this is removed, simulating a bolt, and the handler has ninety seconds in which to get hold of the dog at the earth entrance. For ME the dog must qualify four times. In this test there is a nearby unscented den to distract the dogs. The main tunnel contains two obstacles, one of which narrows the tunnel and the other is a loose object, to test the dog's flexibility and determination. The entrances are partially blocked and two terriers walk off-lead to locate them. One dog is then allowed in, while the other is staked nearby and then the situation is reversed. While the terrier is 'working' it will hear thumping, simulating digging. The dog is eventually removed through a door in the quarry area. Borders are the most successful breed in these AKC tests and claimed the first SE and the first ME titles issued.

Chapter Eight

JUDGING THE BORDER TERRIER

THE ASPIRING JUDGE

There may well come a time when you are invited to judge. However, it takes many years to consolidate your own ideas on the breed, which comes through owning and campaigning many dogs, and it is better to decline to judge until you have sufficient experience. Then, do not be too ambitious, but start with a few classes at a small show. Both the KC and the AKC publish guidelines to judges which are essential reading for a new judge. Every judge should be familiar with the Breed Standard and understand basic canine anatomy. Learning the Standard by heart is helpful because any part can be recited when the judge is confronted by a problem. By knowing the Standard the judge will recognise a virtue, even though there may be only one dog in the entry with this virtue. Unsure judges might penalise a virtue simply because it is different. Re-read the Standard before every judging appointment. It is surprising what small points come to light, even when one thinks one knows it thoroughly. There is no point in pre-judging a show by wondering what dogs will be there or by forming pre-conceived judgements on them. Judges find that prejudices are thrown aside when actually going over dogs, because judging from the ringside is very different to judging the actual dogs.

ARRIVAL ON THE DAY TO JUDGE

Dress should be neat and practical and comfortable for judging. Ladies should bend in front of a mirror to make sure they are not revealing too much when in a judging position. Gentlemen should wear clothes that do not flap into the dog's face when bending forward, so no open jackets or loose ties. Dangling jewellery and strong perfume should be avoided. Smoking or drinking alcohol in the ring is not appreciated. Feet take a hammering when judging, so wear well-worn-in shoes. Do not forget the wet-weather gear, plus a change of footwear and clothing for when you are soaked.

Allow plenty of time to arrive at the show well before judging so that you are not flustered. Announce your arrival to the secretary who will give you your judging book. Have a look at this over a cup of tea to see how the entry falls. It is helpful to know, in a big entry, just how the entry is spread over the classes so that one can pace one's judging accordingly.

When judging outside the UK a small notebook is useful because there may be no judging book, and in the US it is handed in after judging. British judges feel lost without a judging book. Both judge and exhibitor feel uncomfortable if they meet at the show before judging, but this is bound to happen. Pretending you have never seen each other before is a bit silly. It is quite in order to say "Good morning" but better not to hold any conversation. It goes without saying that a judge does not look at the catalogue before judging.

RING PROCEDURE

Avoid conversation with the exhibitors in the ring. Never address an exhibitor by name; "sir" and "madam" is polite and sounds better than "Joe" or "Debbie". Asking the age of exhibits is permissible in Britain, but not in all countries. Remember that some exhibitors are absolutely petrified, so a pleasant manner from the judge helps to put them at ease – even if the judge is petrified, too! Panic not if you are struck by an attack of butterflies: this will go as soon as you get your hands on the first dog and become engrossed in your task.

Never look up the lead at the exhibitor as the dogs go round the ring. The ringsiders always notice this bad habit. Memorise the dogs by a feature of the dog, rather than by the colour of the handler's clothing or where the dog stands in line. Circumstances change during a class and a judge using such aides-mémoire comes unstuck. Do not rely implicitly on the steward's reliability as to the placings of a dog coming forward from a previous class. Stewards have been known to make mistakes. If in doubt, check the judging book.

Go to the ring about five minutes before judging is due to start, introduce yourself to your stewards, decide where you would like the judging table, where you want the dogs to stand and which way you will move them, dependent on the terrain of the ring. A dog moving down a slope towards the judge reveals a great deal about conformation. Decide where the sun will travel during your time in the ring. Looking into the light can be very tiring and makes it difficult to see the dogs.

Work out your ring procedure and then stick to it for each dog. That way you will not forget to look at a point. On no account be rough with the exhibits. My own method is first to mark the dogs present and absent in the judging book. Then I take a quick look at general balance and expression. I do not generally move the class around the ring at this stage because it tells me little to see dogs running up each other's tails, or looking back over their shoulders or moving at the wrong pace for that dog.

As each dog goes onto the table I look first at the outline and balance from the side, noting how the weight of the dog is carried, then I walk to the front to see the expression and front. Only then do I examine the head in detail, look at the mouth and feel the underjaw. Next I feel the shoulders, check the elbows, legs and feet, run my hands along the rib-cage to feel the depth and how far back the ribs are carried, feel the loin and coupling, and then examine the hindquarters, and also check the quality of bone from hock to foot. I run my hand the full length of the tail and then check the testicles of a male. The coat and pelt are then felt, the dog spanned and picked up and hand-balanced. I never lift the dog off the table.

If there is a point I want to check again, I go back to it while the dog is on the table, sometimes to savour something good, sometimes to see why something is incorrect. If a bite has been doubtful on the first glance I will always take a second look, opening and shutting the jaws, as sometimes this apparent fault can merely be caused by the way the dog is clenching the jaws.

I prefer to see a dog moving straight away from and back towards me rather than in triangles. I like to see the dog turning at the end of the ring and to see side movement on a dog when it is moving straight. I go to the side to see this. Some exhibitors are not very good at straight-sided triangles – besides, one cannot see the dog doing a smart about-turn on a triangle. Since these were devised to save time, it seems pointless to move a dog in a triangle and then up and down. Having gone over and moved each dog, I then take a good look at every dog again. I have a pretty good idea which dogs interest me at this stage, but I like another look and a mental assessment of every dog to make sure none is being overlooked. I really do discuss them silently with myself at this stage, what I liked and what I didn't about each one.

In a class where there is a clear-cut result, I then place the winners from left to right, where the

Ready for the judge: Betty Rumsam handling Janet Melly's Ch. Hugo of Hassage. Judge, T.A.G. Knight.

A tough decision: Anne Roslin-Williams weighing up the merits of Kate Seemann's Ch. Am. Ch. Thoraldby Free Guest and Elizabeth Crisp Blake's Am. Ch. Ryswick Remember Me, both being handled to perfection.

ringside can see them if possible. A large class may need reducing by sorting the sheep from the goats, making a cut and keeping in those dogs who have something going for them. Sometimes some are moved again, maybe around the ring all together. Rather than fiddling with two dogs, if a decision is close, I will leave them, mentally sort out another placing, and then come back to look at the problem with fresh eyes. If the problem is still there I ask myself which I would choose for work and which I would be robbing if I did not put it up. This has never failed me yet.

Try not to judge on circumstances but on the sterling worth of the dog. By this I mean: Do not penalise a dog for something the handler has done wrong. Judging is to find the best dog – not the best handler, the most beautiful dog, the best showman, the most obedient dog or the best coat on the day. Some judges try to make line-ups of one type, which can be a disaster if there are a lot of bad dogs of one type and few of the correct type present. Similarly dangerous is trying to judge with a view to the Group judge. This could produce a wrong winner. All that is required is that the dogs are judged according to the Breed Standard. Other thoughts, such as encouraging newcomers, putting down big winners, settling old scores, repaying favours, being kind to children or old ladies, not putting up dogs owned by one's friends or closely connected with you, sharing out the prizes, or putting right past mistakes, are all equally dishonest and unfair. If one exhibitor has a string of dogs all better than anyone else's, this should be rewarded, not penalised by thinking 'that's enough'. In other words, *judge the dogs*.

It is expected that a judge will write a report for the dog press, so make a note on the winners of each class, or on the first and second at Championship or breed club Shows, while they are in front of you. A few abbreviations to recall the dog are usually sufficient. There will be some worthy dogs in the awards who may be more difficult to recall than the outstanding ones or ones with obvious faults. Make detailed notes on these less memorable ones. Remember to write positive notes as well as the faults. When writing the report, try to balance the good with the bad, explaining why A beat B without being destructive in your criticism. A tape recorder is not as reliable as simple written notes. Should it fail, the judge has nothing to help recall the dogs for the report.

When marking the judging book, avoid passing comment to the exhibitors. They are at a disadvantage, not being allowed to argue with the judge. Having completed the judging and signed all the slips, make sure that there are no slips retained in the judging book. Remember to thank the stewards. Don't hang around – some exhibitors will feel sore and disappointed and it is better not to discuss the judging until time has passed, if at all. Never apologise to an exhibitor for not placing a dog higher.

Why judge? A serious breeder needs to assess other people's stock by going over them to realise their virtues and the failings in one's own stock. Only by judging does one get a true picture of other people's stock, and one's own. Judging is a responsibility. A good judge, by rewarding the correct dogs, helps, albeit in a small part, to keep the breed on the right lines. If one does not enjoy either judging or exhibiting, there is no need to do it. People tend to forget that it is not compulsory.

RECORD KEEPING

An exhibitor should keep a record of class wins for each dog in order to calculate eligibility for a class as the dog wins its way out of certain classes. A judge must keep detailed and accurate records of every show judged. Precise information on this is required by the KC, should a judge be invited to award CCs. It is advisable to keep the catalogue as well as the judging book.

Chapter Nine

HAVING FUN WITH YOUR BORDER

Alert by nature, active in build, the Border, with that ready-for-anything attitude coupled with a high degree of intelligence, is an ideal breed with which to participate in activities other than shows, terrier work or terrier racing. Border owners can, and should, have a great deal of fun with their dogs. The more the dog and owner do together, the closer the understanding between them, to the mutual benefit of both.

THE BORDER'S STAMINA

Being a country dog, Borders particularly love country pursuits. They make ideal riding, walking, or running companions, being virtually indefatigable when adult, and they are an ideal size for camping or caravanning, taking up little space for themselves or their all-important food rations.

An example of the breed's stamina was shown at an officially organised and monitored endurance test, undertaken in Holland, by twenty Borders who were trained for fitness beforehand. They accompanied a bike, at a trot, for 20 km over different types of terrain, at a regulated speed, with 'pit-stops' for a rest and water. On completing this, after a short rest, they were put through a simple obedience test to show that they were still *compos mentis*. The judge, who was used to larger working breeds, was a shade sceptical on first sight of these small dogs, but was very impressed when all twenty completed without any difficulty. The lovely remark of a child, who saw the convoy of trotting Borders, is a classic: "Mummy, look, a group of Turbo Terriers!" Some Borders also took part in a Dog Triathlon there – 120 metres swimming with the dog on a lead, 12 km with the dog trotting beside a bike, and 1200 metres running. They acquitted themselves well.

BEATING FOR THE GUN

Apart from the pleasures of a normal country walk, some Borders enjoy beating– flushing out game – for shooting. Their good noses find every bird or bunny. However, this is not what they were bred for and some are gun-shy, some tend to 'peg' the game instead of flushing it, and they may not be able to resist setting off in hot pursuit after it. Also their colour is a definite hazard with trigger-happy guns, particularly in poor winter light. Some have surprisingly tender mouths when retrieving, others cannot resist crunching and shaking the bird or rabbit, presenting it rather more than oven-ready! In some parts of the world, people are starting to shoot deer with the help of Borders. The working partnership of a Border with a sight-hound is efficient, and can provide great sport. The running-dog will course the rabbit or hare while the Border will use brains to cut the prey off as it runs to a hedge or wall. One bitch of mine was adept at pegging a hare in its seat before it ever ran, and another caught several mallard which came up onto the bank of the lake to eat bilberries.

*Viltspar: Int. Nord.
Ch. Bannerdown
Monarch
acknowledging the
line.*

*Photograph courtesy:
Margareta Carlson*

THE TRACKING BORDER

Tracking blood trails, Viltspår, is an important job at which Borders excel in Sweden, where there are a great number of traffic accidents involving elk. Any elk wounded through an accident, or when being hunted, must be tracked and shot. By law, every elk hunter must have at least one trail dog. The dog is always worked on a long line attached to a harness. Borders hunt the trail silently. Training is done through the Viltspår Club. To be put on the official list to be called out by the police, and to receive the Hunting Association badge, the dog must gain first or second prize in the open class at an official test, during which the dog must withstand gunfire and be tested working overnight in the forest. The Swedish Supreme Champion, in 1990, against all breeds in this work, was a Border, Frasse, owned by Inger Björner. The first dog of any breed to become a Norwegian Champion in this field was a Border, Sw. Norw. Ch. Brackenhills Tiffany, who was three times Viltspår Club Champion in Sweden.

In America, there are two kinds of tracking competitions, one run in the country over natural terrain, and a newer one, run over variable surfaces in towns and cities, on pavements, roads, grass and paths. These events are officially recognised by AKC. At them, dogs can earn TD and VST qualifications after their name. To date five Borders have qualified TDX (Tracking Dog Excellent). In the UK there is no official tracking work for Borders, but good fun can be had privately by laying a trail with a scent rag or fresh animal skin, over increasing distances.

THE SPORT OF AGILITY

The elementary training undertaken for the Canine Good Citizen might be taken further with a view to competing in Agility or Obedience work. Agility is a dog sport which has really taken off all over the world. Borders love it, taking part with obvious enthusiasm, sometimes too much so! Mini-Agility is for dogs measuring fifteen inches or under, which includes Borders.

Run over an obstacle course, Agility is completed at speed with the owner running beside the dog, so both must be fit. Mini-Agility jumps are set at fifteen inches maximum height, with a long jump of no more than two foot eight inches, with a nine inch maximum height. There are a variety of obstacles to be negotiated, including an A-Frame (up and down which the dog must walk, making foot contact at the points marked at the base of each side), a hoop, weaving poles, a see-saw, a raised narrow 'dog-walk' plank, a tube tunnel, a collapsible tunnel and a table onto which

Sw. Agility Ch. Rabalder Hit-och-Dit: Both dog and handler must be fit to compete in Agility.

Photo courtesy: Anna-Karin Bergh.

the dog must jump and lie for the count of ten. In any form of competitive work with the breed, it is no good taking it too seriously. From time to time, the Border will play the gallery, thinking up something awkward or amusing to do to demonstrate independence of spirit. Loss of concentration seems to be a breed failing and if something more interesting appears, such as a person eating a hamburger by the ringside, or the dog in the next ring looking as if some company was needed, the Border will 'do its own thing' and join them. One brought the house down by going and sitting stoically under the lady judge's long skirts because an order had not been understood. A sense of humour is definitely needed by the handler.

Agility competitions range from classes for starters upwards, with jumping competitions, classes for pairs, time-fault eliminations and classes for junior handlers. Rosettes are given for clear rounds and for placings. There are no titles in the UK. Borders are doing really well in this sport. Sw. Ch. Rabalder Svengom was Supreme Champion in Sweden. There is one Agility Excellent qualified Border in the USA and the breed is doing great things in Agility in Finland also.

Besides the internationally accepted type of competitive Agility run by the United States Agility Association, where the titles Agility Dog (AD), Advanced Agility Dog (AAD) and Master Agility Dog (MAD) may be earned, a rather less competitive form of Agility was started. This was designed to be easily portable, set up in smaller ring spaces, with less formidable obstacles and a slower time. This lower-key type is run by the National Club for Dog Agility in the US.

Fly-ball, an off-shoot of Agility, is becoming increasingly popular. The dog negotiates a series of hurdles to a reach a box, releases a ball, catches it, and then returns to the handler – all at top speed – as this is a team relay game. Training for Agility, Obedience and Flyball should be done through a local club. Both Agility and Flyball are entertaining spectator sports.

OBEDIENCE

Obedience is more serious. The Border can perform well in Obedience but will be unlikely to have the smart, immediate response to an order and the finish of some other breeds. The exercises, which include Heelwork (on and off the lead), Stays, Recalls, Retrieves, Scent discrimination and response to hand signals become increasingly difficult as the dog progresses. There are several stages of competition, ranging from pretty elementary ones at Exemption Shows, through to Test C at Championship Shows, where CCs may be won. It can be done with Borders. There have been

*ABOVE: Am. Ch. Luvemur's First Edition UD, TD,
owned by John and Laurale Stern.*

RIGHT: A smart retrieve.
                        Photo courtesy: Anna-Karin Bergh.

three Obedience Champions in America, one in Finland and several in Sweden. Working trials include a greater variety of tests. The lowest class is CD, which comprises three sections: obedience, agility and nosework. The agility course for Borders comprises a four-foot scale, a two-foot clear jump and a six-foot long jump. To qualify for entry into a Championship Trial, a dog must win an overall average of 80% and no less than 70% in all sections. In the Championship stake, the CD award is made to those obtaining 70% or more in each group, and the CDEx to those with 80% or more. This can be done. Betty Orin's Foxwyn Northern Lass CDEx proved it.

The Utility Dog Stake is as far as it is possible to work a Border in the UK, because Working Dog (WD) and Tracking Dog (TD) stakes involve jumps not graded for small dogs. The extra requirements for UD are steadiness to gunshot plus tracking. Jumps are the same size as in the CD, and awards made in the same way.

In America there are four Obedience awards: Novice (CD) involving on and off-lead heeling, off-lead recall, in-sight group sits and group downs; Open (CDX) adds retrieves, a broad (long) jump, a drop to the recall and out-of-sight group sits and group downs; Utility (UD) does hand-signal heeling, scent articles, glove retrieve, moving stand and directed jumping. Three qualifying scores of 170 out of a possible 200 under three different judges are required for the UD award. There is also a UDX award. Up to the end of June 1995 Borders in America earned 338 CDs, 108 CDXs and 34 UDs. The American OTCh. (Obedience Trial Championship) is earned beyond UD. The title requires high scores and 1st or 2nd place scores at Open and Utility levels, in competition against all breeds. Near-perfect scores and several years of experience are required to achieve this. The three Borders which have done so to date are OTCh. Pete UD with Floyd Timmins, OTCh. Ketka's Fine O'Pinyon UD with Anne Galbraith, and OTCh. Woodlawn's Cheery Woody UD with Richard Gilman. In 1995 Cotswold Wutizzi Babas UDTX earned a unique position, having earned CD, CDX and UD obedience qualifications and TD and TDX tracking qualifications, the first Border to achieve this in the USA.

The art of showing: Daniel Alpe taking part in a Junior Handling competition.

JUNIOR HANDLING

This is something for young Border enthusiasts to enjoy either with their own dog, or one which they borrow on a regular basis to brush up the art. Not all Borders are ideal for this. Some are so dour that they will give little extra to their handler. Others are most obliging and do really well. Borders feature regularly in the top awards at the JHA competition in the UK. The Kennel Club Junior Organisation membership is open to youngsters between the age of eight and eighteen. This encourages interest and activity across a broad spectrum of the dog world, with regionally organised activities. There is plenty on offer for a junior with Border to take part in, including KCJO Stakes Classes, which are judged on breed points rather than handling skills, Agility, and an annual camp for juniors with dogs.

BORDERS HELPING HUMANS

Pets as Therapy (PAT) is another field in which Borders are giving excellent service. PAT dogs visit hospitals and residential homes of all sorts, with their owners, on a regular basis. They brighten many lives through these visits, being welcome visitors to those who love dogs but who are no longer able to own one. Dogs can manage to break through the communication barrier of withdrawn people when human contact has failed. This work is being recognised worldwide and many Borders are involved. To be accepted as a PAT dog in the UK, the dogs must undergo a temperament test to ensure that their characters are outgoing, friendly and reliable, and suitable for the work involved, which is meeting a number of people in a short time and being petted and talked to – and, of course, the odd biscuit is slipped to the welcome visitors!

Working with the deaf is something else at which the breed seems good, although it is still early days, with just a few Borders having been trained so far. Two have successfully 'passed out' of their training as Hearing Dogs for the Deaf in the UK and are now working with their recipients. Trainers have found the breed to be bright, active and fairly easy to train for this. Because of their

Therapy dog:
Hazel Wichman
with Von
Hasselwick
Turtle Dove in
the USA.

high level of activity, Borders are likely to be placed with a similar type of active recipient. Wearing the official yellow jacket of a qualified HDFTD, the dog may accompany the human to places where dogs are normally banned.

Search and Rescue is another serious occupation serving man at which Borders are proving adept. In America, Nancy Hook and Steephollow Megan are members of a Search and Rescue team. S and R dogs search for lost people by air scent, not tracking, in any sort of terrain. Having found the person, they return to the handler, whom they take back to the found person. This is arduous work.

In Sweden the potential of the breed for finding people trapped in ruined houses is being realised. Several Borders work in this field and are ideal, being able to squeeze underground where larger breeds cannot go. Sw. Ch. Kickans Kunniganda works as a Security Service dog and is the first Border to carry the qualifications TJH (BEV). This is the type of work normally done by German Shepherd Dogs, so Kunniganda had dispensation for size. Both these categories of work are officially recognised by the government and the dogs may be called upon in an emergency.

THE COMPANION BORDER

Boating in various forms is enjoyed by many Borders who have a natural, almost cat-like balance. The Goodridge family's Molly learnt to windsurf at six months, quickly gaining her sea-legs on an unrigged board. She was then taken out with the sail up and would happily relax while the board was taken back and forth on the lake. She was always eager to get back onto the board, unlike her sister who tried once, fell in, and could never be persuaded to repeat the experience. Molly also enjoys a gentle sail on the sea, close to the shore, but is not taken far out because it would be too dangerous for her.

There are so many ways of having fun with a Border companion. One of my nicest occupations is gardening with Borders in attendance – my idea of bliss, combining two of my favourite things. And there is nothing like taking a Border out for opening up conversations with strangers who either are attracted by the dog and want to know more or who know the breed already and just have to speak to the dog – and to the owner, of course, but that is out of sheer politeness!

Chapter Ten

THE BORDER'S COAT

The natural-looking coat of the Border does not require trimming, i.e. cutting or clipping, but it will require stripping out by hand twice a year, otherwise the dog will look shapeless and feel uncomfortable and itchy wearing layers of dead coat. A Border puppy looks smooth and sleek, although the topcoat will feel hard, until about three months of age. Then the puppy coat will stand off in a frizz or halo which can be removed easily by hand, using finger and thumb to pull it off with a sharp tug, a few hairs at a time. Always follow the direction in which the hair grows when pulling any off. There will be a tidy new jacket underneath which will last until the pup is about seven months old, when it will become open and long, technically called blown. When the long hairs start to form a natural parting and fall apart in clumps of hair, the dog is ready for stripping again. Each coat the youngster grows will be harder and coarser than the last, until about the third or fourth jacket, when the true firmness of the adult coat will be felt.

The coat varies in texture at different stages of growth. When newly stripped, the new coat is soft, then hardens as the coat grows in. As the coat goes over, it tends to become softer. The new coat is at its best about eight weeks after stripping. After a further four weeks or so, the coat will start to become full, until it is once more blown.

Texture and colour are definitely linked. Many reds look marvellous when in new coat, but this only lasts a few weeks then, whoosh – it has blown. A coat of this particular colour and texture is nigh on impossible to keep going after that. Some light-coloured reds, and grizzle and tans, have soft coats; conversely some of those colours have excellent coats. Dark grizzle and tans, and blue and tans are, generally speaking, the easiest coats to keep going. Blue and tans are like pick-and-come-again vegetables as their coats can be topped off without any noticeable difference.

A smooth-coated adult is wrong. Smoothness denotes a single coat, a bad fault and untypical of the breed. A smooth coat may be handy to live with, requiring no stripping, but lack of undercoat affords that terrier no protection against cold and wet. The working Border needs a full double jacket. I'll bet the terrier sitting tied to a spade handle on the fell top in a drizzle or blizzard never complains of too much undercoat, something which I have heard modern Border breeders do because the dense undercoat made their youngster difficult to present for show.

HAND-STRIPPING

The very thought of this is a deterrent to some novice owners who feel that hand-stripping must be done by an expert at a grooming parlour. Rather than neglect the coat, it is better to book the Border in twice a year to be hand-stripped. But it is not difficult to learn how to do this relatively simple task, which can save a lot of money and inconvenience. Using finger and thumb undoubtedly produces the best result but some people find it easier to use a penknife or trimming

Ready for stripping.

knife. Any knife used must be blunt, or it will cut the coat instead of pulling it. Avoid trimming knives which incorporate a blade. I use one with a serrated edge, and a new one is run across a stone several times to blunt the edge before use.

Let the coat grow until it is long and parting before stripping, as it will come off much easier then. If the dog has strong hairs which do not part but just need tidying up, count your blessings. Take account of the climate and do not strip the poor dog if the temperature has just plummeted after a heat wave. If the heat wave has arrived and the dog is in full coat, take some off. Sometimes I make the initial inroad into stripping by taking a little off all over, particularly in winter. Even though the dog might look a bit rough for a few days, and I pray no-one comes to visit the kennels during that time, it both breaks the back of the job and acclimatises the dog gradually. A steady table at which one can work comfortably when standing, placed outside because hair billows everywhere, is best, although one can work with the dog on one's lap or with both dog and human on the floor. Don't wear good clothes – they will become interwoven with Border hair.

First, comb the dog thoroughly all over with a fine-toothed comb. Then, starting behind the shoulders, with finger and thumb or knife and thumb, pull a small tuft of hair sharply in the direction in which it lies. If done correctly, the dog will not mind and the hair should come off easily. Continue down the spine until there is a broad strip plucked as far as the root of the tail. This strip should consist of soft, furry undercoat of a different colour to the top-coat. This undercoat should be left in, not stripped out.

By taking the tail down gradually, a third at a time, starting from the thick end, the pleasing thick carroty effect is retained. Doing the whole tail at one session, as a professional stripper must do, leaves a rat-tail. There is no need to have a rat-tail except when a bitch has a full moult after having her litter. To tidy the long, straggly hairs under the tail, part them underneath the tail so that they fall to left and right of it. Pick out those which extend beyond the full width of the tail. The long twist of hairs on the tip of the tail can be picked out, one at a time, using fingernails. This is easy if the swirl of the tail is straightened out between two fingers. The tail should taper, finishing in a thick point. Cutting across with scissors gives an incorrect blunt finish.

It is easier to pluck the sides if the dog is trained to lie first on one side and then the other.

The coat is easier to strip when it is rubbed up the wrong way.

Pull a small tuft in the direction in which the coat grows.

Use a blunt stripping knife to pull the coat in the direction in which it grows.

It is easier to work on the body when the dog is lying down. If the head is held flat, the dog cannot move.

Follow the direction of the swirls when pulling the trouser hair.

Hygienically trimming the hair around the rectum.

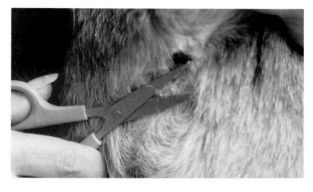

Part the hair underneath the tail and pull out the long tufts on either side of it.

Gradually strip the tail starting from the root. In this way, the tail need never be reduced to a thin whip.

Taking the long hair off the skull.

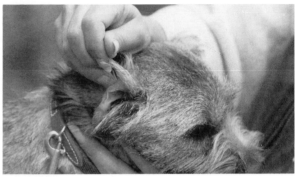

Long hair should be removed from the inside of the ear.

When the long hair is removed, it allows the air to circulate.

Tidying the hair around the head and ears results in a keener expression.

Removing the long whiskers also helps to improve the expression.

The finished head: The skull shape is clearly visible and there are enough whiskers to give the correct expression.

After stripping, run the stripping knife through the coat to remove loose undercoat.

Trim the hair of the foot upwards.

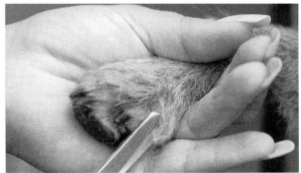

Remove the long hair on the back of the pastern with the stripping knife or with finger and thumb.

Trim the heel upwards.

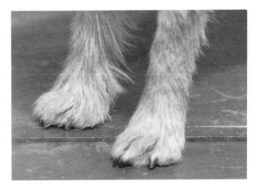

One foot tidy, the other requires attention.

The finished result showing the shape and lines of the dog.

Otherwise, one has to sit or crouch to be lower than the standing dog in order to get at an angle to see what one is doing. Similarly, it is helpful if the dog will lie on its back while the chest, lower ribcage, tummy and inside the thighs are done. A dog who struggles to get up cannot do so if the head is held down flat to the surface. Not having anyone to help me, I adopt a three-handed hold by keeping the head down with one hand while holding the hindlegs with my elbow, which leaves me a hand to work with.

The tummy and inside of the hindlegs and inside the elbows are sensitive areas to strip because the skin is looser there and the hair tends to be softer. By holding the skin taut of the area on which one is working, one can pull against it without hurting. Some dogs just cannot bear this area being pulled; it is kinder to cut the hair. The skin on older animals, like humans, becomes flabbier and looser with increasing years. On my oldies, and those which are extra sensitive about their tummies, I use thinning scissors which do not leave obvious cut marks on the hair. Straggly hair on the male's sheath and the hair in front of it, which may be sprayed with urine, are unhygienic and smell musty, so should be kept short, as should any trailing hairs on the bitch's vulva. The area around and below the rectum should also be kept stripped or cut short for hygiene.

The hindquarters are done from the rear, usually with the dog standing up. My dogs learn to oblige patiently from an early age but, when doing those for other people, whose dogs have been unwilling participants in the stripping game, I have found that a short lead with collar attached to a hook or handle above, will hold the front of the dog just as well as another person. Obviously the dog is never left unattended when thus tethered, as a leap off the table could be fatal. When stripping, keep following the intricate whirls on the hindlegs, neck and chest. The hair will come off easily if pulled in the right direction, that in which it grows. Hair on the lower part of the trousers, the elbows and the chest may not yield, in which case leave it to grow for another week or so. The long hair up the back of the hindlegs should be pulled off gradually. Cutting leaves very harsh lines and, next time around, the dog will grow curly pantaloons.

Fringes on the back of the front legs have to be picked out, a few hairs at a time. The point of the elbow is hard to do, growing very thick hair, but this will come away if worked at patiently. Cutting looks terrible. Surplus hair around the feet is easily removed but that on top of the foot should be just reduced. If the foot is denuded on top it will look flat. A purist would pick off hair around the foot to shape it. However, with a sharp pair of scissors, the size for cutting a bandage, this can be shaped with upward cuts, a little at a time.

The head I tend to keep tidy always by pulling off odd hairs as I talk to the dog. Skulls are kept clean because I love to see this beautiful feature of the breed. A silky topknot must be pulled gently, a little at a time. Being fluffy, this hair is difficult to remove. There is usually no undercoat beneath, just pink skin. Cutting makes the topknot worse. The Border's military whiskers are very attractive but need keeping within bounds on some dogs. Spikes of hair sticking up in front of the eyes can grow into the eye and cause irritation, so they should be taken out regularly. Long hair on the outside of the ears is usually removed between two fingernails. The thick growth of hair under the earflaps, on the cheeks, can be finger-and-thumbed away, paying particular attention that the actual ear opening is free from hair. This is gently picked out. Never use any cosmetic hair-remover on this or any other part of the dog.

Rubbing the hair the wrong way so that it sticks out enables one to make a thorough job when stripping or working on any specific area. A chalk block rubbed through the coat prior to stripping makes the hair easier to grip. About a fortnight after stripping, the dog must be gone over again, picking out any hairs which may have been missed previously. Rubbing the hair up the wrong way helps one to spot them.

After stripping, run a blunt serrated knife through the coat, in the direction it grows, which will bring out any loose undercoat. Repeat this from time to time until the new top coat is growing through and there are no ridges of undercoat sticking up, then leave well alone. Brushing stimulates coat growth. The brush is hardly ever used on my Borders unless I am trying to encourage a coat to grow. I comb them instead of brushing them in the normal course of grooming.

Most Borders appreciate being stripped and indicate how good they feel afterwards, without that heavy, hot coat, by belting around with unmistakable glee. While stripping my Borders I talk to them throughout, apologising and making a joke of it if I make a mistake, giving them breaks to run around and relax during the long process and generally trying to make it pleasant for them. It can't be too awful because there is usually a queue at my feet saying "me next, please". My regular show-goers, who are attended to weekly, show or no show, know that the feet are trimmed last. "One-two-three-four" and off they leap. Too bad if I want another look or a tweak.

THE GROOMING SHOP

If your Border is to be trimmed by another person, establish what this entails beforehand. Very few people do a complete hand-strip nowadays but strip with a sharp knife, which cuts the hair, and finish the difficult parts with scissors. Some are skilful indeed and the initial effect is pleasing but the longterm effect is not so pleasing when the coat starts to grow. Cutting alters the texture and, eventually, the colour of the coat, which will become softer and crinkly, then curly, and lighter in colour. Many Borders are clipped with electric clippers at grooming parlours, which is preferred by some owners. This keeps them tidy, done frequently, but the effect is smooth and the coat becomes woolly or silky and eventually has almost white hair. Whatever the method, make sure the operator has done a Border before. I once had friends call in, nearly in tears, with their nice Border who had been stripped and was returned to them looking like a cross between an Irish Terrier and a Miniature Schnauzer. It took months of regular visits to me to restore her to resemble her previous self, and a full year before she looked right again.

STRIPPING FOR SHOW

It is no good attacking a Border's coat the day before a show and expecting it to look the part. When done by experts, show preparation is a gradual process, planned stage by stage, culminating in a perfectly finished animal. The aim is a fit animal, wearing a uniform all-over jacket with a good depth of undercoat and a close-fitting, harsh, tweedy top-coat which looks natural, while showing off the lines, shape and good points of an individual dog to best advantage. Good feeding and proper exercise result in a fit dog whose general well-being is reflected in a good coat. Good coats are fed from inside the animal.

First, decide which shows you aim to have the dog looking 'spot on' for. If these fall at a time when the dog is bound to be blown in coat, or short of coat after a litter, this may be physically impossible. Normally a bitch will look superb from about twelve weeks after her litter. Count the weeks backwards from the first of the selected shows and plan to strip the coat eight or nine weeks before the show. Once the dog is back in coat, the coat should last for four to six weeks before starting to lift prior to blowing. In winter it will take longer for a coat to grow back. In the days when Crufts was held in early February, we in the cold north of England knew that, unless the jacket was removed by the first week in November, we had no hope of it being back for Crufts. Trying artificially to force a coat to grow, through the use of lamps and jackets, does not work. A covering of hair may result but never of correct texture or depth, and the future cycle of coat growth is confused. Having decided when to strip the jacket off the body, decide the order of stripping of the other parts: the tail, the legs, the feet, the neck, the shoulders, the hindquarters, the head. Think what effect is needed. A lighter-boned dog will be enhanced by heavier leg-hair, while a heavy-boned dog will look better with less hair on the legs. Prior to the body, I tend to strip the legs, fore and aft, right down in order to have a good growth of hair on which to work. The same applies to the feet, but I just pick off the hair on the top of the foot: denuded knuckles tend to make the foot appear spoon-shaped and flat. Constant cutting alters the coat so I try to grow the feet right out and pick off old cut hair around the toes. Actual trimming of the foot I leave until the day before the show. I do them before every show.

If the tail is started upon in advance of the body, there will be a good thick tail to complement the new coat. So often one sees a Border in lovely coat whose tail will not be right until after the coat has blown. To present a shapely neck and shoulders, these are left a week or so after the body to be taken down. Look carefully at the head before removing any hair. Optical illusions are caused by too much hair in the wrong place, whereas hair left on can be used to disguise weakness in the head. Should the whiskers become wild and straggly and too long, remove the longer ones with finger and thumb about a fortnight before the show. This gives the natural look time to re-establish itself.

The expression of a Border requires some eyebrows left on. If taken back too harshly above the eye the expression is untypical. Long Mandarin moustaches can create a down-faced appearance. Too much hair on the eyebrows, coupled with long spikes in front of the eyes, can give a false impression of a deep stop. Too much cheek-hair can make a bully head. Long hair on top of the skull can create the appearance of an apple skull. Take the hair off the skull as far back as the occiput to emphasise the otteriness of the skull; this will also start the neckline at a pleasing angle. Hair at the back of the underjaw should be removed, thus emphasising the strength of the underjaw, not making it appear chinless and weak, while making the head appear ottery rather than deep through and also enhancing the neck. Ear carriage can adversely be affected by tufts of hair on the back of the cheeks or inside of the ear. Sore and itchy ears also affect ear carriage. The fine fringes of hair around the edge of the ear are easily picked off between two finger nails making the ear appear smaller.

FINAL PREPARATION FOR SHOW

The final preparation is given to the coat a day or two before the show on the eight weeks growth of, we hope, superb coat. Study the dog, both set up and on the move, to see what parts can be improved. Every dog requires slightly different preparation to enhance the virtues and to try to detract the eye from the faults. Maybe the neckline could run into the withers better? Does the neck look short? Is there a lump of hair on the rump causing the dog to appear to run up behind and the tail-set be low? Can the hair on the shoulders be thinned down to advantage? Is the layback of shoulder lost by lumps of hair?

By carefully picking at hairs, these details can be corrected. Similarly faults, such as not very straight front legs, or too straight hindlegs, can be disguised a little by judiciously leaving certain hairs and removing others. This will not fool a good judge but at least the dog is presented as well as possible. Borders can be made to look leggy or dumpy through hair being either removed or left on. Unfortunately the sequence of judges with a preference for leggy or dumpy does not always follow a convenient order. It is easy to make a Border look tall by removing hair but this cannot be put back to suit the next judge!

Having finished the preparation, including trimming the feet and taking the long hairs off the tail tip, watch the dog in action. Uneven swirls on the trousers, or hair on the inside of the hocks giving the appearance of being cow-hocked, can be rectified. After each show prepare immediately for the next by taking hair off here and there. Maybe some needs to come off the ribs or legs. Do this well in advance so that the alterations blend in, thus keeping the coat going longer than if nothing is done to it. Neglect this tweaking and pruning for more than a few days and the shape is lost until the next time round.

When trying to keep a dog in the ring we all try to keep a coat going when it is past its best. Whether to take it off and start again or try and keep it going a little longer is a familiar quandary to most of us. How many times do we get home from a show and remove the coat, only to find the dog looking much nicer than at the show? Sometimes the new coat underneath the top-coat is visible. Other times, taking the coat off is a complete gamble. There may be a nice surprise awaiting or just an undercoat. Short cuts in coat preparation using clippers, razors and sharp knives are not recommended unless it is an 'all-or-nothing' job and the dog is required to look immaculate just once. The after-effects are horrific, requiring months of picking out each cut hair by hand.

ROLLING A COAT

This describes bringing a new coat through the old one so that the terrier is never out of coat, which can be done successfully with Borders of certain colours and good coat texture. I managed to do this with Pearl-Diver, a rich grizzle and tan, for eighteen months. He did not always look perfect to my eyes but was presentable enough to keep him in the ring. The coat needs regular attention, conscientiously picking out the longer hairs all over at least twice a week. This enables the new coat to come through the top coat. If done unevenly, lumps and bumps result which leave holes in the coat when removed. Any mistakes show more on light-coloured coats so it is easier to roll a darker-coloured coat.

BATHING

Borders are not normally bathed before a show as this softens the coat. Sometimes the little treasures roll in delightfully disgusting substances, in which case a bath may be unavoidable. In hot, dusty weather a bath can remove some of the dust lying on the skin, causing itchiness. Try not to bath a Border less than a week before a show, to give the coat a chance to settle down again. Coats may become grubby, being slightly greasy. As I have mentioned in the chapter on Showing, a chalk block rubbed through the coat the wrong way will dry-clean the coat quite well. Brush all the chalk out with a stiff brush and the dirt will come off too. All trace of chalk must be removed before a show. Spirit on a cloth will clean the coat beautifully.

GREASY COATS

Some Borders are prone to very greasy coats, particularly in winter. These are usually kennel dogs, which fuels the theory that this condition might be caused by coldness. The grease sticks the undercoat together and the coat looks tatty and spikey. The first remedy is to try and treat the cause by making the dog warmer and by increasing the diet. Bathing with a medicated dog shampoo can help but I still maintain that cleaning the skin with a solution of three parts surgical spirit to one part Dettol on a cloth, every few days, is the best treatment.

POVERTY COAT

An adult who has had a serious illness, or a puppy who has had a major set-back, may grow a very thin and poor coat which is termed a poverty coat. This will not improve until it has grown out and a new coat has been grown.

SOFT COATS

Constant stripping may improve a soft coat slightly, which will probably grow in a little harsher each time, but nothing beats breeding for and selecting for the correct coat. A soft coat is a nuisance as well as being incorrect. It is difficult to present for show.

OVER-PRESENTATION

Sad to say, the majority of Borders shown are over-presented with smooth outlines, devoid of the tweedy, workmanlike look. Straight scissor lines are to be seen up the trousers and under the tummies and tails are chopped around unskilfully. The Border shown in what used to be considered the correct show jacket is now penalised for being over the top, in need of stripping. The breed is fast losing the natural look. A few connoisseurs still try to present their dogs properly. When a dog is never seen in full coat but constantly being honed down to the undies, it is difficult to assess the true coat from a breeding point of view.

The weekend before writing this I watched a class at a Championship show, where the majority of exhibits were shown freshly stripped. In the old days these would have been left at home until they were back in coat. It pleased me that the winner was shown in full coat, a proper tweedy job, yet the lines of the dog could clearly be seen. Full marks to both exhibitor and judge. Obviously with Borders in their country of origin being over-presented this has been emulated and taken further in other countries. The slick presentation of the breed is anathema to those who appreciate the Border as a workmanlike terrier. Judges could be equally impressed by the same good dogs properly presented.

COLOUR INHERITANCE

The various colours of the breed are described in the chapter on the Breed Standard. Genetically, the colour of Borders falls into the agouti category. The inheritance of colour in the breed is very complicated for the layman to understand. The basic rule which breeders do need to know is that blue and tan is recessive, so two blue and tans mated together can only produce blue and tans. Mating blue and tan to blue and tan for generations loses the silver from the coat, resulting in black and tans. Blue and tans are erroneously referred to as being ticked. Ticking is clusters of light hairs in a dark coat, or dark hairs in a light coat, or on the skin. The blue and tan Border has banded hairs and it is the silver in the banding that causes the blue colour, not ticking.

Bright reds with black masks were common when I started showing, forty years ago. Now they are seldom seen. The true wheaten appears to have been lost. I saw two wheatens in my very early showing days. Some years ago I was the guest of Marius and Erica Bons in Holland and there were two apparently wheaten puppies playing outside my bedroom window when I looked out at the view – an exciting view indeed! They were light gold. However, a few years later, when judging an assessment, I was asked by the owner of a rather washy-coloured grizzle and tan whether this was a wheaten, to which I gave a definite negative answer. This was one of those 'wheaten' puppies.

The liver-nosed Border is rare now. Steve and Carol Dean's Working Certificate holder Strider the Rockranger, born 1984, was the last Border I saw with a liver nose. Taking the registered colour of a Border as a scientific fact is not safe. It is difficult to assess the colour of a young puppy. For instance, my Ch. Leatty Juliet of Law was registered as a wheaten, but she was grizzle and tan. Similar inaccuracies are confusing for would-be geneticists.

Chapter Eleven

PLANNING A LITTER

Every litter born should have been carefully planned. This means considering whether the litter is necessary, how and where the puppies will be accommodated at the various stages, who will be there to whelp the bitch and to look after the puppies – which will require a great deal of time and attention – how homes are to be found for them and, having established all of that, the best sire to use.

WHY BREED?

The first consideration must be whether the bitch is good enough to breed from. She must have a correct mouth, a good temperament, be sound in construction and without any major fault. The aim of breeding should be to produce better Borders, suitable for whatever purpose the breeder uses them for. To breed from a mediocre bitch is non-progressive; she is likely to reproduce her mediocrity. There are more than enough Borders being bred, so why not buy a puppy from a good bitch instead of going to all the trouble, expense and nuisance value which breeding entails? The idea that it is good for a bitch to be bred from is rubbish. Do not be misled into having a litter for the good of her health. Another myth is that breeding a litter is easy money. Borders often have small litters, maybe only one puppy. Caesarean sections are not unknown. It is possible that the only products of one's efforts are a huge vet's bill, no live puppies, a great deal of anxiety and, at the worst, the bitch might die. Rearing a litter is costly. Puppies must have good-quality food. They are only as good as the way they are reared. However, if you really feel that you want to breed a litter and can accept the possible risk to your bitch, the probable stress to yourself and the demands that a litter will put upon both your time and your purse, then go ahead. It is important that both parents of the litter are registered at the Kennel Club or the resultant litter will not be eligible for registration and will be difficult to sell, as they can never be of any use to the breed in the future, however well they may turn out.

WHEN TO BREED FROM THE BITCH

The ideal age to breed a first litter is between eighteen months and two years of age. No Border should be bred from at her first season. She will not be fully mature then. It is preferable not to take a first litter much after two and a half years of age, as this could invite whelping problems. The Kennel Club will not normally register puppies born to a bitch after the age of eight years, or after she has bred six litters.

The best puppies tend to be produced by bitches at the start of their breeding careers. Six litters is a lot for one bitch to produce. My own bitches produce a maximum of two litters each, usually just one if this has produced a satisfactory successor to the dam. Plan your life around the litter

Ch. Loiriston Amber, owned by Peter and Maureen Thompson, bred by Ron and Fiona Wheatley. Amber, a Group winner, exemplifies the wisdom of breeding from a top-class bitch who is correctly constructed. She is the dam of six British Champions, one American and one International Champion.

before mating the bitch. A pregnant or nursing bitch cannot be dumped in boarding kennels to fit in with holidays or family commitments. The vista ahead is nine weeks of pregnancy, eight weeks of constant attention and endless meals to the litter, then another four weeks at least of frequent little meals should a puppy be kept.

PLANNING THE LOGISTICS OF THE LITTER

Before the bitch is mated, mentally rehearse the phases of rearing the litter. The whelping quarters should be in a quiet place, away from other dogs and the comings and goings of the family. It is more convenient if this can be a quiet corner of the house. For years I used to struggle out through the night, in all weathers, to the whelping kennel. Now all whelpings are in the house – much more comfortable for me and I can monitor what is going on the whole time.

The whelping box should be solid in construction as the bitch may push and lean against the sides and it would be disastrous if she tipped the box over. I use a wooden box of a size in which the bitch can lie out flat with sides high enough to keep out draughts. Underneath this are slats to raise it off the floor slightly. The front is lower than the sides. When the puppies become in danger of falling out, I screw an extra piece of wood across the front to contain them until they are old enough to be able to get back in. A hinged front which lets down as a ramp is useful. Inside the box is a wooden strip, nailed about three inches from the base, which prevents the bitch from squashing any puppy inadvertently. My open-topped box is placed where I can suspend an infra-red lamp above it. If there is no overhead lamp, a box with a lid retains the heat. The litter stays here for about three weeks. As they become mobile I place a puppy play-pen around the whole area to prevent them wandering off into corners. The next move is into a more spacious outbuilding, still with the infra-red lamp for heat. The dam is still with them but has a high-sided box to jump into to escape from them, or a bench to lie up on out of their reach. This building opens into a secure yard and on fine days the door is left propped ajar so that the puppies can wander out and explore. A mown grass run, containing a small open hut for shelter and with boards to sit on, is the next stage. Puppies stay there all day in fine weather. It is essential that growing puppies have plenty of room to run about and play and explore.

CHOICE OF SIRE

With the thought in mind of breeding from a bitch, one looks at every male with new interest – is he the answer to my prayers? The more knowledgeable you become, the more difficult it is to find mates for your bitches. The novice tends to choose a dog on personal fancy, which is no bad thing. The educated eye sees faults which the novice may not. Also, with time in the breed, one knows too much about the ancestors of the chosen dog; these can be remembered instead of just being names on a pedigree.

First, take a good long look at your bitch, the prospective bride. Try to weigh up dispassionately what are her positive virtues, her main faults and her lesser failings. Then look around to find a dog who complements her virtues and can improve maybe upon some fault by excelling in that department himself. Study the dog as often as possible to see what his temperament is like. If he displays any sign of the wrong temperament, forget him and look for another dog. Mating together two wrongs will not produce a right – that is, mating an extra long cast bitch to a very short-backed dog will not necessarily produce a puppy of medium length.

Forget about where the dog lives. It is difficult enough to find the right mate without limiting the choice by geographical boundaries. Be prepared to get the bitch to the best available dog rather than to a less suitable one in a more convenient place.

Having made a short list of several possible suitors, write out or ask their owners for a copy of their pedigree. Compare this with that of your bitch. If this means nothing to you, take both pedigrees and ask the advice of the breeder of your bitch, or of other breeders with stock of similar

Sw. Ch. Dandyhow Grenadier, bred by Bertha Sullivan and later owned by Mona Hedman in Sweden. This dog's Champion descendants are legion throughout Britain, Europe, Scandinavia and also across America, chiefly through his sons, the litter brothers Ch. Int. Ch. Duttonlea Suntan of Dandyhow and Am. Ch. Duttonlea Autocrat of Dandyhow.
Photo: Maud M.

Ch. Dandyhow April Fool, owned by Dave and Trak Fryer, bred by Bertha Sullivan: An influential sire.

breeding. They will know whether the prospective parents are too closely related, or not related enough, to merit combining the two pedigrees. The general public likes every name in the pedigree to be different. Breeders like to be able to see a recognisable pattern in breeding, not just a hotch-potch of names and affixes.

The temptation may be to use the dog of the moment, the latest Champion. He may be totally unsuitable, a flash in the pan who will be forgotten in a few years. Far better either to ask the breeder of your bitch for advice, and be prepared to follow this, or to study what patterns of breeding are producing nice stock from bitches of a similar background of pedigree to yours. Sometimes it is noticeable that daughters of a particular dog 'nick' with a certain sire, or that one dog is producing nice progeny to several different lines, in which case go back to the source, the sire, rather than one of his sons.

Having chosen the stud dog, it is wise to ensure well in advance that his services will be available for the bitch by asking his owner whether you would be allowed to use him, please. Not all dogs are at public stud. Some stud dog owners are as fussy about the suitability of the bitch to their dog as the bitch's owner has been. It is a mistake to think that all members of a litter are genetically the same. Breeders sometimes think that because one member of a litter has a fault, all the others must carry the gene for this. This depends on the inheritance of that particular fault.

LINE BREEDING
Line breeding, the pattern followed by most successful breeders, means keeping within a certain family by mating together animals with a common ancestor not too far back in the pedigree, or several lines back to that ancestor. By using this system one consolidates the type and attributes of that dog, who should of course be an animal of merit. The progeny are fairly predictable in type and therefore easy to select for the attributes required. New blood is brought in through the unrelated parts of the pedigree, i.e. the in-laws. It is disappointing for a breeder to see the purchaser of a carefully line-bred bitch throw away years of work by going off at a tangent with a complete outcross. It takes years to recover from this initial mistake; much better to follow the advice of the breeder until one is more knowledgeable about bloodlines.

INBREEDING
This is the mating together of closely related animals – father to daughter, brother to sister. This is not recommended to the novice breeder but must be done only by experts with a thorough knowledge of the stock. This is the way to breed out a fault or to fix virtues. Some clever breeders have inbred successfully, establishing a good line, but have found it difficult to introduce an outcross when one had to be used.

OUTCROSSING
This is the mating together of unrelated animals. The pedigree containing all different names would be said to be outcrossed. A dog bred thus could be good-looking but would be unlikely to make a great sire or dam, being chance-bred. However, a true outcross Border pedigree is unlikely, as most Borders share some common ancestors when the pedigree is traced back far enough. Outcrossing, meaning the introduction of fresh blood into a closely line-bred or inbred line, is something which the breeder must do from time to time, albeit with some trepidation. The first few generations may drop back in quality. A good breeder who has outcrossed with a particular goal in mind will persevere in breeding the outcross into the line, reaping the benefits of it while trying to lose any detrimental aspect of it through selection. Patience and the courage of one's convictions are needed.

TIMING THE MATING

As soon as the bitch comes into season, advise the stud-dog owner. It is helpful to have observed on past heats when she has been cocking her tail when her back has been rubbed or when the cat or another bitch has brushed past her. This gives a clue as to when she might be ready for mating but she may not always follow the same pattern on different heats. The usual time for a bitch to be receptive to a dog is from the tenth to the fourteenth day of her season. There are no hard and fast rules. I had two bitches who were mated successfully on the second day and twenty-third day respectively. At the onset of her season, the bitch's vulva will be noticeably swollen and she will shed drops of brightly blood-coloured discharge. This will become more copious. After several days this becomes less profuse, the colour changes to straw-coloured and the vulva becomes softer; the time is about right. Light pressure above the root of the tail will produce a cocking of the tail to one side when she is starting to stand.

My recipe for success is to wait for two days after the bitch is first standing before trying to mate her. This is somewhat nerve-wracking because there is always the possibility that she might go off in this short time. Some very sexy bitches will stand right through their season, which makes it difficult to judge when they are ready. The tendency is to mate bitches too early, at the first opportunity. This explains the many bitches who are difficult to get mated and who do not tie. Some lose blood throughout their season and, if one is waiting until there is no sign of blood, it is easy to miss them. Some have a silent heat, when there is no sign of blood, yet this is a proper, fertile heat if caught at the right time.

In the case of a bitch who proves difficult to get in whelp, Pre-Mate has proved accurate in predicting the optimum time to mate the bitch. This involves several visits to the vet for regular blood-tests and one must be able to take the bitch to the dog precisely when the tests decree. Of course this scientific process costs money, whereas guesswork does not. But it is well worth the cost and effort involved when the bitch is in whelp after several previous misses. Vaginal swabs taken by the vet have also proved effective in diagnosing bacteria which prevent a bitch from conceiving as well as in predicting when to mate her. Treatment with a course of the appropriate antibiotic is often effective.

The right time to mate a bitch is when she is ready, not at the nearest convenient weekend to that time. Mother nature does not wait for weekends. The bitch should be fit and healthy at the time of mating, free from any infection or parasites, and not fat. She should have been wormed prior to coming into season. As soon as your bitch appears to be coming up to standing, contact the owner of the stud-dog again and make an appointment. Keep the appointment punctually and do not take the entire family for the outing. This is a business appointment.

THE MATING

The bitch should not have been fed a heavy meal before mating and should have been well-exercised before leaving home. Take her on a properly fitting collar and lead, not a slip lead or choke lead. She will probably struggle at some stage of the mating and it is the responsibility of her owner to hold her firmly. Give her an opportunity to relieve herself before reaching the stud dog's home. She may be reticent about doing this on a strange place which is doggy.

The owner of the stud dog will be in charge of the mating and will know the best way of achieving this with the specific stud dog chosen. Stud dogs are all different. Some like help, some don't. The pair will probably be allowed to flirt a bit on collars and leads but it is unlikely that they will be allowed to cavort freely, chasing in a romantic manner over hill and dale. The stud-dog can be put off by a snap from a bitch and can be injured should she roll or twist once they are tied. Once the flirtatious antics are over and the bitch is standing for the dog, who wants to mount her, hold her firmly with one finger through her collar and the other hand supporting the front of her chest.

Be alert for her attempting to bite the dog, wriggle sideways or sit down. She must not. If she persists in trying to bite, a simple muzzle can be made with either a bandage or a pair of tights. Wind this round the muzzle a couple of times, tie a knot underneath and then tie the ends tightly behind the head. This can be removed once the pair are tied and more relaxed, as the bitch seldom tries to bite then, though she still may try to fling herself to the ground. If the dog is thrusting but not getting anywhere, try lowering the bitch's head a little. This action raises the vulva slightly which may be all that is needed. Failing this, look to see where the dog is striking, too high or too low, and use the contours of the ground to position the bitch to compensate for this. A small mat will be just as effective once one has worked out which partner needs to be higher or lower.

Her tail can get in the way. If so, hold it to one side. Usually the dog's handler, who will probably be holding her stifle with one hand to keep her firm, can do this. Cupping her vulva between two fingers and guiding this towards the penis can help. It may be necessary to lubricate her slightly, although the dog will usually do this. Vaseline, clean and new, not from a germ-ridden old jar, is effective but the dog may not like it. Water is good, just as good as grease.

Once the dog has penetrated her, his thrusting rhythm will change to frantic movements. He will be right against her in a tight embrace and his hind feet may be off the ground. Hang on to her tight – this is when she will wriggle hard to free herself. If she succeeds at just the wrong moment she may throw the dog out. She may whine or yell but a few reassuring words should calm her. The dog will want to turn once he is tied. This can be a tricky process as first he lifts one front leg, then the hind leg on the same side, over her back so they are standing back to back. The tie is caused by the bulb at the end of the penis swelling, which locks the two animals together for anything between a couple of minutes to half an hour or even longer. Some dogs never tie, in which case the stud-dog handler may hold the dog on the back of the bitch rather than risk turning him. A tie is not essential to the production of puppies, but it is normal.

Should the bitch succeed in throwing the dog out there is nothing for it but to hope that he will return to his normal dimensions quickly, when it may be possible to try again. Some dogs will not try again, thinking that they have served the bitch. If this has happened, it is not ethical to try another dog, however tempting, because it is possible that sperm have been received by the bitch. Sperm are ejaculated in the first seconds of mating.

Once the pair separate after the tie, pick the bitch up at once and carry her, rear-end higher than the head, back to the car. Do not allow her to relieve herself immediately after the mating. Let her rest in the car while the paperwork is settled. A good mating achieved with a fully co-operative bitch indicates that the timing is probably right and it should not be necessary to have another service. However, most stud dog owners are willing to offer a second service a couple of days later but this should be arranged beforehand. It is unwise to have too many matings spread over too long a period as this complicates knowing when the litter is over-due.

Should the chosen dog fail to mate the bitch, another may be offered from the same establishment. Only accept this offer if you are absolutely happy with the dog, not out of desperation to get the bitch mated. Never use a dog which you don't like or you think unsuitable for that particular bitch. It is better to wait another six months to try another suitable dog than waste time and the bitch by breeding a wrong litter.

THE STUD FEE AND PAPERWORK

The stud fee should have been fixed at the time when the dog's services were booked. This is payable immediately after the first mating, before leaving the premises. The fee is for the service of the dog and is not dependent upon the subsequent birth of a puppy or puppies. Sometimes, in the case of a slip mating or if the dog's fertility is in doubt, an offer may be made by the stud-dog owner to wait until the puppies are born for the fee. This is generous and should be honoured immediately the litter is born.

In some countries the stud fee is paid in two portions: so much at the time of the service and then a fee when the puppies are born. In the event of no puppies being born a free return may be offered to the same dog, or even another in the same kennel. This is generous but not mandatory. In the event of a bitch missing who I thought had been mated at the right time, I prefer to use a different dog next time, rather than waste time repeating the error if something is wrong. I can always come back to that dog in the future once my bitch is proven.

On receipt of the fee, a pedigree of the stud-dog should be issued along with a form completed and signed in the relevant part to say that the mating took place. This being the application form to register the puppies, it should be kept in a safe place. Some stud dog owners will issue this only after the birth of the puppies.

KEEPING THE STUD DOG

Forget the idea that there is a fortune to be made by keeping a stud-dog. Only the top dogs in the breed will get many bitches to them. A nice run-of-the-mill dog may not have any bitch visit him, or just a few of middle quality, because good bitches are taken to top dogs, not to a dog of less quality than the bitch. A male puppy must not be discouraged from showing an interest in sex or this could have a lasting effect. Mating two maiden animals together can be difficult, so it is ideal to have an experienced bitch who has been mated before as a first bride. Young dogs can be terribly stupid and sometimes such a bitch can give them the "come-on" or a nudge in the right direction just at the right time.

It is important to start a young stud the right way. He should allow the bitch to be held and himself to be handled right from the start, otherwise a great deal of time will be wasted in the future. After mating the bitch he needs no special attention, once the owner has checked that his penis has gone back correctly into the sheath, without any hairs or skin being folded back inside. He should be offered a drink of water and put back in the kennel, not put straight back into the pack with other males. No dog should be offered at stud who has a wrong mouth, an untypical temperament or is a monorchid or has something questionable, such as fits. A dog can be used frequently. Over-use as a reason for bitches missing is rubbish. If a dog persistently fails to produce puppies to proven broods with whom he has had a good mating, there may be a reason, so a sperm test might be a good idea. Males have been known to have a temporary loss of fertility. If the dog has missed to several consecutive bitches, it is fair to warn anyone who wants to use him.

The stud dog should be kept fit and not too fat. He will not require any special feeding but maybe a little extra protein would be beneficial if he is in great demand. Usually a dog remains fertile into old age, past the time when the spirit is willing but the flesh weak. My Post-Card was sired, in a litter of three, by Ch. Mansergh General Post when he was aged over fourteen years old. He had officially been retired from stud for years, but stole a mating and sired a litter and was none the worse for it, so his owner, who knew I was longing to try him once more, let me borrow him. It is not done for a stud-dog owner to tout for bitches to come to the dog, apart from placing a stud advertisement.

Chapter Twelve

PREGNANCY, WHELPING AND REARING

The gestation period of the dog is sixty-three days or nine weeks from the time of fertilisation of the ova, which can take place any time from the actual mating to within a four-day period following this. The bitch must ovulate for this to occur. Sperm can live inside the bitch for up to four days. When there has been more than one service, the difficulty is to know just when the bitch is due. Coupled with this is the fact that some families whelp early and some late. So it is no good planning to be in attendance to whelp the bitch precisely nine weeks from the moment she was mated. She could whelp up to a week early or a week late, although both are extremes. Murphy's Law dictates that if there is a really inconvenient moment for a drama, such as 2a.m. on a Christmas Morning, she will whelp then!

IS SHE IN WHELP?

It is natural to be curious as to whether the bitch is in whelp or not, but there is no certain way of knowing this for several weeks. Clues to watch out for are behavioural changes such as becoming a little 'precious', taking care of herself and keeping a little aloof from the other dogs. Her expression may soften, her ear carriage be slightly lower than normal and her feet and pasterns may slacken. The latter is often the first indication. Some bitches become fussy about what they eat for a few days after about three weeks after mating, or may eat more grass than normal first thing in the morning.

The first sure signs are the nipples turning pink, enlarging slightly and squaring off at the edges, noticeable from about three weeks onwards. Following the main meal, and noticeable from four and a half weeks onwards, a ridge of fur sticks up on the flanks. This is a sure sign. But beware the bitch that looks filled out earlier than that – one with a false pregnancy tends to look pregnant too early.

By the five-and-a-half weeks stage there should be no question about it, except to wonder why one was doubtful just a few days ago. If the due date approaches and there is still a question of 'is she, isn't she?' the probability is that she isn't. However, if there is any possibility that she might be pregnant, preparations should be made, just in case. My mother used to say that if you have to wonder whether your bitch is in whelp, she is not. This maxim usually holds good.

It is relatively easy to have a bitch scanned with an ultrasound scanner, a common practice in sheep breeding. This is not infallible but usually gives the right answer. This must be done between thirty-two and thirty-five days of pregnancy. It is painless to the bitch but the upheaval in getting it done might upset her. It is yet to be proved whether or not this invasion can upset the foetus or not. Some people are experts at palpating a bitch with accuracy at three-and-a-half weeks of pregnancy when it is possible to detect the little pea-like knobs. It is also possible to confirm

The in-whelp bitch.

Photo: Bob Hand.

The nipples and hindquarters have been tidied up in preparation for the whelping.

Photo: Bob Hand.

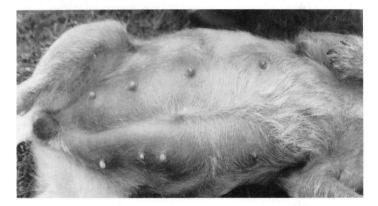

pregnancy by blood-testing. Again, the upset of routine in doing this may traumatise the bitch. It is highly dangerous to X-ray to see whether a bitch is in whelp because this can harm the foetus. My instinct is to leave well alone and not interfere with nature by scanning or feeling. Why people spend money on pregnancy tests is beyond me. All will be revealed in a few weeks anyway. The analogy is X-raying the Christmas presents on December 22nd! Nature often has the last laugh and it has been known for a bitch that has had a definite confirmation of pregnancy to resorb her puppies.

CARING FOR THE PREGNANT BITCH

In the early weeks of pregnancy there is no need to change the feeding regime of the mother-to-be, providing that she is normally fed a good nourishing diet. From about four weeks onwards, whether she appears to be in whelp or not, the ratio of protein to carbohydrate should be increased. When she becomes obviously heavy in whelp her meals should be divided, the normal amount being fed to her but in smaller quantities at a time so that she does not become uncomfortable. She may be fed some calcium in the last few days before she is due.

During pregnancy nothing unusual should be done to upset the metabolism of the bitch. Worming and booster inoculations should have been seen to before she came into season. Normal exercise should be given without her being exhausted, until she becomes too heavy to be able to do this, usually at about six weeks. Avoid lifting her in and out of the car when she is showing heavy in whelp and restrain her from leaping in and out herself. Keep her away from situations where other dogs may bump her. She should take gentle exercise right up to whelping time to keep the muscle tone up. If she has to be lifted, do this by encircling her body in your arms rather than putting any strain on her stomach muscles.

PREPARING FOR THE WHELPING
The whelping quarters, floors, bed, bedding and all equipment should be disinfected in preparation well in advance and dried out thoroughly, then kept sterile. Items needed, which should be assembled before the event as there will be no time to hunt around to find them once whelping starts, are:

The whelping box: The measurements are 22ins by 18ins. The rail is nailed inside, about 3ins off the floor of the box.

A suitable whelping box, as described in the last chapter
At least two pieces of fleecy, acrylic medical vetbed bedding, which is available at pet shops and should be cut to fit the size of the box
An animal thermometer
Several clean towels
Soap
A basin
A pair of sterile scissors
A clock or watch
A note-pad and pencil
A hot-water bottle
A shopping basket or small box
Disinfectant
Glucose
Milk
Brown bread
Rabbit or chicken or fish for the dam

A dropper feeder

A specially formulated puppy milk substitute

A copious supply of newspaper

And, very important, the vet's telephone number written up by the telephone and lots of black coffee or tea to sustain you.

Since whelpings can occur up to a week early, the dam should by then be accustomed to sleeping in her whelping bed in the designated place. If she is moved to a strange place at the last moment she could be upset and may refuse to settle and whelp her litter there. The infra-red lamp, switched off, should be suspended above the bed right from the start so that she is used to this strange thing hanging above her. Needless to say, this must be securely hung, preferably from two different anchors as double insurance against an accident. When the puppies are born the lamp is about four feet above the ground and raised gradually. Put a piece of bedding, disinfected, of the type which she is used to sleeping on, with newspaper beneath it, in her bed to sleep on until she whelps.

THE ONSET OF WHELPING

The first signs of whelping are nest-making, digging in the bed and tearing up newspaper. At this point remove the bedding on which she has been sleeping and give her plenty of newspaper. Nesting can go on, spasmodically, for days. She may also want to excavate holes in the garden, under sheds or hedges. It is important not to allow this at this late stage as she may disappear into an inaccessible spot which she has prepared. It is vital to be able to get at her and her puppies in case of necessity.

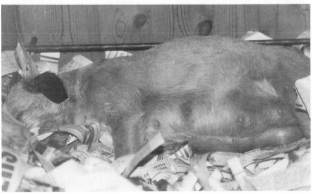

ABOVE: The unmistakable look of a bitch in the early stage of labour.

TOP RIGHT: Nesting can go on for several hours.

RIGHT: Taking a rest: Note the fullness of the nipples prior to whelping.

Photos: Bob Hand.

About twenty-four hours before whelping the bitch's undercarriage will drop. Her enlarged belly will appear to be suspended lower than previously and her teats will enlarge and have milk. When labour is imminent she will pant and shiver, her expression will alter and she will be restless, whining and pacing about. She may miss a meal but, Borders being rather greedy, this is not always the case! Her temperature will drop from the normal 38.5C (101.5F) to about 36C (98F). The digging and paper tearing will become frantic. This can go on for several hours. Drinking water should be available. The floor should be covered with newspaper as she may make quite a mess.

Do not interfere with or fuss her but reassure her if necessary and, if she is obviously anxious that you should be there, sit quietly nearby where you can keep an eye on her but do not look at her too hard, as this may distract her. Make a note of the time of each event. It is difficult to remember these and the vet may need to know, should there be an emergency. Once the contractions start, be with her. A contraction is an unmistakable muscular ripple travelling spasmodically from the front to the back of her body during which she will arch her back and her tail, whether standing or lying, and will appear to be pushing downwards. Contractions become more regular. She may lie in her bed or she may come out and strain on the floor. It is not important that she should be in her bed at this stage. Place a clean vetbed on top of the torn-up newspaper and turn the infra-red lamp on. Puppies need heat, around 70F for the first few days. Place them in the bed as soon as they are born.

THE WHELPING

Within about half an hour or so of the first contraction, the water bag should arrive. This may appear at the vulva looking like a puppy, being dark and rounded, but if gently felt it will not feel solid. Do not attempt to break it. It should arrive producing a cascade of fluid which heralds whelping being well and truly under way. Further straining should produce the first puppy, which should arrive within two hours or so of the water-bag. If the bitch has been straining for that time and nothing has arrived, telephone the vet.

Following a contraction, the puppy should be presented at the vulva contained in a membrane sac. It will probably take several contractions to expel the entire puppy. Should the puppy be suspended from the bitch by the umbilical cord, support the weight of the puppy on the palm of your hand until the placenta, the afterbirth, arrives too. This prevents a possible hernia which might be caused by the weight of the puppy pulling against its navel.

Once the puppy and placenta have arrived the dam will sever the cord with her teeth and clear the membrane sac off the puppy's face. It is important that she should do the latter quickly. If she does not do so, break the membrane with your fingers gently to clear the mouth and nose of the puppy, and wipe excess fluid away from the nostrils and mouth with the corner of the towel. It is vitally important to clear the nose and mouth quickly so that the puppy can breath. Sometimes it is necessary to do this even before the placenta has arrived, particularly if the puppy has been a long time in delivery.

A maiden bitch may not know what to do, although most do by instinct. If she ignores the new-born puppy, clear the puppy's mouth and nose and then sever the cord yourself. To do this, massage the fluid in it towards the puppy and pinch the cord tight between finger and thumb about two inches from the puppy. Then, on the side of the pinched area away from the puppy either cut or pinch with your fingers through the cord. Continue to pinch the end of the severed cord for a few seconds as this reduces bleeding. Take care never to pull on the cord against the puppy.

Clear the sac right off the puppy. Make sure the puppy is breathing, then the puppy should be gently wiped dry and offered to the bitch to lick while you reassure her about the puppy. If she still

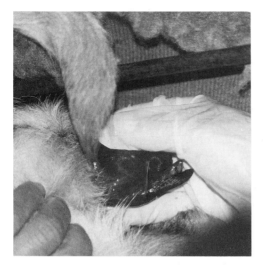

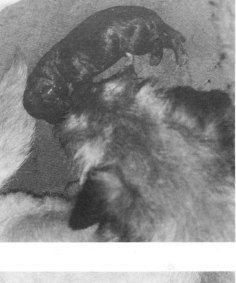

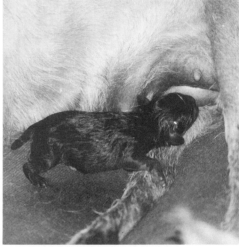

ABOVE: The delivery: Note the characteristic arch of the tail indicating a contraction. This puppy is presented tail first and will need the sac and fluid clearing from the face as soon as possible.

TOP RIGHT The dam cleans the face of the newborn whelp.

RIGHT: The newborn puppy is quick to find its way to the nearest teat.

Photos: Bob Hand.

ignores the puppy, then place the pup on a warm, but not hot, hot-water bottle which is covered by a towel or cloth in a basket or box under the lamp, just beside the whelping box where the bitch can see the puppy. Other puppies can be placed there until the bitch shows signs of interest in them, when they should be put in with her at once.

If the bitch is over-enthusiastic about severing the cord and continues to work on it getting closer and closer to the body of the puppy, gently tell her "that's enough" and try to get her to attend to the face or rear of the puppy. There is no need to tie off the cord. This will soon start to dry off naturally and will fall off in a few days.

It is natural for a bitch to eat the placenta and it is good for her to do so as this contains nutrients important to her health at this time. Try to keep a check that each placenta has arrived, as a retained placenta can cause problems. Sometimes puppies arrive in such quick succession that the dam may not notice the arrival of the latest as she is busy cleaning up the other one. In this case, push the newborn one near to her face to attract her attention but if she still ignores this puppy, start on the whelp yourself.

ASSISTING A BIRTH

It may be necessary to assist in the delivery of a puppy should one appear to be stuck at the vulva and not making progress when the bitch strains. If this seems a straightforward presentation with no legs hooked back under the puppy, grip the puppy's body gently with a towel or cloth and, at the next contraction, gently ease the puppy downwards while easing the vulva back with the other hand. Never pull a puppy straight out but more towards the ground, and never use force but ease the puppy out, always at the time of a contraction.

Should you want to feel inside the vagina to try and straighten the limbs in a badly presented puppy, lather your hands with soap and water, having made sure that your fingernails are short and not jagged. Sometimes by hooking a finger around the puppy it is possible to turn the pup or alter the position of a limb. But rather than trying to do something inexpertly it is much better to call the vet. Normal presentation is for a puppy to be born head first. However, many are born tail first which is alright provided that the birth does not take too long. A breech birth is when the tail is presented first with the hindlegs bent back under the puppy.

During a normal whelping I leave the puppies in the nest with the bitch, although this will be wet and messy. The warmth of the lamp overhead plus the bitch licking them dries the puppies. Fluids pass through the vetbed and are blotted up by the newspaper underneath it. Puppies arrive with irregular intervals between births. If there is an interval of more than two hours between births it is advisable to inform the vet. In the case of a large litter the bitch may take a long rest during the whelping, which can be unnerving for the anxious owner.

It is important to see that every puppy drinks from the dam as soon as possible. The first flush of milk contains colostrum, containing the maternal antibodies which protect young puppies from disease during their first few weeks of life. Colostrum is in the milk only for a few hours. Instinct is for the new-born puppy quickly to find the way to the milk bar. A small puppy may need assistance, particularly if those brothers and sisters who are a few hours older seem much stronger and push the little puppy out of the way, or if the bitch is moving around attending to other arrivals in the nest so that the puppy who is attempting to suck gets knocked off the teat. It may be necessary to open the tiny mouth with one finger and latch it on to the nipple, having expressed a drop of milk thereon first. Make sure every puppy has actually sucked, not just nuzzled at the teat through being unable to latch on.

IMMEDIATE POST-WHELPING

Once the bitch has finished whelping she must be taken out to relieve herself, on a lead so that she cannot get into one of her prepared holes. This is the time to replace all the bedding and to check the puppies carefully and to adjust the lamp if necessary. If no-one is on hand to help, put the dam in a cage or shut her out of the room for a few minutes while you do what is necessary. During the whelping the bitch may take a sip of milk or water. Once she has finished whelping and been out, offer her milk with glucose or sugar and maybe an egg. Then let her settle down in peace to mother her family.

The dam will be glued to her puppies for the first few days and will have to be lifted out to be taken outside, still on the lead, for several days. Meals are best offered to her in her bed to start with. Brown bread and milk or gravy, with white meat (rabbit is a favourite) or fish are offered for the first few days. She may be a bit choosy. If so, offer her the choicest bits by hand, or anything she will eat, until her appetite returns.

ABOVE: A newborn litter, just hours after birth.
Photo: Bob Hand.

RIGHT: The bitch settles contentedly with her litter.

She will need lots of meals, at least four a day, to start with. Keep the glucose going for about three days. Calcium I give from a few days prior to whelping right through until she has weaned her litter. Her food should contain plenty of protein. It is through her own intake of food that she nourishes her puppies. A radio, turned low, in the room with the bitch and her litter will mask extraneous noises of food being prepared, dogs barking and dog leads being picked up which may distract the mother's attention from her puppies.

Should you have to take the bitch to the vet after some puppies have been born, they will be perfectly alright left on their vetbed under the infra-red lamp for a while. Lower the lamp to about three feet above them while they are without their mother's warmth. If you have to take puppies to the vet, place them on a covered, warm, but not hot, hot-water bottle in a basket or box and cover the whole thing loosely with a towel to prevent heat loss from above. It is sensible to have the bitch visited by the vet after she has finished whelping, just to check that she is alright and has really finished.

SIGNS OF TROUBLE DURING THE WHELPING

Should a puppy appear to be stuck about which you can do nothing, or should there be no puppy presented after a long period of straining, or too long an interval since the arrival of the last puppy or since the waterbag, contact the vet. It is awful to have the quandary in the middle of the night as to whether to call for help at an unsocial hour or to hang on in the hope that something might happen. The longer one leaves this when things have gone wrong, the worse it is for the bitch and for the puppies. Prompt action increases the chance of survival of the puppies. A bitch who is not physically exhausted is stronger should she have to have a Caesarean section.

UTERINE INERTIA

Borders can and do have uterine inertia. This is where they either have feeble contractions or no contractions. My theory is that this is connected to their determination to ignore pain. Inertia can be difficult to detect unless you know your Border very well as she may sit bolt upright, staring into space, and only a slight twitch of a hind leg or a quivering of the whiskers will indicate that all is not right. Contact the vet if you think she is not getting on with whelping when she should be doing more. Take her to the vet in this circumstance as the journey in the car – don't try to drive too smoothly – may be enough to get things going. An injection of pituitrin should get things started again. Puppies may be born in the car on the return journey, so be prepared and take a towel and basket just in case.

REVIVING OR HELPING A NEWBORN PUPPY

If a puppy appears to be dead on arrival, but otherwise perfect, it is always worth trying to revive. First wipe away any moisture from around the nostrils and mouth. Then cradle the puppy with the back held firmly against the palm of your hand and the head well-supported between thumb and first finger. Rock the puppy backwards and forwards, head up, head down, quite hard, several times. Or try breathing gently into the puppy's mouth. Another method is to hold the whelp first under a warm (not hot) tap and then under a cold one, repeating the process. The shock may cause the puppy to gasp, which is what is required. Keep working on it. Sometimes it will take twenty minutes or so to get a puppy going. Don't be too gentle. Remember the pup is dead anyway unless you are successful. Rubbing the ribs gently or breathing into the mouth may stimulate breathing. Once the puppy gasps, keep going until you are sure the breathing is regular and independent. Then put the puppy back with the bitch but make sure she licks the puppy to keep it going.

My Champion Toggle was born apparently dead. She looked lovely and I was determined that she should not be dead and worked and worked to stimulate her. It was gratifying to see her come to life after a long struggle of at least twenty minutes. Another thrill was someone bringing a nice Border up to meet me at a show who had been resuscitated at birth through following my instructions.

A puppy who is alive but very cold and weak, should be dried off gently and placed on cotton wool in a box in the bottom of the oven at low heat with the door open, or in a box on top of a stove which has gentle heat to warm the puppy through. Once the puppy looks viable, put it back with the others.

FEEDING A WEAK PUPPY

Occasionally it may be necessary to help a weak puppy by supplementary feeding for a few days. A proprietary brand of milk replacement formulated for puppies is ideal. This should be made exactly as per instructions on the packet. Using either a dropper, a tube feeder specifically made for young animals or an eye dropper, feed the puppy just a few drops at a time. Open the mouth and place a drop on the tongue and once the puppy tries to suck release just a drop at a time, while keeping the puppy's head and neck held up a little. Take it slowly. Do not overfeed the tiny puppy. Literally a few drops every two hours are all that is needed. Increase this gradually as the puppy increases in strength and size. If the puppy cannot manage this way, take up some of the liquid food onto a rolled-up corner of cotton cloth and the puppy will probably manage to suck some off this to start with. Then progress onto a dropper feeder when the puppy is stronger. Until the puppy has the strength to feed from mum again, feeding should be every two hours.

THINGS THAT CAN GO WRONG

ECLAMPSIA: This may occur any time from a few hours after the birth of the puppies until five weeks or so afterwards and has been known to happen in the last weeks of pregnancy. Symptoms are extreme restlessness in the bitch, not settling with her litter, carrying the puppies around, trying to bury them, digging in her nest after whelping, whining, shivering or panting or tremors. Her expression may change, become strange and rather wild-looking, and she may look at you as if she cannot make you out. She will stare fixedly at her puppies, 'watching' them, or stare intently at things that are not there. In extreme cases she may collapse, unconscious. Waste no time. This is a serious condition requiring prompt medical treatment. If not treated she may injure her puppies by flinging them around and her own life is at risk. The condition is caused by the sudden demands on her calcium reserves from her litter. The cure is amazing to witness – like magic. A shot of calcium from the vet and she is herself again within minutes. Just occasionally a second injection is needed but one usually does the trick.

MASTITIS: It will take a few days for the dam's milk supply to be adjusted by natural means to meet the demand. If the milk builds up, this can cause mastitis which is when the area behind the nipple becomes inflamed. Check the nipples, including the two tiny ones between the front legs, regularly to ensure that there is no hardness behind them. They should feel soft and free from hard lumps or swelling behind them or in the milk vein between the nipples. Make sure the puppies are feeding from all the nipples. They may not be able to get their mouths around the larger ones to start with. Try to put the larger puppies on to these to draw the milk off. If they cannot manage, do it gently by hand until they take over. In the case of hard areas I gently ease some milk off two or three times daily until these go but you may prefer to get veterinary assistance. The condition must be alleviated somehow because the bitch will become increasingly uncomfortable, sore and less willing to allow her puppies to suckle. If unattended, infection could set in. In the event of the bitch's milk drying up suddenly before the litter is ready to wean, an injection can probably get it going again.

METRITIS: Metritis or inflammation of the uterus can be caused by the retention of an afterbirth. Symptoms manifest themselves a few days after whelping and are restlessness, as if there were more puppies to be born, a raised temperature and loss of appetite. An evil-smelling greeny-black discharge is another symptom. There will usually be a discharge for several weeks after whelping which is dark red, almost black to start with, lightening after a few days to a normal blood colour and gradually reducing in quantity. There will also be what resemble pieces of pink string coming from the vulva for some time. This is all quite normal but should the discharge ever appear dark-green and foul-smelling, contact the vet at once. Blood on newspaper turns green, but this is not to be confused with a green discharge. Even we old hands tend to panic. Never worry about consulting the vet if in any doubt: any ailment is better treated earlier rather than later. I became concerned when a bitch continued to discharge slightly eight weeks after birth. The vet examined her and reassured me that, although unusual, there was nothing wrong.

DIARRHOEA: Following the whelping, the first motion passed by the dam will be loose, dark coloured and foul-smelling. This is caused by the afterbirths which she ate at the time of whelping and is quite normal. Within a couple of days the motions should be lighter in colour and firmer in texture, but will still be looser than normal because of the unusual quantity of milk which she is drinking. However, should she have diarrhoea after the first few days this is not right so her diet should be considered, in case something could have upset her. If in doubt, contact the vet.

Puppies should not have diarrhoea. Their motions should be soft but not liquid. Should they pass yellow or orange liquid and have permanently wet rear-ends this is serious and they need prompt attention from the vet. Don't waste time hoping they will get over it. Time is important in treating tiny puppies. Blood in their faeces at any time is serious. It worries me that people accept puppies having diarrhoea as normal. It is not. Something is wrong either with the puppy, or with the diet of the dam or the pup. Following antibiotic treatment to either the dam or the puppies, plain yoghurt fed to the puppies, and the dam, will help build up the flora in their digestive systems.

FADING PUPPIES

Puppies who have been born strong and healthy sometimes start to lie away from the others and become noisy, making an unmistakable cry like a sea-gull. This is a noise dreaded by experienced breeders, the sound of a fading puppy. The puppy may take on a flattened look and can be mistakenly diagnosed as having been laid on by the dam. Tell the vet, who may be able to do something about it. But don't be surprised if the puppy dies. Fading can occur any time from about ten days until three weeks old. Others in the litter may fade, others will not. It is very distressing to witness this. The dam will become desperate about the crying puppy. Callous though it may sound, the sooner the puppy dies the better, then the bitch will relax again with her healthy puppies. The silent litter, with occasional grunts or squeaks, is music to a breeder's ears. Noisy puppies indicate that something is wrong.

PUPPIES TOO HOT OR TOO COLD

In our efforts to keep puppies warm we can cause them discomfort by overdoing it. Common sense must be used, and in a heat wave, or when the sun bursts into the room, the heating should be adjusted. In a centrally heated house, extra heating may be superfluous in the daytime but necessary through the night when the central heating goes off. Puppies lying separately, on their backs, are warm, maybe too hot. If they are trying to crawl away from each other and are noisy they are probably too hot. The dam generates heat herself. She may find an overhead lamp and a vetbed too hot. If she tries to scuff the vetbed up, try cutting it in half and removing half so that she can lie on newspaper while the pups lie on the vetbed, which they soon learn to find. Raise the heat lamp gradually and pull the box to one side so that the bare end of the box is away from the lamp and the pups and their vetbed are nearer to it. Puppies that are cold huddle together and may be noisy. Their mother will curl very tightly around them. Noisy puppies may also be hungry. Check that their mother's milk is still plentiful.

AFTER THE CAESAREAN

In the likelihood of the bitch needing a Caesarean section, when taking her to the surgery take with you the shopping basket or a small box, towels and a filled hot-water bottle, plus a towel for the bitch to lie on during the return journey. Be prepared to help the vet, if required, and ask to be in attendance to help with the puppies. These will be weak and the vet will be busy attending to your bitch. If you can warm the puppies on the hot-water bottle and work on any that seem lethargic it will help them on their way. Do not forget colostrum for the pups in the excitement of the drama. Make sure that every puppy feeds within a few hours. Once home, put the puppies into the whelping box under the heat lamp. Introduce the dam as soon as possible, using common sense about this if she is still staggering unsteadily after the anaesthetic. If she is liable to be a danger to her puppies through lack of co-ordination, or does not appear quite right in her head following the anaesthetic, put her in with the pups only under supervision to feed them and then put her nearby, adjacent, in a cage until she is safe to put back with them. Stay with her so she does not get desperate, then put her in under supervision so that you can take control should things go wrong.

TAILS AND DEWCLAWS

Borders are an undocked breed. Their tails are *never* cut. When working, terriers need their dewclaws to scrabble up and down banks, rocks and walls. Most Border breeders leave dewclaws on. Provided that the tips are cut back they present no problem usually. If allowed to grow too long they may break when the dog is leaping up and down against wire and will certainly be a nuisance, snagging clothes. In extreme cases of neglect they may grow round and back into the dog's leg. If they are to be removed, this should be done by a vet when the puppies are two or three days old, well established but not so strong as to make this a big operation. The dam should be removed. It is quickly done, without anaesthetic, and the puppies should be none the worse immediately afterwards. A weakling puppy who is struggling to survive should not have the dewclaws removed as the shock could cause a set-back. Borders do not have dewclaws on their hindlegs. In the highly unlikely event of their having them, they should be removed.

CULLING

From time to time a responsible breeder will have to face up to culling a puppy which may have been malformed at birth, may have suffered brain damage or severe illness or had a mishap, or there may be just too many in the litter to rear them all. Six or seven puppies is quite enough for a Border to rear. Putting the puppy down should be done as soon as possible by the vet, either at your home or in the surgery. In either case, the dam should be removed safely out of sight and sound of her puppies when the puppy or puppies to be despatched are removed from the nest. On no account let her see what is happening. Put her back with the other puppies as soon as possible.

A breeder may be worried to see white toes on newborn puppies. Provided the white is confined to just the toes it will grow out with time. A complete white foot or sock will not. White on the chest or tummy will grow out considerably and is not a fault. So there will be no need to cull a puppy for having white in these places. A white chin does not matter either.

REARING THE LITTER

Having been presented with a litter of live puppies it is up to the breeder to keep them going. Kept at a comfortably warm temperature, on clean bedding and with a well-nourished dam in attendance, they should progress steadily. On no account should other dogs be allowed to visit them. Remember that Borders are terriers and, however sociable, could make a terrible mistake when confronted with tiny, squeaking, crawling puppies. The presence of another dog could upset the dam, causing her to kill or injure her puppies in her anxiety.

As the puppies become more active they will start to fall out of bed. If they cannot get back in they may become chilled, lying on the floor. A strip of vetbed outside the box will not only break their fall but give them warmth until a human comes to their aid. If the front of the box will let down, this should be lowered and each puppy shown how to get back to bed. A board screwed across the front of a fixed-fronted box will contain the puppies a while longer but once they start to fall over this it should be removed and a few bricks placed against the outside corner of the box to make a ladder. Each puppy must be shown how to scramble back up the ladder several times. They soon learn.

At four days old this puppy is nicely filled out and looking well.

Photo: Bob Hand.

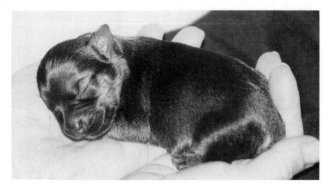

The eyes are starting to open. This puppy is fourteen days old.

Photo: Bob Hand.

At about three weeks of age a litter in the house can become a bit too smelly to live with. If they are to be moved outside, do this on a comparatively warm day, having hardened them off gradually in the house beforehand. If necessary, bring them in at night for a day or two. My puppy kennel is warmed with an infra-red lamp for a couple of hours before the pups are moved into it. I keep the infra-red lamp on at night for background heat for several weeks, suspended fairly high and not necessarily directly over the puppy bed. A tea-chest makes a warmer puppy bed than an open topped box. A heap of puppies on a vetbed in a tea-chest keep quite snug. Free-standing heaters are dangerous in a puppy kennel, or any other kennel. They can be knocked over and wires and plugs are a dangerous temptation.

Puppies' eyes open gradually between ten to twelve days old. Little slits appear at first which gradually open fully in a couple of days. Members of a litter do not always open their eyes at exactly the same time. All puppies should be checked to see that their eyes are opening. If for any reason they have discharging eyes (which they should not have unless ill) this will gum their eyelids together. These should be gently wiped clean with lukewarm water on cotton-wool. At first puppies' eyesight is weak and their eyes will appear blue, which is quite normal. They darken in due course. Keep bright lights away from their eyes.

Opening the eyes is the first milestone on the way to becoming a proper dog. Once they can see, the litter develops rapidly, both mentally and physically. They become more adventurous and start to play. Before long you will be rewarded with the first unmistakable wag of the tail, a great moment, similar to the first smile of recognition from a baby.

FEEDING THE PUPPIES

Shortly after their eyes are open I start to feed my puppies. This removes some of the strain on the bitch. Also, should anything go wrong, such as her milk drying off, the puppies are partially weaned. Feeding tiny puppies is extremely messy. Food gets everywhere, so be prepared for this. Mine start on human baby food, cereal or rice based, preferably made up with milk to the consistency of thick soup. All puppy food has the chill removed. Remove the dam for at least an hour before trying to feed the puppies. If they have just fed from her they will not want any more food. In turn, each puppy is held, on newspaper on the floor, in one hand while with the other hand food is presented by rubbing it on the muzzle with the fingertips. The puppy will lick this off and

The Border Terrier bitch will carry on feeding her puppies for as long as she has access to them.

Photo: Bob Hand.

will then take a bit more. It will be a day or two before the puppies can lap. By placing the dish right under the nose and bringing up a stream of food with one's fingers to the pup's mouth one can encourage lapping. Start with just one meal a day until they are eating a little. Then increase this to two, then three, then four, to meet the demand. Feed any left-overs as perks to the dam. Never leave unfinished food down with puppies. Once the litter starts to eat properly they must be watched while feeding to see that every puppy is getting food. If there is a wide divergence in the size of the puppies, a smaller one may get pushed out of the dish by the stronger siblings. In this case allow the less strong one to have first go in the dish.

MENU FOR THE LITTER

Having started on baby food, lean minced beef can be added, once the puppies are eating. Goat's milk is excellent for puppies and freezes well. My puppy diet is as follows:

Breakfast: cereal, goat's milk, minced beef plus calcium and vitamin D or multi-vitamin supplement added occasionally.

Lunch: rice pudding, a little goat's milk, sometimes with a scrambled or coddled egg.

Afternoon: brown bread, which is soon replaced by a plain puppy biscuit, soaked in gravy or water, plus a little meat, fish or tinned meat.

Supper, last thing at night: warmed baby food with goat's milk.

From about six weeks old I replace the cereal with a 'complete' food, cut small and soaked overnight in goat's milk. Some people rear on complete diets which they find convenient. If this is fed dry it is essential to keep fresh water available to the puppies at all times. Since these diets are carefully formulated to be perfectly balanced they should be fed according to the

Weaning can be a messy business.
Photo: Bob Hand.

instructions on the packet. Feeding puppies a varied diet enables them to change diets in their new homes without too much difficulty. A puppy fed entirely on one type of food may refuse to eat anything else.

WEANING

As the puppies become less dependent on their dam for food she will spend less time with them and should be able to get away from them when she wants to, from about three weeks after having them. A shelf or deep-sided box will provide refuge for her from which she can emerge to administer to them when necessary. At about the same stage she should be taken out from them in the daytime for a few hours, going back to clean them up after they have been fed. It is natural for her to vomit her own food for the puppies, so she should be kept well away from them for a while after she has fed.

She should stay with them at night until they are six or six-and-a-half weeks old. When to take her away depends very much on the weather and on the puppies. Common sense must be used but my aim is to have the litter weaned by about six weeks. Her milk starts to dry off as the demand decreases. For her comfort, allow her a quick visit to the pups after she has officially left them, for a couple of days just before she is put to bed and then maybe once again, having missed a day.

WORMING

Puppies need worming as soon as possible, which is when they are three weeks of age. The modern syrups and pastes specifically for worming small puppies against roundworms are gentle to use compared with the purges of days gone by. However it is vital to follow the dosage exactly and to weigh each puppy. This is said from the heart, as I once carelessly gave what I thought was the right dose rather than taking the trouble to fetch my spectacles to read the small print on the bottle and I nearly killed a lovely litter through over-dosing them. They were very ill.

Keep the dam away until the results of the dose have appeared. Each puppy should pass some worms in the faeces later in the day. Try to watch to see who does what, as, should a puppy not pass any worms and the others do, this one will need worming again in a few days' time. The likelihood is that the dose was sicked up quickly. All droppings and worms should be picked up and burned. The litter will need worming again about three weeks after the first dose. This takes planning because this may be about the time of the first parvovirus inoculation and obviously these two shocks to the system must be administered at least a week apart. The dam must be wormed once she has finished with the litter and again three weeks after that.

TOE NAILS

The toe nails of the pups, including dew-claws if these have been left on, should be cut regularly starting from about ten days old. These become very sharp little talons which scratch the bitch's undercarriage, causing her soreness which in turn makes her reluctant to feed them because she is tender. They will need cutting about every ten to fourteen days until the litter leaves home and then each puppy will need doing at less frequent intervals for some time. In fact I do all my adults about very four weeks throughout their lives. For small puppies I use a pair of nail clippers for humans which have an end-to-end pincer cut. For adults I use one made for dogs where the tip of the nail is placed through a hole and is then guillotined off.

PLAYTIME

It is essential to play with each puppy from an early age. I start by handling mine right from birth, just a little so as not to fuss the bitch, and always talking to her to reassure her while I do so. Even

It is important to give puppies plenty of space in which to play, and to provide a variety of toys.

before their eyes are open, I stroke and talk to the puppies and pick them up. Once their eyes have opened I play games with the pups. After the last feed at night I spend some time talking to each puppy, also the dam, as puppies are always lively at this time. This is a time free from unexpected interruptions so the puppies receive my undivided attention.

During the day puppies need plenty of room to run about without any danger of crashing into objects. They also need toys: tennis balls, yoghurt pots, plastic bottles, cardboard milk cartons, old slippers, small blocks of wood, or an old brush all provide entertainment. Once the pups start to destroy anything plastic rather than rolling it around, remove it, as eating plastic is dangerous.

My pups hear the radio from the day they are born. I am not quiet around puppies, they need to become accustomed to noise. To call them I clap my hands as well as shouting for them. Tip-toeing quietly around them does them no favours. Puppies should not dash up and down steps and stairs as this can spoil their fronts.

SELLING THE PUPPIES

A lesser-known breeder may have difficulty in selling a litter, particularly males. The idea of having lots of puppies to sell for cash may actually backfire and the reality may be lots of lovely puppies, which no-one wants, eating steadily into the bank balance. Don't count on those people who have told you that they would love a puppy from your bitch. More often than not they have a dog already when you approach them. If a well-known sire has been used his owner may be able to pass on a few enquiries but this is not part of the bargain of using the dog. The secretary of a breed club of which one is a member may be able to help, but again this is not a certainty. Advertising may be the only way to sell the puppies. State the age, sex, colour, breeding of father and mother, price and the area in which you live. An advertisement reading "Border Terrier pups, delightful pals, suitable show or work, tel. XYZ" tells one nothing.

It is difficult to vet homes but do try to establish that the enquirers really want the puppy – *all* members of the family – and that the puppy will not be left at home alone all day while everyone is out at work, that the garden is fenced and that the family have thought out how the dog will be kept and who will be responsible. Before parting with the dog do emphasise that, in case of difficulty, the new owners must contact you, the breeder, in the first instance. This should prevent the dog, in case of changed circumstances, being passed on.

LEAVING HOME

At about seven and a half or eight weeks of age the puppy will be ready to leave home and start a new life. By this time the pup should have been wormed twice, had a first parvovirus inoculation, which should have been given not later than one week before the puppy leaves home, be free of lice, fleas and other parasites, have clean ears free of mites and have had the toe nails cut just beforehand.

The new owners should be handed a pedigree, the Kennel Club registration certificate and transfer signed by the breeder, a vaccination certificate and written instructions on how to feed the puppy. Changing homes is quite stressful for the puppy. To make the transition as smooth as possible I provide a few days' supply of 'iron rations' of the various meals and food which the puppy has been used to eating. It is sensible to keep the new puppy on food to which the digestive system is accustomed to start with, then gradually change onto whatever the new owner prefers.

The new owner must be advised as to what inoculations the puppy has had and when to start the next stage of this. The warning that the puppy must be confined to the home and garden until fully inoculated must be remembered – no going out onto doggy ground or visiting, and no dogs coming in from outside to meet the new puppy. Many breeders will insure the puppy for the first six weeks following purchase. If the Kennel Club transfer form is sent in promptly after the purchase of the puppy, there is a similar arrangement through the Kennel Club.

CUTTING THE APRON STRINGS

Having sold the puppy with the advice that if there are any problems or queries you are there to help, you must sever the apron strings. The puppy is no longer the breeder's property and the breeder has no lien on it, unless the puppy was sold on specific terms. The new owner may spay or castrate the puppy and may breed from the puppy to any mate of their choice, or sell the puppy. Some breeders seem to have the strange idea that, although the puppy has been purchased, in some way this is still their puppy to interfere with or use to suit a breeding plan.

It is nice when contact is kept between breeder and new owner. Don't we all love the photos at Christmas? I am glad to see my puppies when they visit as adults with their human entourage. But we must not interfere in the normal course of events.

Chapter Thirteen

THE BORDER TERRIER IN BRITAIN

In writing about the leading kennels I have concentrated on those consistently and currently to the fore in the show ring. There are other good kennels which steadily produce good stock which may not reach the top spots because they are not campaigned enough and, of course, those which quietly produce good workers, the unsung heroes of the breed. The UK is known for 'backyard breeders', people with just a handful of dogs who have the skill for producing a string of good ones out of them. Nowadays these breeders could probably best be described as 'fireside breeders' as many so-called kennels keep their dogs as house dogs. Visitors to famous kennels are sometimes disappointed to find just a few Borders of good quality and think the others must be hidden away somewhere!

The Champion title won in the UK is highly valued throughout the world and is difficult to acquire, because it is always won amid large entries and in competition with Champions. For that reason there are comparatively few Champions made per year. There are now twenty-eight Championship Shows a year with CCs for Borders. From 1920 until the end of June 1995, there had been 508 British Champions made as compared with 1490 American Champions made since their first one in 1941.

LEADING KENNELS

ASHBRAE: ARTHUR AND ELAINE CUTHBERTSON
The line was founded in 1973 with Suki Suzette of Ashbrae, of predominantly Dandyhow bloodlines. Ch. Ashbrae Anouska and Ashbrae Aurora were bred in the first litter, sired by Ch.

Ch. Ashbrae McNally: The sire of Champions.

Ribbleside Ridgeman. The line descends through Aurora whose daughter, Thoraldby Tipolina, produced Ch. Ashbrae Jaffa, sired by Ch. Int. Ch. Duttonlea Suntan of Dandyhow. A repeat mating gave Jean Clark's Am. Ch. Ashbrae Sunnimaid and Ashbrae Fleet, who sired Ch. Gem of Valmyre. Ch. Ashbrae Jaffa sired two British Champions and had international influence through his son, Am. Ch. Traveler of Foxley, grandson, Ch. Int. Ch. Thoraldby Glenfiddich, and great-grandsons, Ch. Another Scot and Int. Ch. Fin. Working Ch. Double Scotch.

Ashbrae Candie, grand-daughter of both Jaffa and Aurora, to a son of Ch. Gem of Valmyre, gave Ch. Ashbrae McNally, Ashbrae Young Fay, CC winner, and Fin. Ch. Fin. Working Ch. Ashbrae Dexter. McNally sired Ch. Irton First Footer, owned by the Fryers and Ch. Irton Hogmanay at Ashbrae and Irton Reveller of Ashbrae, a CC winner, both owned by Arthur and Elaine. Young Fay produced Int. Ch. Ashbrae Archie, owned by the Saaris in Finland.

BANNERDOWN: PAM CREED

The foundation bitch, Derwood Tia Maria, was bred by Maureen Wood and was a daughter of Ch. Mr Tims and Oxcroft Gin. She produced Ch. Bannerdown Viscount, Int. Nord. Ch. Bannerdown Monarch and Bannerdown Bush Sprite, dam of two Champions for Sylvia Clarkson, Sprignell. Tia Maria was grandam of Maureen Wood's Ch. Bannerdown Capricorn. The most famous dog in the kennel, Ch. Dandyhow Silver Ring, by Ch. Dandyhow Shady Knight, was bought as a puppy. Ring sired three British Champions, all bitches. His son, Clipstone Dash, sired four British Champions. Andy Berg's Am. Int. Ch. Sprignell Woodsmoke, a Silver Ring son, sired many American Champions. Kris Blake's Am. Ch. Trailsend Bewitched, a Ring daughter, was the dam of many American Champions.

Bannerdown Lady Abigail, a Ring daughter, was the foundation of Nan de Boer-Huben's successful 'of the Whiskered Gentry' kennel in Holland. Another of his daughters, Int. Nord. Ch. Bannerdown Butterscotch, produced several Champions in Sweden for Margareta Grafström. Ch. Dandyhow Marchioness, made up here, gave the litter-brothers Chs. Bannerdown Boomerang and Cavalier, the latter of whom appears behind several Champions and is grandsire of current show stock in the kennel.

BEENABEN: BRIAN BAXTER

A kennel with an Oxcroft foundation, the dog, Forest Samson, bred by Jack Price, was litter-brother to Ch. Oxcroft Vixen. He sired out of a bitch by Dandyhow Nelson, brother to Napoleon, Ch. Beenaben Brock in 1976. Dandyhow Marcia to Forest Samson produced Beenaben Bargain whose daughter, Ch. Mansergh Toggle, produced three British Champions. Marcia to Ch. Am. Can. Ch. Ryswick Ranger (Dandyhow – Oxcroft breeding) produced Beenaben Broom whom Jack Price used on Oxcroft Milkmaid to breed Ch. Banff of Beenaben. Banff and Bargain produced Bugibba who, put back to her grandsire, Broom, gave the litter-mates Ch. Beenaben Bertie and Ch. Beenaben Broidery. Bertie sired Int. Ch. Ashbrae Archie.

BREHILL: FRANCES WAGSTAFF

To have bred five bitch Champions in direct line is the proud record of Frances Wagstaff, who started showing in the late fifties. The line was established from Ragus Dark Secret, bred off Dandyhow lines by Marjorie Bunting and Lesley Crawley. Her daughter by Ch. Dandyhow Nightcap, Ch. Brehill Wayward Lass, produced Ch. Brehill March Belle whose daughter, Ch. Brehill April Lass, gave Ch. Brehill Maybelle who was the dam of Frances's first blue and tan, Ch. Brehill Gloster Girl.

Brehill March Secret of Kelgram, litter sister to March Belle, was a foundation for Sam and

Ch. Brehill Gloster Girl: The fifth Champion bitch in direct line to be owned and bred by Frances Wagstaff.

Photo: John Hartley.

Heather Mitchell's Kelgram line, their first Border. The secret of this small and highly successful kennel is to concentrate on campaigning one exhibit at a time.

BROCKHOLE: HARRY DEIGHTON

Harry Deighton shows rarely but his affix is well-known. He bred Ch. Brannigan of Brumberhill, out of Fine Lady, in the famous litter which also contained Careless Wispa of Brumberhill and Biddy Blue of Milnethorpe. Out of Careless Wispa, Harry's daughter, Ann, bred Ch. Blue Dun and Aust. NZ Ch. Brigand, both of Brockhole and Lynsett, both owned by Lynn Briggs and David Shields in England. Brigand went to Elaine Davies, Australia, and sired many Champions 'down under'. Fine Lady, put back to her son Brannigan, produced Brockhole Barnacle Bill. Careless Wispa to Ch. Milnethorpe Noble Sportsman at Bretcar, a Biddy Blue son, gave German Ch. Langenby Lass at Brockhole and Bright Beacon at Brockhole. Bright Beacon to Barnacle Bill gave Brockhole Blue Ribband at Quatford out of whom Val Furness bred Ch. Quatford Kardinal.

BRUMBERHILL: STEWART McPHERSON

Ch. Brumberhill Blue Tansy, bought as a pet in 1980, was Stewart's first Border and the foundation of the line. By chance, Stewart lived in the same village as Ted Hutchinson who immediately spotted the potential of Tansy and encouraged Stewart to show her with Ted handling her. Many of the subsequent Champions from this kennel were co-owned by Stewart with Ted. By

Ch. Brumberhill Bewitched winning runner-up in the Group, South Wales, 1994.

Photo: Dog World.

laying down a careful pattern of line-breeding back to Ch. Wharfholm Warrant, Ch. Int. Ch. Brumberhill Blue Maestro was produced, three generations down from Tansy. Maestro won four CCs as a puppy but could not claim his title until his fifth which came after he was twelve months old. He won nine in all, then went to Holland where he was shown in the ownership of Erica Bons and Stewart. He sired eight Champions in Holland.

Out of his dam's litter sister, both bred by Ted, Maestro sired Ch. Brannigan of Brumberhill and the bitches, Careless Wispa of Brumberhill and Biddy Blue of Milnethorpe, both of whom produced a Champion. Brannigan's achievements in the show ring are unlikely to be equalled by another Border. He won Reserve BIS at Crufts, 1988, and BIS at the prestigious National Terrier Club Championship Show the same year – the only Border to achieve either of these 'plum' wins. He was, and still is, the only Border to win BIS at an all-breeds Championship Show in Britain, Driffield 1986. He set a new breed record, winning thirty-one CCs from thirty judges. He won seven Groups and was six times Reserve. He qualified three years running for the final of the Pedigree Petfoods Champions Stakes, to date the only Border to have qualified. As a sire he rates joint second in breed history, along with Ch. Billy Boy and Dandyhow Brussel Sprout, with ten British Champion progeny. He sired Sw. Ch. Fin. Working Ch. Cheltorian Midnight, an influential sire in Sweden and Finland, Dutch Ch. Villathorn Tiger's Eye and Am. Ch. Plushcourt Gangster and Am. Ch. Cheltorian Mischief of Brumberhill.

Ch. Blue Maverick of Brumberhill, by Maestro out of a Michael daughter, was somewhat unlucky to stand in the shadow of his older three-quarter brother, Brannigan, but did remarkably well, winning twelve CCs, no mean achievement in the Brannigan era. Maverick's daughter, Ch. Blue Lace of Brumberhill, came from a half-brother-sister mating on Maestro and won twelve CCs. Tansy's daughter, Brumberhill Blue Mist, the paternal grandam of Brannigan, to Ch. Mansergh General Post, who carried several lines to Ch. Wharfholm Warrant and also brought in outcross blood, gave Ch. Brumberhill Bittersweet, Reserve Terrier Group, Darlington 1987, and Can. Ch. Brumberhill Bright Spark, a Group winner. Bittersweet to Brannigan produced Ch. Dutch Ch. Brumberhill Bedevilled and, in a later litter, Ch. Brumberhill Bewitched, Reserve Terrier Group, South Wales 1994. Bedevilled and Ch. Dutch Ch. Ribbleside Rogue, a Brannigan son who was made up here, both went to Erica Bons. Brumberhill Blue Print, CC winner, was bred by Ted out of Brannigan's daughter, Ch. Mansergh Denim, by Wilholme Regal Reform, a CC winning grandson of Careless Wispa.

CLIPSTONE: JEAN, FRANK AND ELSPETH JACKSON
Frank and Jean had the affix for years and then Jean and Elspeth, who shares her parents' interest in the breed. Jean and Frank's first Border was purchased in 1964. Their first Champion was Ch. Am. Ch. Clipstone Hanleycastle Bramble. However, it was Clipstone Dandyhow Lady, daughter of the two famous producers, Dandyhow Brussel Sprout and Ch. Dandyhow Soroya, who founded the current line. She produced Sw. Ch. Clipstone Clover and, in a later litter, Ch. Clipstone Carrots and Ch. Int. Nord. Ch. Clipstone Guardsman. Clover and Guardsman went to the Bombax kennel in Sweden. Ch. Llanishen Illse of Clipstone was the dam of Ch. Clipstone Comma whose son, Clipstone Dash, sired four Champions, three of them bred at Clipstone. Ch. Clipstone Cumin, by Dash, sired six British Champions including Ch. Stonekite Charisma of Clipstone. Cumin's full brother, Sw. Norw. Ch. Clipstone Ceriph, was a sire of note in Sweden, owned by Tomas Larssen.

An important bitch here was Dandyhow Creme Caramel of Clipstone. Mated to the Swedish import Ch. Int. Nord. Ch. Bombax Xavier she gave Ch. Clipstone Cliquot. Xavier, son of Sw. Ch. Clipstone Clover, was co-owned in England by Jean Jackson and Carl Gunnar Stafberg and is the only imported Border to win a British title. Creme Caramel went to the Bombax kennel, as did Ch.

Int. Nord. Ch. Llanishen Reynard who was made up by the Jacksons. Ch. Cliquot was the first in a direct line of Champion bitches: Cliquot, Chasse, Tearose and Soft Soap.

Ch. Durham Red Clipstone, descending from a sister of Chasse, joined the kennel and was made up quickly. His CC-winning daughter, Starcyl Penny Red Clipstone, whose dam went back to Clipstone blood, was bought in. A son of Durham Red, Val Furness's Ch. Quatford Kardinal, won Reserve in the Group at Border Union, 1995. To date, the Clipstone kennel has owned or bred nineteen British Champions and is renowned for outstanding bitches, notably Illse, Chasse, Charisma and Soft Soap.

DANDYHOW: BERTHA SULLIVAN, KATE IRVING

The pedigree of the large percentage of present-day Border Terriers can be traced back to Dandyhow ancestry to some degree or other. The kennel, started by Bertha Sullivan in 1950, has made or bred more British Champions than any other, thirty-one to date. Even more significant is the number of British Champions owned by other people to have a Dandyhow parent or parents. Leading kennels

Ch. Stonekite Soft Soap by Clipstone: One of the lovely bitches for which Clipstone is renowned. Pictured with Jean Jackson.

Photo: Gerwyn Gibbs.

throughout the world have a predominantly Dandyhow base. Kate Irving, the daughter of Brin and Bertha Sullivan, has a separate interest in the affix. Her husband, Ronnie Irving, is a third generation Border breeder and grandson of the legendary Wattie Irving. Ronnie had several well-known Champions including Ch. South Box whose name figures in Dandyhow pedigrees.

Before having an affix, Bertha used the initials BS on her dogs. The first Champion she made, Ch. Am. Ch. Dandyhow Bitter Shandy, won her crown in 1960 and was later owned by Kate Webb

Ch. Dandyhow Cleopatra: A great favourite and a top winner.

(later Seemann), Shelburne kennel, USA. Ch. Dandyhow Shady Knight, universally acknowledged as one of the all-time greats in the breed, held the CC record with twenty-four, was the first Border to win a Group in the UK (at the East of England Championship Show, 1971) and is the all-time leading sire in the breed in the UK with twelve British Champions. His sire, Dandyhow Brussel Sprout, sired ten. Knight's son, Ch. Dandyhow Nightcap, sired six.

Three Shady Knight sons proved to be important sires overseas: Bob and Ruth Ann Naun's Am. Ch. Dandyhow Bertie Bassatt in America, Minka Crucq's Int. Ch. Dandyhow Knight Errant in Holland and Krister Giselsson's Int. Nord. Ch. Llanishen Ivanhoe in Sweden. Shady Knight's full sisters, Dandyhow Sweet Pickle and Sweet Polly, were important broods in Julia Geijer's Juniper kennel, Sweden. Dandyhow Observer and Sw. Ch. Dandyhow Grenadier went to Mona Hedman's Tallarnas kennel and both sired many Champions in Sweden. Ch. Norw. Sw. Ch. Dandyhow Scotsman, Reserve in the Group at Crufts, 1982, later went to Anne Tove Strande, Norway. Anna-Karin Berg from Sweden used him with considerable success on her Rabalder line.

Grenadier's influence is carried chiefly through his sons, Ch. Int. Ch. Duttonlea Suntan of Dandyhow and Am. Ch. Duttonlea Autocrat of Dandyhow, a leading sire in the USA, owned by Nancy Hughes, Trailsend kennel. Scotsman sired Ch. Blue Doctor, himself the sire of Champions, and the following bitches who are the foundation of, or directly behind the foundation of, the kennels mentioned. Tipalt Scots Lass of Dandyhow was the dam of Ch. Dandyhow April Fool on whom the Irton kennel, owned by Dave and Trak Fryer was founded, and was also the dam of Dandyhow Meg Merrilees, a foundation of Jayne Brown's Orenberg kennel. Tipalt Early Riser was the dam of Irish Ch. Astra of Opinan, the foundation of Arthur Sneeden's Opinan line. Tipalt Glenmelt Lady was the dam of Tandem Matamba, the foundation of Margaret Curtis's Matamba line. Scots Lass was also influential on the Dandyhow line, Cleopatra carrying three lines to her.

Ch. Dandyhow Cleopatra, an outstanding Border and a Champion many times over, won BIS at several breed club Championship Shows. Unfortunately, due to Ronnie's position on the KC General Committee, Cleopatra was unable to be shown at Crufts as an adult. Her daughter, Dandyhow Bright Sparkle, won Reserve in the Group at Driffield, 1995, on the day she won her first CC, aged eleven months. Her sire, Am. Ch. Dandyhow Brass Tacks accompanied the Irving family to, and returned with them from America where they lived for a few years.

Some famous sires from Dandyhow, apart from those already mentioned, were Saracen, Bolshevik, Napoleon, Ch. Spectator, Ch. Silver Ring (owned by Pam Creed), Ch. Crofter and Ch. Valmyre Magician. The brood bitches included Ch. Soroya who was the dam of four Champions, Cobbette, and Solitaire who were each the dam of three Champions, Ch. Margery Daw whose name appears behind many good Borders, and Marjorie Staveley's Hot Chocolate, dam of two Champions. Overseas Champions include: Am. Ch. Herdsman with Kris Blake and the Nauns; Am. Ch. Top Notch with the Nauns, USA; Ch. Am. Ch. Forget Me Not with Nancy Hughes, USA; her sister Int. Ch. Fleur de Lis with Minka Crucq, Holland; Sw. Norw. Ch. Tom Fool with Anne Tove Strande, Norway; Sw. Fin. Ch. Skye Blue in Sweden with Mona Hedman.

DIGBRACK: GEORGE ROBSON

A line of European winners stems from Barleycorn of Digbrack, who was bred off Dandyhow lines by Elaine Hislop. Her son, sired by Thoraldby Night Owl, Ch. Int. Ch. Digbrack Barley Sugar was exported to Wiebke Steen, Germany. Barleycorn to Dandyhow Silver Scott produced Digbrack Brandy Snap and Bramble, the dam of Ch. Digbrack Rambler. Doubling on Bramble gave Digbrack Topaz, the dam of Int. Ch. Digbrack Candy Tuft, who proved a wonderful brood for the Foxforest kennel, Finland. Hanne Sonne, Denmark, imported the full brother to Topaz, Dk. Ch. Digbrack Barley Mo whose son is Sw. Norw. Ch. Dandyhow Tom Fool. Bernd and Brigitte

Krafzik, Germany, imported Int. Ch. Digbrack Jet Way, a Barley Sugar and Bramble son, who sired several Champions, including Int. Ch. Elfe-Highness von Lärchenbruch, a well-known winner owned by Bernd and Brigitte. Brandy Snap produced Ch. Borbeck Electron and Borbeck Beta by Irton who was the dam of Raeburnfoot Isla at Irton, CC.

DORMIC: MICK AND DOREEN RUSHBY The first Champion here was made in 1981, Ch. Grenze Galanthus of Dormic, by Ch. Foxtor Blue Jester out of Grenze Srikalight, a Step Ahead daughter. Dormic MacAndrew, a CC winning son of Cheltor Michael, to Galanthus produced Dormic Moody Blue who was the dam of Ch. Cinnamon of Dormic. The sire of Cinnamon, Ch. German Ch. Thoraldby Tiptoes, came to the kennel holding two CCs and won his crown here. He sired eight British Champions before joining the Tillners' kennel in Germany. NZ Ch. Head Waiter at Dormic, a MacAndrew son, and Dormic Mood Indigo, a Galanthus daughter, went to the Patterdale kennel in New Zealand and together produced NZ Ch. Rushby of Patterdale. Most of the Dormic Borders hold Working Certificates.

DYKESIDE : MARJORIE STAVELEY Dandyhow Hot Chocolate, a Nightcap daughter, produced Ch. Blue Doctor and Ch. Dykeside Gordon Ranger who were sired by Ch. Norw. Ch. Dandyhow Scotsman and Ch. Dandyhow Crofter respectively. Blue Doctor sired Marion Danks' Ch. Bushnells Turtle and Jean and Frank Jackson's Ch. Stonekite Soft Soap by Clipstone, while Gordon Ranger sired Margaret Curtis's Champions Matamba Houdini and Rosemary. Sw. Ch. Dykeside Jock Scott was bred from Dandyhow Melian of Dykeside, sired by Am. Ch. Dandyhow Brass Tacks. Melian was also the dam of Am. Ch. Dykeside Kristina, by Gordon Ranger, who also sired Fin. Ch. Kelgram Owen Tudor.

FARMWAY: MADELENE ASPINWALL This kennel, founded in the late fifties, has had great influence on the breed across the world. The first Champion, Ch. Covington Dove, was bought holding two CCs. Madelene made her up the first time she showed her. The line today descends from Dove. Ch. Farmway Red Robin, her grandson, was the first home-bred Champion, born in 1962. In all there have been seven British Champions at Farmway and so many overseas that it is difficult to recall them all. Many kennels are based on the Farmway line. In the home kennel were that great character Ch. Farmway Fine Feathers, Ch. Farmway Snow Kestrel and Ch. Farmway M'Lady Robin, truly a connoisseur's bitch.

Ch. Farmway Snow Kestrel: A sire who stamped his type – a very influential dog worldwide.

Ch. Snow Kestrel stamped his progeny. He sired three British Champions including the famous sire, Ch. Lyddington Let's Go. Aune Luoso's Int. Nord. Ch. Farmway Southern Hawk was a very famous Kestrel son, out of Hanleycastle Sally. A great winner and sire, Southern Hawk was the first Border to win a Group in Finland and sired the first Border to win BIS at an all-breeds Championship Show there, Int. Ch. Rabalder Milda Makter. Other Kestrel progeny overseas were Int. Nord. Ch. Farmway Kestrelstar and Am. Ch. Farmway Roadrunner, both out of Ch. Thoraldby Star Appeal of Lairdarch whom Madelene owned, Can. Ch. Farmway Cherry Wren, Am. Ch. Farmway Snow Song, Sw. Ch. Farmway Snowmerlin, and Fin. Ch. Fin. Working Ch. Farmway Snow Dove. Betty Rumsam's Wilderscot and Steve Dean's Tyrian kennels both had Farmway foundations. Three Tyrian Champions descend from both Snow Kestrel and M'Lady Robin.

The Border in New Zealand owes much to Madelene who exported to Rosemary Williamson NZ Champions Farmway Swinging Chick, Tui, White Dove and Red Raven. Red Raven made history by being the first Border to win BIS at an all-breeds Championship Show there. Jim Graham's first Otterhead litter was bred off Farmway Swansdown. A strong bitch line has been bred for generations by Madelene – the Dove line. The good brood bitch, Dusky Ice Maiden at Kelgram, was a daughter of Snow Kestrel and Twilight Tara who was by Fine Feathers out of Farmway True Dove. The litter-brothers, Dutch Ch. Farmway Flamebird, Fin. Ch. Farmway Firebird and Sw. Norw. Ch. Farmway Thunderbird are out of Septimus Dove. Other overseas Champions are Belg. Lux. Sw. Ch. Farmway Bluewing, Int. Nord. Ch. Farmway Early Bird (brother to NZ Ch. Swinging Chick), Nord. Ch. Farmway Seagull, Am. Ch. Farmway Lookensee Hawk and Am. Ch. Farmway Miss Feather.

FOXWYN: RON AND KATH HODGSON

Ron and Kath's first Border joined their other terriers in 1975. The first Champion here was Ch. Thoraldby Yorkshire Lass who made history by being the first Border bitch to win a Terrier Group, which she did at Driffield Championship Show, 1978. She had won Reserve in a Group the previous year. Ch. Foxtor Blue Jester was made up in 1980. He proved an influential sire, appearing in the pedigrees of many Champions. The female foundation of the line was Cover Girl and the line descends through her daughter by Ch. Step Ahead, Foxwyn Celebrity Girl. Blue Jester with Celebrity Girl produced the dam of Ch. Foxwyn Shoot A Line, sired by Cheltor Michael, a Blue Jester son. Shoot A Line's son, Ch. Lynsett Trouble-Shooter was bred by Lynn Briggs who co-owned him with the Hodgsons. Am. Ch. Foxwyn Blue Line, a Shoot A Line daughter, is owned by Nancy Brown. A half-brother and sister mating on Trouble-Shooter, carrying a further line to Blue Jester, produced the litter mates Ch. Foxwyn First Choice and Ch. Foxwyn Lucky Shot. Trouble-Shooter sired Ch. Blue Dun at Brockhole and Lynsett and NZ Aust. Ch. Brigand at Brockhole and Lynsett, an influential sire in New Zealand and Australia. Foxwyn First Option, a son of Ch. First Choice, went to Chuck and Charlotte Pollard, USA, in 1995.

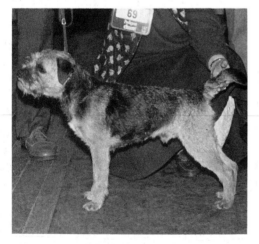

Ch. Foxwyn Lucky Shot winning BIS at the Border Terrier Club Championship Show 1991.

Photo: M. Baird.

HUTCHINSON, TED: NO AFFIX

It would take a chapter to record all the Champions handled by Ted for their owners or those whose breeding he master-minded. He started showing Borders in 1949, handling the Dryburns for Helen Vaux. Much later, he co-owned Ch. Warfholm Warrant with Barbara Holmes. Among Ted's charges was Harold Jenner's Ch. Am. Ch. Final Honour, a Warrant son, the first Border to win Reserve in the Terrier Group at Crufts, in 1973, after which he was bought by Nancy Hughes, Trailsend kennel, USA. Ch. Step Ahead, a Final Honour son, co-owned by Harold Jenner and Ted and handled by Ted, broke all previous records, establishing a new breed record with twenty-six CCs and winning four Groups. Cheltor Michael, a sire whose name appears in many pedigrees, was shown by Ted for Lady MacAndrew and was a Step Ahead grandson. Undoubtedly the most famous Border to be campaigned by Ted was Ch. Brannigan of Brumberhill, co-owned with Stewart McPherson. Brannigan went Reserve BIS at Crufts and beat Ch. Step Ahead's record of both CC wins and Group wins. No-one could deny that Ted has a natural flair for Borders, being a master at presenting and handling them, with a talent for producing Champion after Champion. Line-breeding has always been his policy. His genius lies behind many successful kennels of today.

IRTON: DAVE AND TRAK FRYER

The great influence in this kennel comes from its first Champion, Ch. Dandyhow April Fool, the last son of Ch. Dandyhow Nightcap to be shown. Born in 1985, he was made up the following year and won his sixth CC at the age of eight. He won Reserve in the Group at Peterborough, 1986. His immediate Champion progeny include Ch. Valmyre Magician of Dandyhow, Ch. Borbeck Electron, Am. Ch. Hollybridge Raffles, Am. Ch. Hollybridge Royal Jester, and Am. Ch. Dandyhow Brass Tacks who has Champion progeny both sides of the Atlantic. The April Fool son, Am. Ch. Hollybridge Raffles, excelled in Working Trials, gaining many working qualifications

Lochmaddy Mist at Irton, a Ch. Blue Doctor daughter and the Fryers' first show Border, to April Fool produced Irton Firecracker, the dam of Ch. Irton Wildfire. Opinan Baubo by Irton, an April Fool daughter, mated to an April Fool grandson, Ch. Ashbrae McNally, was a union that really 'clicked', producing Ch. Irton First Footer, Ch. Irton Hogmanay at Ashbrae, Irton Reveller at Ashbrae and Irton Ransom at Hollybridge, all CC winners, whelped in two litters. Ransom's son, Hollybridge Royal Ransom, owned by Nancy Hogg, won his first CC from the puppy class in 1995. His sire, Ch. Raeburnfoot Royal Mail, is by Ch. Valmyre Magician of Dandyhow. Borbeck

Ch. Irton First Footer: One of four CC winners bred by Dave and Trak Fryer out of their Opinan Baubo by Irton sired by Ch. Ashbrae McNally – a union that 'clicked'.

Photo: Carol Ann Johnson.

Beta by Irton, sister to Ch. Borbeck Electron, produced Raeburnfoot Isla at Irton who was another CC winner in 1995, which was a year to remember with Ch. Irton First Footer winning the CC at both Crufts and the Border Terrier Club Show on consecutive weekends.

LYNDHAY: TONY AND ANN TOMLINSON

The affix came from Tony and Ann's first show dog, Ch. Am. Can. Ch. Lynhay Daz, born 1987, who won eleven CCs before joining Georgette Toesca's Glendory kennel in the USA. Sired by Daz and out of Otterkin Blue Ribbon at Basvale, Joy Gordon produced Dutch Ch. Wee Blue Rustler, the first Border to win the Terrier Group in Holland. A repeat mating of Daz with Blue Ribbon gave Tony and Ann's Ch. Without Equal at Lyndhay, exported to Gunnel Eckvard in Sweden, and Ch. Dazzle 'em Lyndhay, the sire of Ch. Nettleby Wicked As It Seems.

MANSERGH: ANNE ROSLIN-WILLIAMS

The affix was originally owned by my mother, Mary Roslin-Williams, who then gave me a separate interest in it. This kennel had working origins, my father carrying the horn for the Kendal and District Otterhounds for many seasons. Our Borders were first and foremost workers in those days. The first Border registered with the affix was born in 1948. Ch. Leatty Juliet of Law, the kennel's first Champion, was made up in 1959. The present line descends from Ch. Mansergh April Mist and Ch. Nord. Ch. Mansergh Rhosmerholme Amethyst, who went to the Juniper kennel in Sweden. Ch. Int. Ch. Mansergh Pearl-Diver won the Terrier Group at the Scottish Kennel Club, 1981. He sired three Champions before joining Ted Hunt and Minka Crucq's of the Half House kennel in Holland, where he sired more.

Three generations of Champion bitches: Ch. Froswick Button of Mansergh, Ch. Mansergh Toggle and Ch. Mansergh Denim.

To date there have been 17 British Champions bred or made up in the Mansergh kennel. A line of six Champions in direct descent is unusual in the breed: Ch. Mansergh Sergeant Pepper, Ch. Mansergh General Post, Ch. Int. Ch. Mansergh Pearl-Diver, all males, then Ch. Froswick Button of Mansergh, Ch. Mansergh Toggle and Ch. Mansergh Tassel. Toggle produced three British Champions: my Ch. Mansergh Denim and Betty Judge's Ch. Mansergh Doublet at Plushcourt in one litter and my Ch. Mansergh Tassel and Int. Ch. Mansergh Tontine, owned by Ted Hunt and Minka Crucq, in her second, and last, litter. From Denim, Ted Hutchinson bred, in two litters, Blue

Print at Brumberhill, CC winner, and Pilot Officer, who went to Holland. Doublet sired Susan Wilson's Olderhills Oberon who won Reserve in the Group at Southern Counties, 1995.

MATAMBA: MARGARET CURTIS

From her foundation, Tipalt Glenmelt Lady, Margaret Curtis, bred in 1985, her first Champion, Ch. First Time Matamba, and Tandem Matamba. In two litters, sired by Ch. Dykeside Gordon Ranger, Tandem gave Ch. Matamba Houdini and Ch. Matamba Rosemary. Matamba Christina, Houdini's litter-sister, to Ch. Bushnells Turtle produced Am. Ch. Matamba Picasso, owned by the Werbelows, Tweedhill kennel, USA.

Ch. Matamba Rosemary: BOB Crufts 1995. Owned and bred by Margaret Curtis. Photo: Trafford.

Ch. Nettleby Mullein: The bitch CC record holder. Owned and bred by Terence and Jena Tuck.

NETTLEBY: TERENCE AND JENA TUCK

Tez and Jena started in Borders with the purchase of a puppy in 1979 as a rabbiting pal. This puppy, bred by Sylvia Edmunds, became a leading show dog and sire, Ch. Lyddington Let's Go, the sire of seven British Champions. His daughter, Ch. Nettleby Mullein, is the current bitch CC record holder with eighteen from different judges. Kris Blake's Am. Ch. Nettleby Nighthawk, Mullein's full brother from a later litter, earned Gold ROM, siring many American and Canadian Champions. Irish Ch. Nettleby English Rose is out of Mullein's daughter, Nettleby Morgause. Ch. Nettleby Wicked As It Seems is by a Let's Go grandson out of a descendant of both Mullein and her full sister, Lupin. These last mentioned two Champions won their crowns in 1995.

OTTERKIN: KATHY WILKINSON

The foundation bitch was Sutoby Foxy Lady of Otterkin, a CC winning blue and tan bred by Joyce Robinson and sired by Cheltor Michael out of Grenze Gloxinia, a Ch. Step Ahead daughter. In 1984, Foxy Lady produced the litter-sisters, Otterkin Blue Brocade and Bouquet, sired by Ch. Int. Ch. Brumberhill Blue Maestro. Blue Brocade was a remarkable brood. To three different sires she produced Champions or CC winners. By her half-brother, Ch. Brannigan of Brumberhill (doubling on Maestro) she gave the litter-sisters, Ch. Otterkin Singin' The Blues and Ch. Otterkin Tapestry, the latter owned by Joyce Robinson. A repeat litter produced one puppy, Joy Gordon's

Ch. Otterkin Blue Note: A typical Otterkin.

Otterkin Blue Ribbon of Basvale, dam of two British and one Dutch Champions. Singin' The Blues produced Ch. Otterkin Blue Note by Scots Guardsman. Otterkin Blue Angel, Jane Parker's CC winning blue and tan, came from a CC winning Blue Brocade daughter, Otterkin Ruby Tuesday, and was also sired by Scots Guardsman. Bouquet won two CCs and two Reserve CCs, then an accident prevented her being shown again. Mated to Otterkin Pioneer, the CC winning son of Blue Brocade by Cheltor Michael, she gave Dutch Ch. Otterkin Valentina, also Otterkin Red Alert of Redbrush from whom Jane Parker bred Ch. Conundrum Anticipation.

OXCROFT: JACK AND JULIE PRICE

The Oxcrofts, well-known as doughty workers as well as high-class show dogs, have been carefully line bred for generations. This is one of the few modern day kennels which could be said to have a distinct line and an instantly recognisable kennel type. Many Oxcrofts have Working Certificates. The foundation bitch, Daletyne Magic, was put to Milkbank Tarka, a well-known worker with the Dumfriesshire Otterhounds and litter-brother to Ch. Marrburn Morag. This produced Oxcroft Rocket in 1964, a well-known worker and the first CC winner for the kennel. Breeding back to Rocket and the Daletyne line, with the occasionally introduced judicial outcross, Jack bred: Gordon Knight's Ch. Oxcroft Moonmagic, sire of five Champions: my Ch. Oxcroft Pearl of Mansergh, dam of a Champion; Andrew Willis's Ch. Oxcroft Tally, dam of a Champion;

Ch. Oxcroft Rogue: A typical Oxcroft with a true otter head.

Ch. Oxcroft Vixen who was Jack's first Champion; Ch. Oxcroft Rocker, sire of four Champions; Frank Wildman and John Bainbridge's Ch. Ragsdale Blueberry, dam of a Champion; Brian Baxter's Ch. Beenaben Banff, dam of two Champions; and Ch. Oxcroft Rogue. Ch. Oxcroft Rocker spent his final years in Germany with the Tillners who also took his son, German Ch. Oxcroft Trader, the sire of Rogue, and several other Oxcrofts. Oxcroft Rocky sired many good ones, including two Champions. It is somewhat confusing to find three famous sires, which feature in pedigrees of so many Champions and workers, named Oxcroft Rocket, Oxcroft Rocky and Ch. Oxcroft Rocker!

PLUSHCOURT: BETTY JUDGE

An unusual kennel for modern times, housing between fifty and a hundred Borders of which about twenty are stud-dogs, the Plushcourt line was founded in 1982. A broad base of bloodlines was introduced in the purchase of five foundations: Farmway Tawny Pipit of Plushcourt, Dandyhow Elizabeth of Plushcourt, Delightful of Plushcourt who was a Ch. Foxtor Blue Jester daughter, Loving Spoon of Plushcourt, and the dog, Langpool Nuts in May of Plushcourt, the last two being by Pearl-Diver. These lines have been tried in many combinations here and other lines introduced. The first Champion was bred out of Tawny Pipit, namely Ch. Plushcourt On Target, who gave Irish Ch. Plushcourt Tactic of Rathvarig, sired by Ch. Mansergh Doublet at Plushcourt who was Betty's next Champion. Elizabeth and Nuts in May produced the 'E' litters which could be said to be the true foundation of the line, since just about every Plushcourt in the kennel descends from this combination. Encore, Emblem and Elation all produced CC winners.

Int. German Ch. Plushcourt Extravagance went to Germany to Diana and Jörn Tillner who bred several Champions from her including Int. Ch. Malepartus Anthony. Int. German Ch. Plushcourt Echo also sired several title holders. Ch. Plushcourt Blue Hero descended from Elizabeth, Nuts In May and Loving Spoon. He sired three British Champions to date, also the brothers Blue Owl at Plushcourt, a dual CC winner co-owned by Betty with Andrew and Wendy Mooney, and NZ Ch. Brindleoak Hooligan at Plushcourt. The Mathesons' Can. Ch. Plushcourt Brain Wave is by Hero out of Plushcourt Embrace.

Ch. Lyrical of Lexing at Plushcourt won the Group at WELKS 1993, only the third bitch to achieve this in the UK. Rainsbarrow Buzzard at Plushcourt, an outcross, joined the kennel. He holds two CCs and is the sire of a Champion. Plushcourts are in many countries. Overseas Champions include: Am. Ch. Plushcourt Gangster who is by Brannigan out of Plushcourt Garter

Ch. Lyrical of Lexing at Plushcourt pictured after winning the Group at WELKS in 1993 – one of only three Border bitches to win a Group in Britain.

who is a daughter of Doublet and Encore; the litter-mates, NZ Champions Plushcourt Dewdrop and Distinction; Int. It. Ch. Plushcourt Royal Bond; Int. Am. Mex. Ch. Plushcourt Kinglet; NZ Ch. Plushcourt Scarlet Ribbons who is by Doublet out of Plushcourt Secret Romance. Dewdrop, Distinction, Royal Bond and Kinglet are sired by Secret Romance's brother, Plushcourt Royal Warrant, whose sire Plushcourt Run The Gauntlet was litter brother to Garter. Dewdrop, Distinction and Royal Bond descend in the bitch line from Delightful.

RHOZZUM: MARIE SHARP

Although there has not been a British Champion from this kennel for a few years, it must be included by virtue of the influence in many countries of Rhozzum exports. The kennel was founded in 1971. Eignwye Society Girl was the foundation of the line which has produced many good workers as well as winners. Ch. Rhozzum Tudor and Ch. Rhozzum Zodiac were bred here. The dual CC winner Rhozzum Tenor went to Krister Giselsson in Sweden and produced Champions and good workers. Aust. Ch. Rhozzum Venture, owned by Gordon Knight in England where he won two CCs, went to Robert Bartram in Australia and sired twenty Champions. In Denmark, Dk. Ch. Dk. Working Champion Rhozzum Victor and Int. Dk. Ch. Dk. Working Ch. Rhozzum Night Owl are behind good dual purpose stock, Night Owl having sired a Dual Champion himself. Fin. Ch. Fin. Working Ch. Brackenhills Samuraij was bred by Krister Giselsson, Sweden, in a litter imported in utero and sired by Moordown Wayne of Rhozzum. Aust. Ch. Rhozzum Argos went to Carol Maciver, Australia, in 1994.

SPRIGNELL: SYLVIA CLARKSON

Sylvia Clarkson's Sprignells must be one of the oldest established kennels still active in the breed. She owned her first Border in 1943 but Sprignell Scylla, born 1955, founded the line. Five generations on from her came Ch. Sprignell Selina, sired by Sprignell Sceptre out of Bannerdown Bush Sprite. Ch. Sprignell Spice, a Selina daughter, produced Sprignell Sirius who sired Ch. Knightstone Golden Nugget of Sprignell. Bannerdown Bush Sprite to Ch. Dandyhow Silver Ring gave Diana Swales and Suzanne Coupé's Ch. Sprignell Crystal Bell, foundation of the Grabbist line. Andy Berg's Am. Int. Ch. Sprignell Woodsmoke, a ROM sire with many Champion progeny, was a Selina son, sired by Silver Ring.

THORALDBY: PETER AND MAUREEN THOMPSON

From the first litter bred from their first Borders, Peter and Maureen bred Ch. Thoraldby Miss Mandy who set this internationally known kennel off to a flying start by breeding four Champions sired by Ch. Step Ahead, including the first Border bitch to win a Group, the Hodgsons' Ch. Thoraldby Yorkshire Lass. Thoraldby Miss Magic, sister to the four Champions, produced three British Champions including Ch. German Ch. Thoraldby Tiptoes who was made up by Mick and Doreen Rushby and later owned by Jörn and Diana Tillner in Germany. Tiptoes sired eight British Champions and has been used with success in Europe. Ch. Am. Ch. Thoraldby Free Guest, a Tiptoes son out of Ch. Loiriston Amber, was exported to Kate Seemann, USA. He sired Ch. Int. Ch. Thoraldby Glenfiddich who sired four British Champions before joining Wiebke Steen and Christopher Habig's kennel in Germany where he became the first Border to win a Group in Germany. Betty Judge's Ch. Lyrical of Lexing at Plushcourt was another Group winner sired by Tiptoes.

Miss Magic to Ashbrae Aurora gave Thoraldby Tipolina, dam of Ch. Ashbrae Jaffa. Miss Magic was also the dam of Pat Quinn's Am. Champions Thoraldby Magic Chip and Magic Moment who was exported in whelp to Ch. Ashbrae Jaffa, which produced the famous sire Am. Ch. Traveler of

Foxley. Another of Pat Quinn's Foxley foundations was Am. Ch. Wee Gee Gemstone, out of Ch. Thoraldby North Star. Thoraldby Early Bird was another Step Ahead and Miss Mandy daughter. To Thoraldby Night Owl, a Miss Mandy son by Ch. Foxtor Blue Jester, she gave Thoraldby Mary Poppins who was the foundation of Ron and Fiona Wheatley's Loiriston line.

Ch. Loiriston Amber, bred by the Wheatleys, owned by the Thompsons, was a great show bitch, winning twelve CCs and one Terrier Group, SKC 1983. More important, she was a splendid brood as well, holding the British record with six British Champions: four sired by Tiptoes – Ch. Am. Ch. Thoraldby Free Guest, Champions Tolomeo, Noble Flyer and High Flyer – and two by Ch. Int. Ch. Thoraldby Glenfiddich – Champions Golden Glen and Forever Amber. Am. Ch. Thoraldby Thyme, owned by Pat Quinn, and Int. Ch. German Ch. Thoraldby Another Amber, owned by Wiebke Steen, are Amber daughters.

Ch. Sw. Norw. Ch. Baillieswells Auchentoshan, made up here, bred by Tony Milton, carried Loiriston Jet, sister to Amber, on both sides of the pedigree and also ten lines back to Ch. Miss Mandy. Auchentoshan sired two British Champions before joining the Bombax kennel in Sweden with his daughter out of Another Amber, Sw. Norw. Ch. Thoraldby Shady Lady. To date there have been eighteen British Champions owned or bred by Pete and Maureen, all descending from Miss Mandy.

Among the overseas Thoraldby Champions are Am. Ch. Uncle Sam; Am. Ch. Pretty Woman and her sister Am. Ch. Ebony Eyes (by Ch. Thoraldby Trillion out of Ch. Thoraldby Star Appeal of Lairdarch); Am. Champions Tomahawk and Tom Jones, litter-brothers by Stirkhill Ironside out of Thoraldby Pebbles; German Champions Thoraldby Tinkerbelle and Sassy Lassie and Austrian Ch. Tallan. Jim Kane owned Pretty Woman and Tom Jones; Kate Seemann owned Tomahawk and Ebony Eyes.

TYRIAN : STEVE DEAN

The kennel was founded by Steve's late wife, Carol, on a predominantly Farmway base. All the Tyrian Champions descended from Carol's first show Border, Burchett's Rocky, a Ch. Farmway Snow Kestrel son. Rocky sired Strider the Rockranger, the sire of the first Champion here, Ch. Ragsdale Cock O' Roost at Tyrian whose dam was Farmway Ravishing Raven. Ravishing Rock Raven, litter sister to Strider, produced the dam of Ch. Am. Can. Ch. Lynhay Daz. Also out of Ravishing Rock Raven came Ch. Tyrian Midshipman. Cock O' Roost sired Tyrian Bluebeard who, out of Farmway Snow Bunting at Tyrian, produced Ch. Tyrian French Dressing. Snow Bunting to Midshipman produced Tyrian Red Alert, the dam of Champions for the van Hasselwick kennel, USA. Snow Bunting to Ch. Am. Can. Ch. Lynhay Daz produced Tyrian Dazzler, Reserve in the Group, Bournemouth 1994. French Dressing to Cock O' Roost gave Norw. Ch. Tyrian Sunset Strip.

Ch. Tyrian French Dressing.
Photo: S. Pickerin.

TYTHROP: JANET LEE The first Champion bred by Janet was Debbie Bass-Pickin's Ch. Basvale Blue Warrior, in 1986, out of Good Sport, who was bred at Brumberhill. From Peter and Maureen Thompson, Janet bought Ch. Thoraldby Golden Glen as a brood, being a daughter of the famous Ch. Loiriston Amber, and made her up. Soda Symphony and Skipton Spice were litter-sisters sired by Ch. Am. Ch. Thoraldby Free Guest, an Amber son. Janet sold Soda Symphony on breeding terms and had back from her Ch. Wintergarden Rhapsody in Tythrop, winner of Reserve in the Group, WELKS 1994. Skipton Spice produced Tythrop Cinnabar, the dam of Ch. Tythrop Cinnamon at Copestaff, bred by Janet, owned by David and Carole Webster.

Ch. Wilderscot Fireworks: Sire of Champions.

Photo: Fall.

Janet Lee with Ch. Wintergarden Rhapsody in Tythrop, runner-up in the Group at WELKS 1994.

Photo: Dog World.

WILDERSCOT: DAPHNE (BETTY) RUMSAM The foundation was Farmway Blue Dove who came on breeding terms from Madelene Aspinwall. Wilderscot Daisy, Blue Dove's granddaughter, produced two Champions: Ch. Wilderscot Beau Belle, born 1974, who was sired by Am. Ch. Farmway Dandyhow Beaujolais, and Ch. Wilderscot Silver Jubilee, born 1977, who was sired by Ch. Dandyhow Silver Ring. Silver Jubilee won Reserve in the Group at East of England, 1980. Blue Dove to Ch. Int. Nord. Ch. Clipstone Guardsman gave NZ Ch. Wilderscot Bandsman, behind many Champions in New Zealand and Australia. Ch. Silver Jubilee to Wilderscot Persimmon gave Ch. Wilderscot Morning Star and Am. Ch. Wilderscot Silver Shadow, owned by Diane Jones, Jollymuff kennel. Beau Belle's daughter, Farmway Belle L'Oiseau, produced several American Champions. Ch. Wilderscot Fireworks, grandson of Ch. Morning Star, sired Ch. Penforest Countryman and Janet Melly's Ch. Hugo of Hassage, both of which Betty handled to their titles for their owners. The litter-brothers Dutch Ch. Farmway Flamebird and Sw. Norw. Ch. Farmway Thunderbird were sired by Fireworks.

ABOVE: Ch. Another Scot.

TOP LEFT: Int. Ch. Fin. Working Ch. Double Scotch.
An interesting comparison of two famous litter brothers, both big winners and well-known sires.

LEFT: The first, and only, British and Irish Champion, Ch. Fairfoot Mrs Charity Barnum, owned and bred by Jean and John Taylor.

OTHER KENNELS OF NOTE Other kennels always to be reckoned with are BAYWILLOW owned by Marion Reeves, whose most famous dog, Ch. Baywillow Sundazzler, sired several CC winners including NZ Ch. Baywillow Sun An' Air; BIDDESTONE, Anara Hibberd, owner and breeder of the litter sisters, Champions Biddestone Poetry and Porcelain, and breeder of Fr. Ch. Biddestone Pickled Pepper; FAIRFAX, Mo Holmes, breeder of Ch. Fairfax Bumble Bee; KELGRAM, Sam and Heather Mitchell, owners of Ch. Kelgram Lauren Marie, breeders of Fin. Ch. Fin. Working Ch. Kelgram The Minstrel, Fin. Champions Kelgram Owen Tudor and This's Mist at Ulaani as well as several UK CC winners; ORENBERG, Jayne Brown, breeder and owner of Ch. Orenberg Nightfreight, breeder of Ch. Orenberg Emperor and breeder and co-owner of Am. Ch. Orenberg Tigerlily; PONTBECK, Chris, Bill and Lisa Gray, owners and breeders of Ch. Canny Crack of Pontbeck whose grandson, Ch. Another Scot, winner of fourteen CCs, is co-owned by Bill Gray and Janet Alexander; RUBICON, Ruth Jordan, whose mother and daughter Champions, Rubicon Rarity and Reserve, descended from the foundation of the line, Rayndale Rubicon, born 1965; STARCYL, Rita and John McCrystal, breeders of their own Ch. Starcyl Bracken and the Jacksons' CC winning Starcyl Penny Red Clipstone and of the successful exports Am. Ch. Starcyl March On, Am. Ch. Starcyl Lendl and his son Aust. Ch. Starcyl Rising Light; and VALMYRE, Val Myers, owner of Ch. Gem of Valmyre out of whom she bred Ch. Valmyre Magician of Dandyhow.

Chapter Fourteen

THE BORDER TERRIER IN NORTH AMERICA

It was more than twenty-five years after the Border was officially recognised in the UK that a small band of enthusiasts first mooted the idea of a breed club in America, in 1946. The first AKC registration was in 1927. There had been a few Borders imported prior to that. Harry S. Cram imported a couple bred by Messrs Dodd and Carruthers, and Mr Massey brought in some bred by Wattie Irving and John Renton in the thirties, but it was not until William MacBain imported Am. Ch. Pyxie o'Bladnoch of Diehard in whelp to Ch. Foxlair in 1937 that the foundation of the breed was laid. Pyxie became the first American Champion in 1941. Her double-grandson, Am. Ch. Diehard Dandy, was the first American-bred Champion. Dr Merritt Pope's Am. Ch. Philabeg Red Miss, a Pyxie granddaughter, was the first American-bred bitch Champion. William MacBain's Diehard kennel and Merritt Pope's Philabeg kennel were important in the early days of the breed.

Marjory Van der Veer and Margery Harvey, whose Dalquest kennel produced 44 Champions and provided foundation stock for several other kennels, obtained their foundation, Am. Ch. Philabeg Red Bet, a Red Miss daughter, from Merritt Pope in 1947. They imported several Portholmes including three Gold Register Of Merit (ROM) sires, one of which was Ch. Am. Ch. Portholme Macsleap, and also stock from other UK kennels.

The Border Terrier Club of America was formally organised in 1949 with ten members, including Dr and Mrs Merritt Pope, William MacBain and the Dalquest ladies. Marjory Van der Veer was secretary of the BTCA for 32 years. The BTCA currently has almost 800 members with about the same number of registrations per annum. The first Specialty was held in 1959 with 31 entries. Dalquest's Am. Ch. Portholme Mhor of Dalquest won BIS. In 1986, two Specialties were held. From the seventies onwards eight regional breed clubs gradually came into being, running their own events, including Specialties. The BTCA Specialty is now known as the National Specialty.

Two leading kennels came to the fore in the mid fifties which, with Dalquest, were leading kennels for many decades – Kate Webb's Shelburne kennel and Marion DuPont Scott's kennel, which followed Border tradition by not having an affix. Both ladies imported good stock from the UK and bred good ones, too. Marion DuPont Scott's first import was Am. Ch. Carahall Cindylou and her kennel produced three Gold ROM sires and one Gold ROM bitch among the many Champions. Her line comes down behind many lines today through Am. Ch. Shuttle, the great brood bitch.

SOME MILESTONES IN BREED HISTORY
In 1952 Merritt Pope's Am. Ch. Raisgill Romper of Philabeg was the first Border to be placed in a Group. In 1956 Ch. Am. Ch. Lucky Purchase, owned by Kate Webb (Seemann), was the first to

win British and American titles. In 1969 the first to win CDX was Am. Ch. Cinjola Toluidine Daisy CDX, owned by Francis and Maxine Hoyne. In 1972 Am. Ch. Chief of Lothian UDT, owned by Nancy Hughes, was the first to earn a Tracking title, also the first to earn a Utility Dog title. Also in that year Marg and Harvey Pough's Am. Ch. Bandersnatch Snark gained the first Certificate of Gameness and Dale Gourlie's Am. Ch. D.G's. Wattie Irving of Dalquest became the first Group winner. In 1975 Marion DuPont Scott's Am. Ch. Shuttle was the first bitch to win a Group. In 1977 Ch. Am. Ch. Workmore Waggoner, owned by Kate Seemann, was the first Border to win BIS All Breeds and Am. Ch. Avim Dainty Girl, owned by Pat Quinn, was the first to gain a Working Certificate. In 1978 Ob. Ch. Pete UD, owned by Floyd Timmons, became the first Obedience Champion.

Register of Merit (ROM) awards are awarded by the BTCA to sires and dams who have earned their place in breed history by producing a certain number of Champion progeny to at least two different mates. This is, since 1991, for males: Gold, twelve; Silver, nine; Bronze, seven; and for females: Gold, nine; Silver, seven; Bronze five progeny respectively.

OTHER ACTIVITIES FOR BORDERS

The BTCA encourages owners to participate with their Borders in other activities apart from showing them. Their Versatility Award is given at two levels, from points amassed, which are allocated to titles gained in categories covering Obedience, Tracking, Field, Agility, Flyball, Search and Rescue, Certified Therapy Dog, Canine Good Citizen Test, Temperament Test and in the Show ring.

LEADING KENNELS

When writing about the leading kennels it is not possible to credit dogs with all their titles gained, space being restricted. It is creditable that many owners are taking part with their Borders in diverse activities.

BANDERSNATCH: MARG AND AMANDA POUGH

A bitch from Dalquest, purchased in 1963, was the start of this kennel where Borders have long been expected to do more than look nice. The foundation, Mex. Ch. Dalquest Jody of Town Hill, was of Portholme bloodlines and was put to Ch. Am. Ch. Portholme Macsleap. This produced Am. Mex. Ch. Bandersnatch Brillig, dam of three Champions, and Bandersnatch Beamish who went to Mrs DuPont Scott and produced three Champions including Am. Ch. Bull Run, the sire of the famous Am. Ch. Shuttle. Brillig, to Mrs Scott's Am. Ch. Espresso, produced Am. Ch. Bandersnatch Snark, the first Border to earn the Certificate of Gameness.

Am. Ch. Bandersnatch Conundrum CDX.   Photo: K. Booth.

Am. Ch. Hanleycastle Roxana was imported and produced Am. Ch. Bandersnatch Mome Rath who, to Am. Ch. Dalquest Border Lord, gave Am. Ch. Bandersnatch Border in Blue, holder of a Working Certificate. By Snark, Roxana gave Am. Ch. Bandersnatch Frabjous Day, also a Working

Certificate holder. Snark with Border in Blue gave Am. Ch. Bandersnatch Jubjub Bird CDX, the dam of four Greenbriar's Champions. Border in Blue, to Am. Ch. Scooter, grandson of Bull Run, gave Am. Champions Bandersnatch Triumph and Harley D. Three Champions were produced out of Bandersnatch Black Magic including Am. Champions Bandersnatch Conundrum CDX and Magician, who were by Am. Ch. Traveler of Foxley. Am. Ch. Conundrum Red Jacket was out of Black Magic by Am. Ch. Thoraldby Tomahawk and she gave Am. Ch. Bandersnatch Tuxedo. Am. Ch. Bandersnatch Kachina joined the kennel.

BEHM: ANITA MORAN

Alaska is probably not the most convenient place from which to try to campaign and breed dogs, yet Anita's kennel has produced twenty-seven Champions, all but two bred by her, in the past ten years. The foundation, Am. Can. Ch. Jocasta Just Hollywood ROM, co-owned with Debra Blake, her breeder, is rated the second greatest brood in breed history in the USA, with fourteen Champion progeny. Her sire was Am. Can. Mex. Int. Ch. Sprignell Woodsmoke ROM, and her dam Am. Ch. Jocasta Just Sara ROM. Hollywood was the dam of the first JE titled Border and she, herself, was the second.

Am. Can. Ch. Behm Allegretto: One of fourteen Champions produced by Just Hollywood. Photo: Hellard.

Her daughter, Am. Can. Ch. Behm Allegretto ROM, was twice Best Puppy in Show (Canada). Am. Can. Ch. Behm Devlin and Am. Can. Ch. Behm's Happy Gangbuster are both BIS winners. Am. Can. Ch. Behm Prime Rate won three Groups in 1995. Am. Ch. Behm Jocasta Just Gambit is a Versatility Award Qualifier, and the youngster, Behm's Wild Alaskan, has been particularly successful with good puppy wins. Am. Ch. Craigend Wansbek, a blue and tan daughter of Aust. Ch. Craigend Cheviot Piper and Craigend Snapdragon, bred by Robert Bartram, was the first Australian-bred Border to become an American Champion. Plushcourt Guessing was imported in whelp to Plushcourt On the Run in 1995, co-owned with Debra Blake. Just Gambit and Just Cheviot compete in Agility and Working Trials.

BEVER LEA: TERI BEVERLY

Teri's first Border was Am. Ch. Barrister Just Because CDX, acquired in 1981. The foundation bitch, from whom most of the Bever Leas descend, Am. Ch. Glenburnie's Becky Thatcher Bronze ROM, obtained from Nancy Hughes, produced five Champions, including Am. Ch. Krispin Natty Gann, multiple Group winner, and Am. Ch. Bever Lea Polly Pureheart Gold ROM, who has produced eight Champions to date including the Gold ROM earner Am. Ch. Bever Lea Krispin Magician, Am. Ch. Bever Lea Secret Agent ROM with multiple Group wins and Am. Ch. Bever Lea Bewitching Brew CDX. The foundation stud, Am. Ch. Krispin Scotland Yard ROM, obtained from Dail Corl, sired eleven Champions including the Number one Border in 1993 on group points, Am. Ch. Bever Lea Krispin Not Guilty, and Am. Ch. Bever Lea Choc Full-O-Nutkin with qualifications in several types of work. Redletter days were when Am. Ch. Glenburnies Becky Thatcher went BOS at the BTCA National Specialty, 1987, when Am. Ch. Bever Lea Bewitching Brew went BOW at the BTCA National Specialty, 1991, and when Am. Ch. Krispin Scotland Yard went BIS at Piedmont Kennel Club, 1992. To date there have been thirty-five or more Champions. No imports have been made. The kennel has owned or bred eight dogs with CG or earth dog titles.

Am. Ch. Bever Lea Secret Agent ROM (Am. Ch. Krispin Scotland Yard – Am. Ch. Bever Lea Polly Pureheart). Photo: Sosa.

CALIROSE: VICKI AND JAMES SABO

The foundation was Am. Ch. Miss Taggart of Foxley, bred by Pat Quinn from her Thoraldby imports, in 1986. By Am. Ch. Woodlawn's Dusky Gentleman, who had a Foxley-bred sire, she produced Am. Ch. Calirose Gussied Up, Best in Sweepstakes at the 1990 National Specialty and only the third BIS All Breeds winning Border bitch in the USA, which she achieved twice, which is unique. From her eight puppies, five became Champions, earning her the Bronze ROM. Her daughter by Am. Ch. Nettleby Nighthawk, Am. Ch. Calirose Collectible, WB at the 1992 Specialty, produced Am. Ch. Charisma at Rochar, co-owned with Helen Vance and sired by Dusky Gentleman (her grandsire). Collectible also produced the litter-mates

Am. Ch. Calirose Gussied Up: Only the third Border Terrier bitch to win BIS in the USA, which she achieved twice.

Am. Champions Calirose Bee in My Bonnet, Prize Patrol and Feisty Swashbuckler who were sired by Am. Ch. Otley's Touch of the Desert, whose sire carried much Foxley blood and whose dam was a double Am. Ch. Duttonlea Autocrat of Dandyhow granddaughter. The three litter mates all won their titles from the six-to-nine months puppy class. Prize Patrol went on to Group placements and Bee in My Bonnet went on to win Groups.

Am. Ch. Krispin Calirose Bentley (Dusky Gentleman ex Am. Ch. Steephollow Little Nell) won Reserve WD from the six-to-nine months puppy class at the 1989 Specialty and two years later went BOB there, owner-handled, as he also was for his Group Win – quite an achievement. He sired three Champions out of Miss Taggart. From twenty-six puppies bred so far at Calirose, thirteen became Champions. An addition to the kennel was the puppy who became Am. Ch. Jam Session at Calirose, carrying several lines to Autocrat. The six Borders in residence all receive Obedience and Agility training although not necessarily for competition.

CYMRI HILLS: CATHERINE (KATE) MURPHY

Am. Ch. Highdyke's Tish of Cymri Hills, bred by Camilla Moon in 1979, was the foundation here, a Step Ahead granddaughter and Shady Knight great-granddaughter. She produced four Champions to Waggoner and one to his son, Am. Ch. Cymri Hill's Captain Marvel, whose dam, Am. Ch. Polydorus Pulco, was co-owned by Kate with Bob Naun. An interesting import was Am. Ch. Maxton Merry Mac, one of the rare Borders going back to neither of the current main-stem lines, Dandyhow or Wharfholm. To Am. Ch. Cymri Hill's Custom Maid, a Tish – Waggoner daughter, he gave Am Ch. Cymri Hill's Colleen Mac.

Am. Ch. Cymri Hill's Bonnie Kate, by Am. Ch. Rockferry Bomber Boy out of Am. Ch. Cymri Hill's Clover Mint, owned by Judith Rivers, was my BOB winner when I judged at the NW Connecticut Dog Club in 1995. She is the dam of Am. Champions

Am. Ch. Cymri Hill's Bonnie Kate, owned by Judith Rivers. Bred by Kate Murphy, Bonnie Kate is the dam of four Champions to date, from her two litters.

Photo: Tatham.

Redgate's Bonnie Bess, Oldstone Redgate Sterling and Oldstone Redgate Silver Star. Clover Mint was also the dam of Am. Ch. Cymri Hill's Buster Browne, a big winner for Gloria Connelly.

DICKENDALLS: KENDALL HERR

This affix, famous in Labradors, also graces a good line of Borders, founded with Am. Ch. Lothlorien Smidgeon who gave two Champions by Waggoner and one by Am. Ch. Wilderscot Silver Shadow, who was imported by Diane Jones, Jollymuff, also a Labrador breeder. Am. Ch. Jollymuff Crispy Critter, by Am. Ch. Sprignell Woodsmoke out of the full sister to Smidgeon, produced six Champions including Am. Ch. OTCh. Dickendalls Microchip. Am. Ch. Dickendalls G Whiz to Am. Ch. Dandyhow Bertie Bassatt gave Dickendalls Jollymuff Busby, the dam of two Todfield Champions and also the grandam of the famous sire, Am. Ch. Todfield Trafalgar Square. Am. Ch. Dickendalls Heartbreaker TDX, out of Crispy Critter by Am. Ch. Oldstone Ragrug, gave five Champions including Am. Ch. Dickendalls Heartstopper TDX. Recent Champions are Am. Ch. Dickendalls WYSIWYG and Am. Ch. Dickendalls Flash Gordon, both co-owned by Kendall with Paul and Lori Rudy.

FOXLEY: PAT QUINN

Pat started in Borders in 1974 and imported all her foundation stock from the UK. Her second Border, Am. Can. Bda. Ch. Avim Dainty Girl was the first Border to be awarded a Working Certificate and Hunting Certificate, won BOS at the 1977 Specialty and had Group placings in Canada. She also lost her life, sadly, saving Pat from a deadly snake. Unfortunately she only produced dog puppies so Pat had no bitch from her with which to breed on. Am. Bda. Ch. Weegee Gemstone, a Cheltor Michael ex Ch. Thoraldby North Star daughter, was imported from Bill Gillott and co-owned with Camilla Moon. From Peter and Maureen Thompson Pat imported Am. Ch. Thoraldby Magic Moment Bronze ROM, by Michael out of Thoraldby Miss Magic, and Am. Pr. SA. Int. Ch. Thoraldby Magic Chip Gold ROM. These three founded the Foxley line, behind so many American Borders.

Magic Chip with Gemstone produced Betsy Finley's Am. Ch. Foxley Bright Forecast Gold ROM, the sire of twenty-two Champions among which was Am. Ch. Woodlawn's Dusky Gentleman, himself the sire of thirty-five Champions to date. Magic Moment arrived in whelp to Ch. Ashbrae Jaffa and this produced Barbara Kemp's Am. Ch. Traveler of Foxley Gold ROM with

Pat Quinn's Am. Ch. Foxley Briarpatch.

41 Champions to date. Magic Moment had two Group placings. A later import was Am. Ch. Thoraldby Thyme, daughter of Ch. Loiriston Amber sired by Ch. Germ. Ch. Thoraldby Tiptoes. Am. Ch. Foxley Briarpatch is a recent Champion with a Group placing. Pat has made eight Champions and bred a further ten. Her dogs are worked in AWTA Trials and all have their Certificates of Gameness with the exception of the two youngest. They are worked at home on natural quarry, mainly rats around farm buildings. Groundhogs do not come as far south as Alabama. Terrier owners in the deep South have to be very careful in letting their dogs go to ground as earths and holes are a haven for hibernating snakes.

FREILANCE: PHIL AND SHARON FREILICH
An exciting show dog started Phil and Sharon in Borders in 1989, Am. Ch. Krispin Tailor Made, the winner of BOB at the BTCA Specialty 1994, three times BIS All Breeds, and more than a hundred Group placements. He is a Gold ROM sire with some twenty-five Champions to date. Am. Ch. Krispin Finders Keepers, Silver ROM, the foundation bitch, has also been a strong influence on the line, and her daughter by Am Ch. Tailor Made, Am. Ch. Freilance Diamond in the Rough, went WB and BOS under Brian Staveley at the 1993 Specialty. Am. Ch. Freilance Shooting Star is a recent Champion. To date there have been eleven Champions here. The import Otterkin Miss American Pie is on her way to her title. The Freilichs take part in Earth Dog Work, Obedience (CDX) and Agility with their Borders.

Am. Ch. Freilance Shooting Star, owned by Phil and Sharon Freilich.

Photo: Cook.

HIDEAWAY: LYNN LOOPER
From Barbara Kemp came, in 1987, Am. Ch. Steephollow Wood Nymph, the foundation of this kennel which has been remarkably successful at the National Specialty. Wood Nymph was the dam of five Champions. Put back to her grandsire, Am. Ch. Traveler of Foxley, she produced Am. Ch. Hideaway's Cocklebur, the 1991 BTCA Sweepstakes Winner, who, to Am. Ch. Hollybridge Raffles, gave Am. Ch. Hideaway's Toad Flax, Reserve WD at the 1993 Specialty, aged six and a half months. Putting Toad Flax back to his grandmother, Wood Nymph, produced Hideaway's Poison Oak, winner of the Sweepstakes at the 1995 Specialty, from 96 entries. Am. Ch. Hideaway's Ocimum Basilicum TDX, out of Bessie, earned all his titles before the age of two and earned his TD and TDX titles on his first attempts – a notable feat. To date there have been nine Champions from Wood Nymph and Cocklebur.

KETKA: CAROL SOWDERS

The start here was a puppy from Dalquest, Dalquest Ketka's Kritter, who to Am. Ch. Beaverwoods Bold Blaze gave four Champions – the first of the countless Ketka's Champions. One of these was Am. Ch. Ketka's Gopher Broke, co-owned with David Tinker, and the dam of nine Champions and another, Am. Ch. Ketka's Beaver Woodchip. Another foundation bitch was Am. Ch. Little Fir Rob Roy's Robin, a daughter of Am. Ch. Farmway Dandyhow Likely Lad. To her half-brother, also by Likely Lad, Am. Ch. Rob Roy Buckler, she gave Am. Ch. Ketka's Swashbuckler Gold ROM with 23 Champions to his credit. Swashbuckler's daughter, Am. Ch. Ketka's Short Circuit, Group winner Gold ROM with eleven Champions, including Am. Ch. Ketka's Barrister's Speed Trap whose dam, Am. Ch. Express was owned by Carol. Express was from Mrs DuPont Scott's famous line. Speed Trap to Am. Ch. Concorde, full sister to Express, produced the famous sire, Am. Ch. Seabrook Spriggan. Short Circuit with Spriggan produced eight Champions including James Ham and Larry Saganski's multiple BIS winning Am. Ch. Ketka Qwik Charge of Dalfox, Gold ROM sire with over 30 Champions, whose son was Am. Ch. Feorrawa Ketka's Cagney, multiple BIS winner and sire of 18 Champions. Cagney's son, Am. Ch. Ketka's American All Star, sired 11 Champions. Honourable mention must be given to Am. OTCh. Ketka's Fine O'Pinion UD, owned by Anne Gilbraith, one of the select band of Obedience Champions. Her dam, Am. Ch. Ketka's Sure As Shootin', carried several Hanleycastle lines. To Beaver Woodchip she gave Fine O'Pinion and Am. Ch. Ketka's Poplar Demand, the sire of seven Champions.

KRISPIN: DAIL KORL

The foundations of this line were three excellent producers, the two bitches, Am. Ch. Lothlorien Rosemary and Am. Ch. Steephollow Little Nell, and the male, Am. Ch. Woodlawn's Dusky Gentleman. The line from them bred on to produce top winners as well as top producers. Dusky Gentleman, a Gold ROM sire with 41 Champions, and Little Nell, BOB at the 1989 Specialty and Gold ROM dam with nine Champions, together produced eight Champions. These included the Silver ROM sires, Am. Ch. Krispin Scotland Yard, co-owned by Dail with Teri Beverly, and Am. Ch. Krispin Travel'N Man O Otley, owned by Debbie Pomeroy; also the well-known sire, Am. Ch. Krispin Calirose Bentley and Am. Ch. Krispin Smart Alec, a big winner for Paula and Garry

Wolf. Travel'N Man sired the Freilichs' Gold ROM sire Am. Ch. Krispin Tailor Made, himself a multiple BIS winner and BOB at the 1994 Specialty. Among his 25 Champions came the multiple Group winning Am. Ch. Krispin Tailored to A T, owned by Betsy Kilpatrick, Cindy Peebles and Henry Odum. To A T was out of a Dusky Gentleman – Rosemary daughter, Am. Ch. Krispin Whuzzle. Am. Ch. Krispin Jack B Nimble, owned by Jessica Cortez, is another top winner and is sired by the Bronze ROM sire, Am. Ch. Bever Lea Krispin Magician, a Bentley son, out of the Dusky Gentleman daughter Am. Ch. Krispin Natty Gann.

Apart from the influence of the males, the bitches have done well, too. The Gold ROM dam Am. Ch. Krispin Flashdance, sister to Whuzzle, bred eight Champions for the Riverside kennel, all sired by Am. Ch. Ketka Qwik Charge of Dalfox. The

Am. Ch. Krispin Tailor Made, son of Am. Ch. Krispin Travel'N Man O Otley. Tailor Made is owned by Phil and Sharon Freilich.

Photo: Booth.

Freilichs' Am. Ch. Krispin Finders Keepers, a Bentley daughter, earned her silver ROM with four Champions sired by Tailor Made and two by Dusky Gentleman.

LOTHLORIEN: JO ANN FRIER-MURZA

No more than three Borders at a time, including pensioners, are kept by Jo Ann who owns other terriers for companionship and work, but breeds only Borders. Her first Border was acquired in 1974 after working a Bedlington. The foundation of the Lothloriens, Am. Ch. Trail's End Peaceful Bree UD, was bred by Nancy Hughes, out of Ch. Am. Ch. Workmore Brackon sired by Ch. Am. Ch. Final Honour, and attained titles in Obedience and in the field as well as attaining Gold ROM, being the dam of thirteen Champions. Her progeny attained 23 Obedience and 11 field titles. Their successes in the 1970s and 80s encouraged many to attempt these less popular terrier sports. All the current stock descend from Peaceful Bree. Since a stud dog from this line has never been kept by Jo Ann, the bitches have influenced the kennel, which has been line-bred. Their offspring have founded several kennels. In the show ring, Jo Ann is not interested in going beyond attaining a Championship, so Lothlorien Borders with other owners have done better in this respect, although some of the home team have achieved Group placements on the way to their titles. Since 1976, Jo Ann has bred 23 Champions from 18 litters, also the holders of 20 Obedience titles and 24 field titles. Eight of the total of 19 Working Certificates issued to Borders, so far, went to Lothlorien owned or bred ones, and of the eight Hunting Certificates issued to Borders, three went to Lothlorien owned or bred ones.

Jo Ann and Pam Dyer in Canada have collaborated informally for many years, both having the same ideals of retaining the breed's correct temperament and working ability. Am. Can. Ch. Lothlorien Kingsfoil went to Pam and Chris Dyer at the age of six. in 1990 her granddaughter, who is also a Peaceful Bree granddaughter, came back from them as a puppy and became Am. Ch. Jansim Lothlorien Tangle. The Lothloriens are worked regularly to woodchuck, an eight pound earth-dwelling rodent, and to fox and racoon when available, although they are much less common. As well as taking part in AWTA and AKC artificial den trials, Jo Ann enjoys Obedience training and her Borders have earned Obedience titles at many levels over the years.

LUVEMUR: JOHN M. AND LAURALE STERN

This kennel was founded in 1981 with Am. Ch. Woodlawn's Queen Anne ROM, from whom all the·stock descends. She produced seven Champions, one with UD qualification. Am. Ch. Arberdale's Aliage of Luvemur UD, ROM, produced seven Champions, three with CDX. 23 Champions have been owned or bred here. Am. Ch. Luvemur First Edition UD, owner-handled, placed second in a Group, an exciting and memorable win. His AKC Utility Title also qualified him for a Dog World Award, which must be earned in the first three shows with a score of 195 or over. He is the first, and so far the only, Border Terrier to earn this award at Utility level.

Am. Ch. Luvemur Silvercreeks Mr. Max, CDX, owned by Jenni Tollefson, is a multiple Group placing and winning dog, Number five Border in the USA in 1993, while at the same time placing in the top ten on both national Obedience systems. His sister, Am. Ch. Luvemur Bonnie Brambleberry, CDX, owned by Carol Carson, is the only Border to earn a High in Trial in three Obedience organisations, the AKC, the Canadian KC and the United KC, competing against all breeds. She also earned the Chief of Lothian Award for the highest scoring dog at the BTCA Specialty two years in succession. The four dogs currently living with the Sterns have all earned Versatility Awards through the BTCA. The home team has earned four CDs, four CDXs and four UDs and two CGs, and all are certified Therapy Dogs, visiting nursing homes and children's groups two or three times a week.

OLDSTONE: ROBERT (BOB) AND RUTH ANN NAUN

Since their start in 1972, Bob and Ruth Ann have kept the British Border very much in their sights. They show their own dogs, therefore they do not campaign Specials (Champions) with a view to the Group, where a professional handler is needed to have any success. They have bred and made 19 Champions plus a further 12 not bred by themselves, and 17 Oldstone-bred Borders have been made up by other owners.

Their first Champion was Am. Ch. Borderseal Bessie (by Ch. Int. Nord. Ch. Clipstone Guardsman) who, to their imported Bronze ROM winner Am. Ch. Dandyhow Bertie Bassatt, a Shady Knight son, produced Am. Ch. Oldstone Ragrug Gold ROM with 14 Champion progeny. Bertie Bassatt's daughter, Am. Ch. Highdyke Alpha, who was Oldstone owned and bred by Camilla Moon out of her imported Clipstone Cider Rose (Guardsman ex Ch. Llanishen Illse of Clipstone), put to Ch. Am. Ch. Workmore Waggoner produced Am. Champions Oldstone Hadrian, sire of six Champions, Bowmont, sire of three Champions, Poppy, Brampton Sweet, the Group winning Wholly Terrier and the Gold

Ruth Ann Naun with Am. Ch. Oldstone Brass Ring.   *Photo: Tatham.*

ROM winner Highland Rainbow, owned by Julianne Amidon (Woodbine).

The line continued down through Hadrian to Am. Ch. Oldstone Rapscallion who, to the Nauns' imported Am. Ch. Dandyhow Top Notch (by Ch. Dandyhow Crofter ex Dandyhow Tip Top), Bronze ROM, produced Oldstone's Penrith Molasses. Rapscallion to the Irvings' Am. Ch. Dandyhow Brass Tacks produced Bronze ROM winner Am. Ch. Oldstone Brass Ring who, to Penrith Molasses, produced the young Bronze ROM winner Am. Ch. Oldstone Kingcraig, who is still being widely used at stud.

A further addition to the Oldstone kennel was the Gold ROM winner, sire of 20 Champions to date, Am. Ch. Herdsman of Dandyhow, an Uncle Walter son, who is co-owned with Kris Blake. He came to Oldstone late in his stud career and has sired seven Champions so far for the kennel. To Am. Ch. Oldstone Playmate (Brass Tacks ex Rapscallion), owned by Carlie Krolick, he produced the 1993 Specialty winner, Am. Ch. Neverlands Night Watchman. To the Top Notch daughter, Oldstone Soutra, he produced Am. Ch. Oldstone Silver Sixpence, the dam of several Champions. Am. Champions Oldstone Redgate Sterling and Silver Star, the latest Champions here, are by him out of Am. Ch. Cymri Hill's Bonnie Kate, a daughter of Am. Ch. Rockferry Bomber Boy. Other imports owned or co-owned by the Nauns were Am. Ch. Farmway Snow Song, Farmway Sandling (sire of three Champions, co-owned with Hazel Wichman), Am. Ch. Rockferry Bomber Boy, co-owned with Kate Murphy, Farmway Belle L'Oiseau, co-owned with Jean Clark, Bronze ROM with six Champions including the 1993 Specialty WB, and Am. Ch. Stonecroft Tinkerbelle who was sired by Am. Ch. Oldstone Hadrian.

RANTHORN: ELIZABETH CRISP BLAKE

Elizabeth grew up with the breed and was successful in Junior Handling. Her import Am. Ch. Ryswick Remember Me Gold ROM won BOB at the 1988 Specialty, won a Group and had several placings. He was my BOB winner when I judged at Old Dominion in 1986. He is currently rated the fourth leading sire of all time with over 30 Champion progeny of which only three were Ranthorn-bred; these were out of the only litter bred from Am. Ch. Dykeside Kristina. He has been used as a judicious outcross by many of the leading kennels. His son, Am. Ch. Woodlawn's Unforgettable is a Gold ROM sire and his daughters, Am. Ch. Woodlawn's Double Bubble and Am. Ch. Beverlea Polly Pureheart are ROM dams.

ROYAL OAKS: ERIC AND ARDITH DAHLSTROM

It all started with rescuing a Border in 1980 and Eric and Ardith were then firmly hooked on the breed! Their foundation bitch, Am. Ch. Royal Oaks Gilda Ratter, who carried the Dutch Tassel's bloodlines on her sire's side, was purchased, and was followed shortly afterwards by Royal Oaks Wizard of Foxley ROM, purchased from Pat Quinn and bred from her Thoraldby imports, Magic Chip and Magic Moment. The combination of Gilda with Wizard produced five Champions, all owner-handled. So far, 15 Champions have been bred and owned here. The kennel is line-bred on the Thoraldby line.

Eric and Ardith's main interest is in the field. They keep an average of ten Borders, old timers, youngsters and show dogs, but rarely campaign them after they are made up. They manage to do well in both the show ring and work by juggling show and work, it being difficult to compete in the conformation ring with a Border in really hard working condition.

An intelligent looking group of workers: Am. Ch. Royal Oaks Hurricane Hannah, Am. Ch. Royal Oaks Rhatt Butler and their son, Am. Ch. Royal Oaks Rimini Cricket.

SAGA HILLS: KRIS BLAKE

A blue and tan bitch, Am. Ch. Woodlawn's Angel Dusk, by Am. Ch. Woodlawn's Blue Beard out of Am. Ch. Edenbrae Dusky Maiden, and a dog, Am. Ch. Trails End Fur Trapper, by Am. Ch. Duttonlea Autocrat of Dandyhow out of Ch. Am. Ch. Dandyhow Forget Me Not, were Kris Blake's first Champions, both made up in 1983. Together they produced two Champions. Am. Ch. Trails End Bewitched, Gold ROM, of predominantly Dandyhow bloodlines, proved a super brood with nine Champions, three by Trapper and six by Am. Ch. Herdsman of Dandyhow who joined the kennel. Herdsman sired seven Saga Hills Champions including Am. Ch. Saga Hills Mumbly Peg, out of Bewitched, who in turn produced three Champions.

Am. Ch. Saga Hills English Abbey UDT, by Trapper out of Bewitched, joined the Tyneside kennel as did Am. Ch. Hollybridge Red Jester, whom Kris imported. Am. Ch. Nettleby Nighthawk

Gold ROM was a full brother, later litter, to Ch. Nettleby Mullein. He was sired by the famous British stud Ch. Lyddington Let's Go, and bred by the Tucks. Nighthawk won BIS at the 1990 Specialty, gained a BTCA Versatility award, had a Working Certificate, and sired over 17 American, two Canadian and one South American Champion. His son, Am. Can. Ch. Impressions Digby of Palantyne was Canada's top winning Border, 1992, a BIS All Breeds winner and the winner of many Groups. Am Ch. Orenberg Tigerlily, again of Dandyhow lines, was co-owned with her breeder, Jayne Brown, and produced five Champions, all by Nighthawk. Her daughter, by Nighthawk, Am. Ch. Saga Hills Meri Miss Demeanor, produced several Champions.

SHELBURNE: KATE SEEMANN

Since the start in the mid fifties, this kennel has housed many famous Borders including some of the best British Champions, too many to list here. The all-time star of the kennel must be Ch. Am. Ch. Workmore Waggoner. An outstanding show dog, he won the first BIS All Breeds for the breed in the USA, was a Group winner and was five times consecutively BIS winner at the National Specialty. Waggoner sired 27 American Champions and several in other countries. Seven of his Champions were Shelburne-bred.

Am. Ch. Starcyl March On, a double Step Ahead grandson, also had an outstanding show career with six Group wins and many placings. Ch. Am. Ch. Thoraldby Free Guest, a son of Britain's leading brood, Ch. Loiriston Amber, proved another successful import. His son, Am. Ch. Rogue's Resolute, owned by Kate Seemann, was a BIS All Breeds winner. Am. Ch. Dickendalls Pippin, sired by Kate's Am. Ch. Thoraldby Tomahawk, is a good winning bitch for the kennel with a G2 placement. Shelburne Christopher, my WD in NW Connecticut in 1995, is a Free Guest son out of Am. Ch. Campanologia Striding Edge.

STANDISH: JOYCE STANDISH

This kennel's proud claim is producing the all-time leading brood bitch, Am. Ch. Standish's Dynamite who produced 21 Champions by four sires. Her dam, Am. Ch. Standish's Dyn-O-Mite, was line-bred to Am. Ch. Llanishen Senator and also went back to Am. Ch. Shuttle. Dynamite's sire was Am. Ch. Duttonlea Autocrat of Dandyhow, and putting her back to his descendants paid dividends. Half her children went on to produce Champions themselves, and into the next generation, too, and when line-bred back to Dynamite. Out of Dynamite, sired by Am. Ch. Krispin Tailor Made, is Elaine Bron's Am. Ch. Standish's Kissen' Bandit, a multiple Group winner and sire of Champions.

STEEPHOLLOW: BARBARA KEMP

Barbara started in Borders in 1979 but never bred from her first Border. The foundations of her line were Am. Ch. Traveler of Foxley, who was imported in utero by Pat Quinn and sired by Ch. Ashbrae Jaffa out of Am. Ch. Thoraldby Magic Moment, and two bitches imported by Barbara and bred by Wilf Wrigley, Am. Ch. Duttonlea Genie, out of Ch. Duttonlea Steel Blue sired by Duttonlea Tearaway, and Am. Ch. Duttonlea Jenny Wren, sired by Ch. Ashbrae Jaffa out of a full sister to Steel Blue – an all-British foundation.

Am. Ch. Traveler of Foxley won the 1985 Specialty under Peter Thompson. But more important was his stud record – Gold ROM, with 21 Champion progeny to date. To Genie he produced Am. Ch. Steephollow Little Nell Gold ROM. The latest Champion, Am. Ch. Steephollow Sweet William, is by a son of Little Nell out of a daughter of Traveler and Jenny Wren.

The high point in the ring was the National Specialty, 1987, where Barbara with Am. Ch. Tansy of Steephollow and Am. Ch. The Red Baron at Steephollow, both sired by Traveler, swept the board under Walter Gardner – Tansy going WB, BOW and BOB and Red Baron WD and BOS. For good measure Barbara also won the Stud dog and Brace classes! Another great win was Am. Ch. Steephollow Little Nell, litter sister to Tansy, winning BOB at the 1989 National Specialty under Wilf Wrigley. She also had two BOS at the Specialty and in 1991 her son, Am. Ch. Krispin Calirose Bentley, won BOB under Marjorie Staveley at the National Specialty.

With limited breeding, Barbara has produced ten Champions. Her stud dogs have sired 36 Champions to date. Several other people have picked up the line and are breeding to it, especially Lynn Looper whose Hideaway kennel has produced two Specialty Best in Sweeps and a RWD in four years. In the early years Barbara enjoyed ratting with her Borders, but when one day they got onto and killed a young racoon, which are the primary carriers of rabies in the area, she lost interest on learning that her dogs would have been confined to isolation for six months had the racoon been rabid, despite their inoculations. Up until then she did a lot of AWTA Trials and was an AWTA judge. She has done Obedience, winning some basic titles, and is becoming interested in Agility. Four of her dogs are Certified Therapy Dogs, working on a regular basis.

TODFIELD (FORMERLY LITTLE FIR): DAVID KLINE

Two British imports, Am. Ch. Rhosmerholme Belinda and Am. Ch. Falcliff Target, founded the line in 1970. Together they produced Am. Ch. Little Fir Autumngold who, to Ch. Am. Ch. Final Honour, who was co-owned by Dave with Nancy Hughes, gave the Gold ROM sire Am. Ch. Little Fir Gremlin of Ariel, who in turn sired the Gold ROM sire Am. Ch. Solo. By Am. Ch. Llanishen Senator, Autumngold produced another Gold ROM sire, Am. Can. Ch. Little Fir Kirksman, owned by Betsy Findley.

Dickendalls Jollymuff Busby, going back to Belinda, Target and Final Honour, to Autocrat, produced Todfield Tadpole and Am. Ch. Todfield Truffle, the dam of five Champions, and Am. Ch. Todfield Tycoon, sire of 12 Champions, by Trails End Tradesman, an Autocrat Son. To Autocrat, Todfield Tadpole produced the Gold ROM sire Am. Ch. Todfield Trafalgar Square, sire of over 20 Champions. His son, Am. Ch. Todfield Tribute to Otterby, owned by Bob and Arden LeBlanc, Hickory Ridge kennel, sired nine Champions including five for Hickory Ridge.

Truffle back to Autocrat, her sire, produced Ch. Todfield Tzarina, the dam of seven Champions including six carrying the Deswind prefix. Am. Ch. Todfield Terracotta, sister to Trafalgar Square, produced three Deswind Champions. Todfield Tyf of Hickory Ridge was another successful brood, with five Champions for the Hickory Ridge kennel.

TOWZIE TYKE: WAYNE AND JOYCE KIRN

The start of the line was Am. Ch. Cotswold Dee Dee, a daughter of Am. Ch. Scooter and Am. Ch. Llanishen Sophia. Her son by Am. Ch. Seabrook Spriggan, Am. Ch. Towzie Tyke Tweedle-Dee, was placed in eleven Groups and won two. Am. Ch. Towzie Tyke MacAllister, son of Tweedle-Dee and Am. Ch. Krispin Rona of Towzie Tyke, has eleven Group placings, always owner-handled. In all there have been 26 Champions, mostly in the last decade. Two imports have been made, both from Lesley Gosling – Am. Ch. Akenside Noodle and Akenside Overjoyed. The Towzie Tykes take part in CD and Earth Dog trials and Am. Ch. Towzie Tyke Teviot is an expert terrier racer.

TRAILS END: NANCY HUGHES

Nancy Hughes imported some highly influential stock. Her first Border, Am. Ch. Chief of Lothian UDT was by Wharfholm Wipperin ex Am. Ch. Rose Bud of Lothian. He won BOB at the 1972 Specialty and was the first Border to win both the UD and the Tracking Degree. Ch. Am. Ch.

Workmore Brackon was co-owned with Nancy Kloskowski. To Chief, Brackon gave two males, Am. Ch. Beaverwoods Bold Blaze and Can. Ch. Blue Shadow v. Fichtental. Both appear far back in some pedigrees.

Then, at Crufts in 1973, Nancy Hughes purchased Ch. Am. Ch. Final Honour, co-owned with Dave Kline, who sired only three litters in the USA but left his mark through Am. Ch. Little Fir Gremlin of Ariel and Am. Ch. Trails End Peaceful Bree UD. Gremlin, owned by Ken Klothen, sired eleven Champions including Ch. Solo, who sired fourteen Champions including Am. Ch. Stonehaven Challenger, himself the sire of eleven Champions. Bree was the foundation of Jo Ann Frier-Murza's Lothlorien kennel. She was the sole pup in a litter out of Brackon, but she herself produced large litters and was the dam of twelve Champions including Am. Can. Ch. Lothlorien Kingsfoil, herself the dam of six Champions.

After a lot of bad luck in the breeding department, Nancy made a new start, purchasing in 1980 the eight-month-old Am. Ch. Duttonlea Autocrat of Dandyhow, litter-brother to Ch. Int. Ch. Duttonlea Suntan of Dandyhow. What a great dog he turned out to be! He won Best in Sweeps and WD at the 1980 Specialty, BOB at the 1982, 83 and 86 Specialties. He sired 45 Champions and many top Borders are line bred to him. The winner of BOB at the 1995 Specialty, Am. Ch. Wildwood Mountain Laurel, owned by Annette Neff, carries five lines to him.

Ch. Am. Ch. Dandyhow Forget Me Not had four litters, all by Autocrat, producing six Champions. At the 1982 Specialty, Autocrat won BOB with Am. Ch. Trails End Good Gracious, his daughter ex Forget Me Not, BOS. The following year the litter-mates by him out of Forget Me Not, Am. Ch. Trails End Fur Trapper, owned by Kris Blake, and Trails End Tradesman, owned by Dave Kline and Nancy Hughes, won WD and RWD respectively, with Autocrat going BOB. Among Autocrat's most famous progeny are: Am. Ch. Todfield Truffle, dam of seven Champions; Am. Ch. Trails End Barney, sire of nine Champions; Am. Ch. Saucy Debutant of But 'N Ben, dam of five Champions; the amazing brood Am. Ch. Standish's Dynamite, dam of 21 Champions; Am. Ch. Hickory Ridge Oh Danny Boy, sire of ten Champions; Am. Ch. Todfield Trafalgar Square, sire of 20 Champions; Am. Ch. Trails End Buddy of Glenfarm, sire of 17 Champions; Am. Ch. Jocasta Just Behm's Cadence, sire of seven Champions; Am. Ch. Todfield Tzarina, dam of seven Champions and herself out of an Autocrat daughter, Truffle.

In 1982, Polydorus Peski, a Ch. Dandyhow Spectator daughter, was brought over in whelp to Ch. Dandyhow Silver Ring. From this came Kris Blake's Am. Ch. Trails End Bewitched, dam of nine Champions. Peski to Autocrat produced Am. Ch. Trails End Buddy of Glenfarm, owned by Harriet Wallace Haydon and Nancy Hughes, the sire of seventeen Champions.

Am. Ch. Herdsman of Dandyhow was purchased by Nancy in 1984. He joined Kris Blake's kennel and then the Nauns'. He sired Am. Ch. Neverland's Night Watchman, owned by Carlie Krolick, BOB at the 1993 Specialty and BOS at the 1995 Specialty. Herdsman sired 20 Champions to date. It is hard to pick up a pedigree of an American-bred Border which does not trace back to one or more of these dogs. There have been 21 Champions carrying the Trails End prefix.

TYNESIDE: JANE AND STEVE WORSTELL

A companion for their daughter, bought in 1982, was Jane and Steve's first Border. Tyneside started with their second, obtained two years later, Am. Ch. Saga Hills English Abbey UDT, BTCA Versatility Excellent award, bred by Kris Blake. Her daughter by Am. Ch. Herdsman of Dandyhow, namely Am. Ch. Tyneside Tenacity UTD, also qualified for the BTCA Versatility Dog Excellent award. Like her mother she qualified TD, CD, CDX, CG, UD, but also has United Kennel Club Agility II and was awarded High in Trial (Obedience) at the 1990 BTCA National Specialty. Abbey's progeny include three Champions, five CDs, two CDXs, one UD, two TDs, three CGs and one Versatility Excellent. The most influential male is the imported Am. Ch. U-ACh. Hollybridge Raffles UDT, only the second Border Champion in breed history to earn UTD and the first to earn six AKC titles. Apart from his AKC Champion, these are TD, CG, CD, CDX, UD, plus BTCA Versatility Excellent, UKC Agility Champion, AKC Novice Agility and ROM Stud Dog. This remarkable dog, imported from his breeder, Susan Williams in England, was sired by Ch. Dandyhow April Fool out of Dandyhow Sweet Corn. Also from Susan came Am. Ch. Hollybridge Coco TD, who to Raffles produced Am. Ch. Tyneside's River Rag, co-owned by Bob Scott and Jane, WD and BOW BTCA 1992 National Specialty, judge Ruth Ann Naun.

Portrait of a genius: U-A Ch. Am. Ch. Hollybridge Raffles UDT, NA, CG, ROM. Owned and photographed by Jane Worstell.

Other imports are Orenberg Morning Glory and Pontbeck Lady Charlotte, both with promising descendants. All six permanent residents at Tyneside have earned titles in several fields, with their owners being actively involved with them in breed, obedience, tracking, den trials and agility.

VON HASSELWICK: HAZEL AND JENNIFER WICHMAN

The Farmway line has been influential in this kennel which is well-known in both the US and Canada since the Wichmans spend the summer in New Brunswick. Their first Borders were bred by Professor Mettler who was breeding them to aid his study for a book on genetics and was aiming to breed a good-looking Border, intelligent and capable of work. Am. Can. Ch. Von Hasselwick's Dandy was bred by Jennifer and was the result of a careful breeding pattern from Dr Mettler's foundation stock which was basically Farmway. Am. Ch. Farmway Cherry Wren, a Snow Kestrel daughter, to Dandy produced Am. Ch. Von Hasselwick's Mistletoe, the dam of two Champions and Von Hasselwick Frisker CDX, UD.

Am. Can. Ch. Von Hasselwick Gamekeeper, Am. Can. CDX, was acquired in 1987. He was by a Waggoner son, Am. Ch. Shelburne Thistle, who was out of Starcyl Swan Song. Farmway Snow Sparrow, from a half-brother and sister mating on Snow Kestrel, was the next import, from Madelene Aspinwall. Descendants of her with Gamekeeper are doing well in various fields, including Earth Dog. One of their daughters, Navarre's Isabeau, holds the Certificate of Versatility.

Am. Can. Ch. Doonabrig Von Hasselwick Cliff, by Gamekeeper out of Am. Ch. Shelburne Damsel, was bred in Canada. Tyrian Red Alert, carrying several lines to Snow Kestrel, was imported from the Deans. To Gamekeeper she produced Am. Ch. Von Hasselwick Lady Bug and to Cliff, Am. Ch. Von Hasselwick Cricket. Putting a Gamekeeper – Red Alert daughter to a Gamekeeper – Snow Sparrow son continued the breeding pattern followed throughout by the Wichmans, resulting in Can. Ch. Baron Von Hasselwick. Several of this kennel are registered Therapy Dogs. Top Notch is in training as a Hearing Ear Dog. Hazel has also tried Borders herding sheep alongside Border Collies and thinks they have a natural instinct for this.

WOODLAWN: BETSY FINLEY

The foundation stock of Betsy Finley's highly successful kennel, from which current stock descend, were Am. Ch. Dalquest Rebecca of Woodlawn Gold ROM, Am. Can. Ch. Little Fir Kirksman Gold ROM and the English import, Am. Ch. Edenbrae Dusky Maiden, bred by Margaret Edgar. Rebecca descended from the early Dalquest stock. In 25 years, 115 American Champions have been bred here and a further 17 made up by Betsy which she bought in.

The most influential producers for the home kennel have been the Gold ROM earners, Am. Ch. Edenbrae Dusky Maiden, Am. Ch. Foxley Bright Forecast, Am. Ch. Woodlawn's Prime Time and Am. Ch. Woodlawn's Unforgettable. The line has been influential on many other kennels. Dail Corl's Am. Ch. Woodlawn's Dusky Gentleman is a Gold ROM sire of considerable influence.

Betsy Finley's Am. Ch. Woodlawn's Unforgettable Gold ROM (Am. Ch. Ryswick Remember Me – Am. Ch. Woodlawn's Waltzing Matilda). Photo: Ashbey.

CANADA

The first Border was registered with the Canadian Kennel Club in 1930. June Monaghan pioneered the breed in the 1960s, importing good dogs from England of Hawkesburn and Deerstone blood. Her Birkfell breeding can still be found behind Canadian and American Borders. Alice Sinclair, Windrush, was another staunch supporter of the breed. Wendell Palmer, Canaan, has been breeding Borders since the 1970s. There is no breed club extant. Most people belong to the American Border Terrier Club. Registrations have risen from 24 in 1984 to 71 in 1994 – 30 from six litters being registered in the first half of 1995. Several den trials are held each year in the East, the largest one being hosted for the North American Border Welfare which receives tremendous support from Border folk from the US.

LEADING KENNELS

BROOKHILL: BILL WALKEY

Can. Dk. Am. Ch. Behm Jocasta Just Cheviot, a blue and tan son of Am. Ch. Duttonlea Autocrat of Dandyhow and Am. Can. Ch. Jocasta Just Hollywood, was the first Border in this kennel. He spent a year in Denmark with Hanne Sonne where he became a Danish Champion and placed 2nd in a Group. Dk. Ch. Dalshøj Yum-Yum, by Ch. Int. Ch. Duttonlea Suntan of Dandyhow, was brought back with him and a successful litter was bred from these two. Two further Dalshøj bitches by Suntan were bought from Hanne Sonne.

Can. Ch. Brookhills Brummy Wilo The Wisp: Sired by a son of Am. Ch. Duttonlea Autocrat of Dandyhow out of a daughter of Ch. Int. Ch. Duttonlea Suntan of Dandyhow. Owned by Bill Walkey.

JANSIM: CHRIS AND PAM DYER

Coming from Britain, with a hunting background, Chris and Pam are keen on den trials and field work, working their dogs mainly on woodchucks. Since obtaining their first Border in 1980, seven litters have been bred, producing winners of eleven Canadian Championships, six American Championships, 17 Working, 17 Obedience and ten miscellaneous titles. Six Jansim-bred Borders earned Group placements in Canada or the US. High points have been Am. Can. Ch. Jansim Lothlorien Pepper becoming the first of only two Canadian-bred Borders to earn the coveted AWTA Working Certificate (the second was one of her daughters) and Pepper's daughter, Am. Can. Ch. Jansim Pennyroyal, winning Best Opposite Sex at the BTCA Specialty, also Pepper becoming the first Canadian bred and owned Border to earn the AKC Senior Earthdog Title.

Am. Can. Ch. Jansim Dandylion, owned by Chris and Pam Dyer and Jennifer Chambers.

OTHER BREEDERS These include Anita Gerling, TWIGGANI, who bred Am. Can. Ch. Twiggani Double Act Doggie, the top winning Border in Canada for several years running; Al and Joanne Matheson, whose GANNYMEDE kennel includes Can. Ch. Plushcourt Brain Wave; Vic and Maureen Burrell, BRAEMAR, who bred Can. Ch. Braemar's Tilly The Terminator, a leading exponent at Flyball, and Dale and Tracey Keretesh, IMPRESSIONS.

Chapter Fifteen

THE BORDER TERRIER WORLDWIDE

SWEDEN

The Border is the oldest breed in the Terrier Group in Sweden, a country which is undoubtedly the Border Terrier's second home. The breed has been popular and strong there for a long time. The breed club, Border Terrier Sallskapet, founded in 1962, currently has about a thousand members. The first Borders were imported by Anna Bergman from John Renton, in about 1934 – Int. Ch. Happy Thought and Saucy Queen, who won her title aged eleven years. Julia Geijer's first Border was a puppy from these. This line did not continue. It was Mr Leijonhufvud who got the breed going again later with four imports from the UK, from which he bred three Mellby Champions, but this line also died out.

Brita Donner, a Finn living in Sweden, had her first Border from Mr Leijonhufvud in 1950. Seven years later she imported four dogs from the UK which were the true start of the present-day Border in Sweden. These were Sw. Champions Leatty Linkup, Leatty Golden Randy, Todearth Blue Jacket and Jessica of Tharhill. A daughter of Linkup and Jessica put to Blue Jacket produced, in one litter, Brita Donner's Sw. Ch. Monkans My, Julia Geijer's Sw. Ch. Monkans Mymlan, and Gunnar and Carl-Gunnar Stafberg's Sw. Ch. Monkans Mikron. Brita Donner kept her line going and eventually returned to live in Finland, where she continued to breed Borders. Mymlan and Mikron founded what were, for many years, the two leading kennels in Sweden.

The breed club runs the Årets Border, the Border of the Year Show, which attracts a large entry despite having no CCs by mutual consent of club members, plus several open shows in different areas and annual club championships in Viltspår (blood tracking), Obedience and Agility. There have been several Obedience Champion Borders. The breed beats all others in Viltspår and also in Agility, with several Champions. Sw. Ob. Ch. Sw. Ag. Ch. Tojtas Knutte Krut was the first Border to win both these titles.

Sweden comes under the FCI banner. However, at the moment, the International Champion title may be won with four CACIBS won in two Nordic countries instead of the usual requirement of three. This dates from the closure of the borders with Finland but, since these have been re-opened for some time, the situation is likely to be reviewed. Hence the title Int. Sw. Norw. Ch. on recent dogs in Sweden and Norway instead of Int. Nordic Ch. Three CCs won in Sweden are required for a Swedish Champion, one of which is when the dog is two years or over.

Borders may be worked privately and be trained to work through the club up to a certain standard, to badger in an artificial earth, but competition is not allowed. Many go to trials in Norway and Finland to become Working Champions. There were several carrying the Swedish Working Champion title before this regulation.

LEADING BREEDERS

AXBOR: HÅKON AND ULLA AXÉN

Sweden's top breeders in 1994 and 95. Originally the kennel was founded on Juniper stock. Down that line came Int. Sw. Norw. Ch. Axbor Mozart whose sister, Axbor Barbara Streisand, put to Sw. Ch. Rabalder Röde Baronen, produced Anna Lindberg's Int. Sw. Norw. Ch. Axbor Never Give Up, a top winner of 1995, and his sister Sw. Ch. Axbor What Kind of Fool. Sw. Ch. Rabalder Mittiprick started another bitch line here, breeding the litter-mates Int. Ch. Axbor Respectable Lady and Sw. Ch. Axbor Rejoice With Me. A Mozart daughter, Sw. Ch. Bombax Xcalibur, joined the Axbor kennel, winning her crown in 1994.

Int. Sw. Norw. Ch. Axbor Never Give Up: A top winner in 1995, bred by Sweden's top breeders in 1994 and 1995, Hakon and Ulla Axen, and owned by Anna Lindberg.

Photo: Boos.

BOMBAX : GUNNAR AND CARL-GUNNAR STAFBERG

This kennel started in 1961 with Sw. Ch. Monkans Mymlan and, later, Sw. Ch. Monkans Trapper, the foundations of an extremely successful kennel, owned by father and son, who produced a great many Champions, some of which founded other successful kennels. A showy bitch, Sw. Ch. Leatty Panaga Tess, was imported in whelp from England. From her line with that of Mymlan and Trapper came three very famous dogs, Int. Nord. Ch. Bombax Despot, Int. Nord. Ch. Toinis Mikko, Int. Nord. Ch. Bombax Ericus Rex, who was the first Border to win an all-breeds Championship Show BIS in Sweden, and Sw. Ch. Bombax Xantippa, the dam of seven Champions. Int. Ch. Daletyne Danny Boy, brother to two English Champions, was imported along with Sw. Ch. Felldyke Bonnie Hinnie. Danny Boy made a terrific impact, siring 21 Champions. The foundation bitch of the Tallarnas line, Int. Nord. Ch. Bombax Nickname, was by Mikko out of a Bonnie Hinnie and Despot daughter, while that of the Urax kennel, Sw. Ch. Bombax Leonine, was a Danny Boy daughter out of Xantippa. Sw. Ch. Bombax Gossip produced several Champions for the home kennel. She was full sister to Leonine.

British stock imported over the years included Sw. Ch. Clipstone Clover and Ch. Int. Nord. Ch. Clipstone Guardsman, who sired Vice Versa out of Gossip. Clover to Danny Boy gave Ch. Int. Ch. Bombax Xavier who won his title in England, having left his mark as a sire in Sweden. His son, out of Vice Versa, Int. Nord. Ch. Bombax Desperado, sired Int. Nord. Champions Bombax Popcorn and Peebles, out of Dandyhow Creme Caramel of Clipstone, a Shady Knight daughter. Peebles produced good stock for the Redrob kennel, whose foundation was a Xavier daughter.

Down the line came a succession of famous Champions such as Int. Nord. Champion Bombax Blizzard and his son out of Vice Versa, Int. Nord. Ch. Bombax Mastermind who sired Int. Nord. Ch. Bombax Yatsy who was the sire of Fin. Ch. Bombax Nelson. The most recent Bombax Champions descend from Mastermind and the Blizzard lines, through Int. Nord. Ch. Bombax Hunter daughters. After several quiet years, during which time the line kept going, the Bombax kennel is active again, having produced Sw. Champions Bombax Tellus, Xcalibur, and What's On and imported Ch. Norw. Ch. Baillieswells Auchentoshan and his daughter Sw. Norw. Ch.

Thoraldby Shady Lady from England. Bombax Bäska Droppar and Bombax Black Ribbon, sons of Auchentoshan and What's On, have won many CCs.

BORDROCKS: ANN-MARIE AND KAJ BYSTROM
The foundation, in 1980, was Norw. Ch. Urax Gopis, a daughter of Sw. Ch. Dandyhow Grenadier. Her daughter, Int. Sw. Norw. Ch. Bordrocks Ninni produced Sw. Norw. Champions Bordrocks Kunniga Cinka, Cenna and Jocksiga Dante. Int. Sw. Norw. Ch. Bordrocks Wilhelm was also out of Gopis. Out of a daughter of Ninni and sired by Int. Nord. Ch. Rabalder Raka Spåret came Sw. Norw. Ch. Bordrocks Bess-Annie and her brother, Sw. Norw. Ch. Bordrocks Bess Arvid. Bess-Annie, owned by Eric Svensson, won BIS at Årets Border 1994 from Arthur and Elaine Cuthbertson, and BOS there in 1995 from Brian and Pat Baxter.

BRACKENHILLS: KRISTER GISELSSON
The emphasis is on working ability but this kennel has produced and imported stock which has been extremely influential in both Sweden and Finland. Int. Nord. Ch. Sw. Norw. Working Ch. Llanishen Ivanhoe, a Shady Knight son imported by Krister, sired many Champions including Int. Nord. Ch. Nord. Working Ch. Hagmarkens Into and Sw. Fin. Ch. Belinda, both owned by Krister, and also Int. Nord. Ch. Norw. Working Ch. Redrob Titus, owned by Margareta Grafström. Belinda was a granddaughter of Ch. Nord. Ch. Mansergh Rhosmerholme Amethyst. The mating of Into to Belinda's daughter lies behind many kennels including Ottercap and Gibas. Others by Into were the well-known sire Int. Nord Ch. Juniper Kånjak and the famous worker Sw. Norw. Ch. Int. Working Ch. Ametist.

   Sw. Fin. Working Ch. Brackenhills Foxy Lady, a Belinda granddaughter, to Into produced Nord. Ch. Nord. Working Ch. Brackenhills Flodman, Nord. Ch. Brackenhills Flora and Sw. Norw. Ch. Flugan. Another good working dog here was Sw. Fin. Working Ch. Janto, a Kånjak son out of Mansergh Witchcraft. Janto appears in many pedigrees. The Brannigan son, Int. Nord. Ch. Fin. Working Ch. Cheltorian Midnight was imported. He sired twenty Champions. A few years later out came Sw. Ch. Vandameres Dynasty in whelp to Moordown Wayne of Rhozzum. Midnight, to Flora, sired a leading stud dog in Finland, Nord. Ch. Nord. Working Ch. Brackenhills Flagman. Many Champions and Working Champions came from the combination of Midnight with Foxy Lady's descendants. Dynasty and Wayne gave Fin. Ch. Fin. Working Ch. Brackenhills Samaraij and Brackenhills Sahib. Samuraij produced Champions in Finland while Sahib sired Nord. Ch. Norw. Viltspår Ch. Brackenhills Tiffany out of Flugan. Tiffany was the first of any breed to become Viltspår Champion in Norway.

GIBAS: BIRGITTA ANDERSSON
Sw. Fin. Ch. Ottercap Stardust, going back to Krister Giselsson's early stock, was the dam of five Swedish Champions, sired by two dogs, of which the most famous would be Int. Sw. Norw. Ch. Norw. Working Ch. Gibas Kardemumma who, through his son, Margareta Grafström's Int. Nord. Ch. Norw. Working Ch. Redrob Jack The Knight, appears behind many famous Borders of today. Kardemumma sired many Champions. Sw. Ch. Gibas Salvia, a Stardust daughter, produced four Champions, two of which, Kaffe and Koriander, were sired by Sw. Ch. Gibas Korint, who was bred out of Stardust's dam, Sw. Fin. Ch. Nord. Working Ch. Dana.

JUNIPER: JULIA GEIJER
This famous kennel started in 1961 with the purchase of Sw. Ch. Monkans Mymlan, who produced three Champions. Julia had owned the breed previously but circumstances prevented her

from breeding Borders until then. Sw. Ch. Wharfholm Warrantop was imported in 1965. He sired Margareta Carlson's Int. Nord. Ch. Juniper Jerrantop out of Sw. Ch. Juniper Myrra, daughter of Mymlan, and Sw. Ch. Kampavalls Daniel who sired the famous trio, Darius, Dana and Daga – all Working Champions, with Dana and Daga Champions as well.

Four years later, Ch. Nord. Ch. Mansergh Rhosmerholme Amethyst arrived in whelp to Ribbleside Robert The Bruce. Amethyst produced six International Champions to three sires. Her son, Int. Ch. Juniper Klettermus, sired by Int. Nord. Ch. Juniper Juniper who was bred off the Monkans line, was a big winner for Aune and Anja Luoso, Kletters kennel in Finland. To Danny Boy, Amethyst gave Int. Nord. Ch. Juniper Klissandra, the dam of Int. Nord. Ch. Juniper Kånjak, sired by Into. To Margareta Carlson's Int. Nord. Ch. Bannerdown Monarch, Klissandra gave Int. Nord. Ch. Sw. Fin. Working Ch. Juniper Kämpe and Sw. Ch. Juniper Kära Barn.

Two sisters of Shady Knight, from a later litter, were imported in the early 1970s. Dandyhow Sweet Pickle to Int. Nord. Ch. Bombax Ericus Rex, going back on the Monkans lines, gave Sw. Champions Blue Peter and Blue Pericus. To Kånjak she gave Sw. Champions Juniper Pyssimandra, Pyts and Pysen. Dandyhow Sweet Polly, to Sw. Ch. Hanleycastle Rebel, produced Sw. Ch. Juniper Polka and Sw. Ch. Sw. Ob. Ch. Juniper Pollyanna who was the first Border to win an Obedience title in Sweden. By Kånjak, Polly produced a further three Champions and Juniper Palette, the foundation of the Winkis line. To Int. Nord. Ch. Bombax Desperado, Polly gave Pålinett, the dam of Int. Sw. Norw. Ch. Juniper Jönses Daga. Int. Sw. Norw. Ch. Juniper Kånjakspojken came from a daughter of Polly and Sw. Ch. Blue Pericus, and was sired by Kånjak.

OTTERCAP: ULLA AND TOMAS LARSSON Ulla and Tomas are primarily interested in work and have produced many good-looking Borders who work. Their foundation, in 1975, was the Belinda daughter, Int. Nord. Ch. Nord. Working Ch. Dana who, to Into, produced Nord. Ch. Nord. Working Ch. Red Rat and Sw. Norw. Ch. Randy who is behind the Bisus kennel. Sw. Ch. Ottercap Stardust, also from Dana and Into, produced Int. Sw. Norw. Ch. Nord. Working Ch. Gibas Kardemumma. Rhozzum Tenor, 2 CCs, was imported from England in partnership with Krister Giselsson. Out of Red Rat, Tenor sired Nord. Ch. Nordic Working Ch. Ottercap Shot of Love, a super producer with many Champion progeny including Sw. Ch. Ottercap She Loves You, the foundation of the Gibas kennel. Two famous dogs from the kennel were Int. Nord. Ch. Ottercap Abracadabra, out of Red Rat, and Sw. Ch. Ottercap Borderline who was sired by Sw. Nord. Ch. Clipstone Ceriph, a sire of note imported by Ulla and Tomas. A later import was Sw. Ch. Ragsdale Raiment. A successful export was Int. Dk. Ch. Ottercap Wuthering Heights, to Denmark.

RABALDER: ANNA-KARIN BERGH She was the leading breeder for five consecutive years, no mean achievement in Sweden where there are several excellent breeders. The foundation bitch came from Mona Hedman, Int. Sw. Fin. Ch. Tallarnas Låtoss Gissa, who was a daughter of Sw. Ch. Dandyhow Grenadier out of a daughter of Int. Nord. Ch. Daletyne Danny Boy and Int. Nord. Ch. Bombax Nickname – all very good progenitors. Låtoss Gissa bred at least nine Champions by four sires. To Ch. Sw. Norw. Ch. Dandyhow Scotsman she produced a host of Champions, including Int. Sw. Norw. Ch. Rabalder Siffra who, in turn, produced several Champions including Sven Larssen's famous Int. Sw. Norw. Ch. Rabalder Raka Spåret and Sw. Ch. Rabalder Rätt-och Slätt, his sister who was the dam of four Champions.

Raka Spåret was the top winning Border four years in succession, with over 70 BOBs and over 40 Group Placings. He won five BIS including the Swedish Kennel Klub Show. His Champion progeny, to date, include Sw. Ch. Bombax What's On, Sw. Norw. Champions Bordrocks Bess-Annie and Bess Arvid, Sw. Ch. Hoksell Othello, Sw. Norw. Ch. Krysshamns Eagle and Sw. Ch.

Stenkumlets Cornish Ecstasy. Siffra's sister, Sulitema, produced Int. Sw. Norw. Ch. Rabalder Nattens Drottning, the dam of several Champions including Sw. Ch. Rabalder Röde Baron, also a leading sire. Both Raka Spåret and Röde Baron were sired by Int. Nord. Ch. Redrob Jack The Knight.

Låtoss Gissa to Int. Nord. Ch. Farmway Southern Hawk gave Sw. Fin. Ch. Rabalder Milda Makter, top winning Border in Finland for several years and dam of Champions, and Int. Sw. Norw. Ch. Rabalder Mittiprick, dam of Axbor Champions. Rubicon Rhubarb, by Ch. Baywillow Sundazzler out of Ch. Rubicon Reserve, was imported as a stud-dog. Sw. Norw. Ch. Rabalder Rätta Virket is by him.

Int. Sw. Norw. Ch. Rabalder Raka Sparet: The top winning Border in Sweden for four consecutive years. Owned by Sven Larssen, bred by Anna-Karin Bergh.
Photo: Anna-Karin Bergh.

Apart from being the tops in the show ring, Rabalders do well in Obedience and Agility. Two well-known Agility dogs, who competed in the National team in Holland, were Sw. Ch. Sw. Ag. Ch. Rabalder Snusmurik, owned by Christer Gustavson, and Sw. Ch. Sw. Ag. Ch. Rabalder Svängom, owned by Kjell Wahlberg. Svängom was Supreme Champion in Agility in Sweden. Sw. Ag. Ch. Rabalder Hit-och-Dit is another to make a name in that sport.

REDROB: MARGARETA GRAFSTRÖM
Work is important in this kennel which has bred some influential Champions. Margareta's foundation was Int. Nord. Ch. Redrob Viktoria, a daughter of Ch. Int. Ch. Bombax Xavier. By Ivanhoe, Viktoria produced Int. Nord. Ch. Redrob Titus from whom came a strong line of Champion sires in direct descent: Titus, Int. Sw. Norw. Ch. Nord. Working Ch. Gibas Kardemumma, Int. Sw. Norw. Ch. Redrob Jack The Knight, Int. Sw. Norw. Ch. Rabalder Raka Spåret. Another important sire by Titus was Int. Nord. Ch. Sw. Fin. Working Ch. Waggs Alfons Åberg. Jack the Knight came from doubling on Viktoria. Int. Nord. Ch. Bannerdown Butterscotch, by Ch. Dandyhow Silver Ring out of a Bolshevik daughter, was imported in whelp to Ch. Dandyhow Nightcap, breeding Int. Nord. Ch. Yessalina from whom Margareta Carlson bred a line of Qusins Champions. Int. Nord. Ch. Bombax Peebles joined the kennel as had Nord. Ch. Juniper Kämpe. Together they bred Sw. Fin. Ch. Redrob Pay-Kash. Sw. Fin. Ch. Sundalgo Serenade, daughter of Ch. Duttonlea Sue, was another import to breed several Champions for the kennel. Sw. Norw. Ch. Redrob My Kassandra was out of Nord. Working Ch. Redrob Trademark, a Viktoria daughter, and was sired by Kardemumma, a Viktoria grandson.

TALLARNAS: MONA HEDMAN
A super brood bitch gave this kennel a good start, in 1972, namely Int. Nord. Ch. Bombax Nickname, the dam of twelve Champions, including three International ones, one of which, Int. Ch. Tallarnas Nypon Flinga, played an important part in Inger Morgen's Trientalis kennel which has a strong Tallarnas background. Dandyhow Observer, a Shady Knight grandson, was imported and sired four International Champions for the kennel including the sires Nick O'Demus, out of Nickname, and Lille Orkan, out of Int. Nord. Ch. Nej

Då, a Nickname daughter. Sw. Fin. Ch. Sky Blue of Dandyhow, sired by Ch. Int. Ch. Duttonlea Suntan of Dandyhow, and Sw. Ch. Dandyhow Grenadier, Suntan's sire, joined the kennel. Sky Blue with Sw. Norw. Ch. Trientalis Nobilitet, the latter doubling on both Observer and Nickname, produced Int. Nord. Ch. Tallarnas Senaste Nytt, a top winner. Two famous broods for other kennels were the sisters Int. Sw. Fin. Ch. Tallarnas Låtoss Gissa for the Rabalder kennel, and Int. Nord. Ch. Tallarnas Lyck-O-Par for the Rebus kennel. They were by Grenadier out of Nej Då.

Sw. Ch. Farmway Snow Merlin, a Snow Kestrel son, and Sw. Ch. Dykeside Jock Scott were imported. Sw. Ch. Tallarnas Goosi Min, top brood in 1994, was sired by Snow Merlin. Jock Scott has been widely used and sired several Champions. Sw. Ch. Tallarnas Kon-Trolla, by Senaste Nytt out of a Grenadier daughter, was a big winner and also produced good stock. Her daughter, Int. Ch. Tallarnas Tiff-Annie is the leading brood in Denmark, owned by the Hjelme kennel. Her sire, Int. Nord. Ch. Alias Alfred, was by Grenadier out of Nord. Ch. Tallarnas Bonna Fröjd. Sw. Ch. Tallarnas Anais Anais is Tiff-Annie's sister, kept by Mona.

Sw. Ch. Tallarnas Kon-Trolla: A big winner and a producer of good stock, with owner and breeder Mona Hedman.
Photo: Boos.

URAX: CHRISTINA GUNNARSDOTTER
The foundation of the line was Sw. Ch. Bombax Leonine whose daughter by Ch. Int. Ch. Clipstone Guardsman, Int. Nord. Ch. Urax Grima, produced the grandmother of Int. Nord. Ch. Urax Lif. Lif was the dam of Nord. Ch. Urax Gopis, foundation of the Bordrocks line, and Int. Nord. Ch. Urax Gaia. Int. Nord. Ch. Fin. Working Ch. Urax Ilia, out of Int. Nord. Ch. Urax Katla, who was a Grima daughter, is behind the Cerix kennel, while Sw. Ch. Urax Pandora, a Lif daughter, founded the Vandrarstigens line and Urax Gefjon was influential in the Caius kennel.

NORWAY
The breed has never taken off in Norway, despite its success in neighbouring Sweden. There were only 67 registrations from 1990 to 94. However, there is a growing interest with the few dogs that are there being seen regularly in the ring, at Working Trials and in Agility. Stock is based on imports from Sweden and the UK and, lately, Finland. Working Terrier Trials are allowed in Norway so many Swedish dogs go there to compete. Breeders include: Anne Tove Strande, AV SAGA HALL, who owned Ch. Norw. Sw. Ch. Dandyhow Scotsman and owns Norw. Sw. Ch. Dandyhow Tom Fool and Foxforest Red Demon; Brita and Per Oye, SVENOR, owners of Norw. Sw. Ch. Norw. Viltspår Ch. Brackenhills Tiffany; Grethe Wahl and Roar Seem, COQUETDALE, with Tallarnas Nova Scotia and her daughter, Coquetdale Audrey Hepburn; Kim Fangen with Norw. Sw. Ch. Rabalder Tycke Och Smak; and Kirstin and Ronny Bjolbäkk, BORDYSK, with Norw. Ch. Norw. Working Ch. Stubbåsens Gvazdika and Stubbåsens Sputnik, both well-known workers.

DENMARK

Borders are currently the fourth most popular Terrier breed in Denmark, with around 150 registrations annually, a steadily increasing figure. Early breed pioneers were Abigael Juel-Brockdorff in the early 1960s and Lizzie Waage-Jensen, Kennel Thurø, from 1973 onwards. A recent Champion from the Thurø kennel is Dk. Ch. Thurø's Hertug, by Cedarcourt Lonicera out of Thurø's Juvel, made up in 1991.

There is no breed club. Borders are included in the Terrier Club with two breed representatives to the club. The first Border show was in 1983, since when they have been annual events, usually two shows. At the request of Danish breeders, who are anxious that the show-ring should not spoil the breed, in 1990 a rule was made that no Border may win a CC in Denmark without having first qualified at the 'grav prov', the going-to-ground to a fox test. This is the only country with this rule. To become a Danish Working Champion, a Border needs a first prize grading at a show and three CCs in Working Tests to fox. Only one CC is given at each test, and only if the best dog is awarded a first grading. Five tests are held each year.

LEADING KENNELS

BORDERHOUSE: TINA GRUBBE

The line of excellent bitches, big winners in many countries, are well-known. Int. Ch. Arnakke Crazy (Int. Ch. Don von Vogthof – Nille) was the dam of Int. Ch. Borderhouse Anisette sired by Ch. German Ch. Thoraldby Tiptoes. Anisette produced Dk. Ch. Borderhouse Crazy Girl, sired by Dk. Ch. Digbrack Barley Mo. Dk. Ch. Foxforest Taste of Whiskey, co-owned with Tuija Saari, who bred him in Finland, is another member of the kennel.

Int. Ch. Borderhouse Anisette: A top winner in many countries, owned by Tina Grubbe.

DALSHØJ: HANNE SONNE

Hanne started in Borders in 1977 and was the first in Denmark to breed for show and work. She would use no Border for breeding unless the dog would work, and it was largely through her efforts that the breed took off in Denmark. In 1982 she imported Dk. Ch. Hynerbrook Rufus from Joyce Patterson. Rufus, a CC winner in England, by Ch. Llanishen Red Eagle out of a Ch. Bannerdown Viscount daughter, gave the breed a great lift, being the first Border to be placed in a group in Denmark, with a Group 2 at an International Show and several other placements.

The following year, Hanne imported Ch. Int. Ch. Duttonlea Suntan of Dandyhow, winner of many titles and the first Border to win the Terrier Group at an International Championship Show in Denmark. He became the leading sire of both show and workers. Int. Dk. Am. Ch. Amadeus, a famous son of Suntan out of a Rufus daughter, was owned by the late Palle Vinther. Amadeus was the first Border to win BIS at a Terrier Club Show. The following day he won Group 2 at an International Championship Show. Palle took him to the USA where he was made up within three weeks. Hanne imported Dk. Ch. Ragsdale Walnut, sister to Ch. Ragsdale Whynot, from Frank Wildman and John Bainbridge. Her granddaughter, Dk. Can. Ch. Dalshøj Yum-Yum was exported to Canada. Hanne used Can. Am. Dk. Ch. Behm Jocasta Just Cheviot, sired by Suntan's litter brother Autocrat, while he was in Denmark, to breed several Champions. Dk. Ch. Digbrack Barley Mo, son of Ch. Valmyre Magician of Dandyhow, was imported from England.

HJELME: LENE AND OLLE HJELME

Several Champions were produced here before the purchase of Int. Ch. Tallarnas Tiff-Annie from Mona Hedman in Sweden. She is the top brood bitch in Denmark. In her four litters, all by different sires, she produced Champions in the first three, and members of the fourth are on their way.

Int. Ch. Tallarnas Tiff-Annie: The dam of four Champions in three litters, all by different sires. Owned by Lene and Olle Hjelme.

LUTRA: INGER HOLL AND BENGT KVITZAU

This kennel has the remarkable record of three Show and Working Champions in a line. Int. Dk. Ch. Dk. Working Ch. Rhozzum Night Owl was imported from Marie and Philip Sharp. He is behind many good winners and workers, the most famous being his daughter, Int. Dk. Ch. Dk. Working Ch. Thayo, herself the dam of Dk. Ch. Dk. Working Ch. Lutra's Akturus Ajax, owned by Lars Landt. Among Night Owl's other progeny are Bent Peterson's Dk. Ch. Ulrik, who is also a top tracking dog, and Bente Busk's Dk. Ch. Arnakke Doolittle, top winning Border for two successive years.

ROSTGÅRD: DAGMAR HENSEN
Very successful as a breeder of workers, Dagmar Hensen imported Dk. Ch. Dk. Working Ch. Rhozzum Victor, who is behind many winners and workers, from Marie and Philip Sharp. Two Working Champions were bred by Dagmar, who were out of Danpug Apple Rose and sired by Sw. Fin. Working Ch. Transjøns Grytpelle: her own Rostgård's Bonni and Soren Jacobsen's Mack.

THE DUAL CHAMPIONS – SHOW AND WORKING CHAMPIONS
Anker (Hanleycastle Shenandoah – Hanleycastle Jan) owner Inge and Kurt Høyer
Thayo (Int. Dk. Ch. Dk. Working Ch. Rhozzum Night Owl – Andromeda of Atlantis) owner Inger Holl, Bengt Kvitzau
Rhozzum Victor (Ch. Int. Nord. Ch. Llanishen Reynard – Rhozzum Theme) owner Jens Jensen
Rhozzum Night Owl (Rhozzum Volunteer – Rhozzum Milady) owner Inger Holl, Bengt Kvitzau
Lutra's Akturus Ajax (Ch. Int. Ch. Duttonlea Suntan of Dandyhow – Int. Dk. Ch. Dk. Working Ch. Thayo) owner Lars Landt
Dalshøj Kiss Me Kate (Ch. Int. Ch. Duttonlea Suntan of Dandyhow – Dina) owner Hanne Sonne
Dalshøj Kelly (Ch. Int. Ch. Duttonlea Suntan of Dandyhow – Dina) owner Flemming Strårup
Dalshøj Laban (Ch. Int. Ch. Duttonlea Suntan of Dandyhow – Cedarcourt Love in a Mist) owner Palle Thomsen.

In the obedience ring Dk. Ch. Dalshøj Lucifer, brother to Laban and owned by Sissel Bagge-Blindboek, won the titles Obedience 1 and 2 and has been mini-agility Champion. Sissel has imported several Ragsdale Borders from Frank Wildman over the years, including Ragsdale Redcoat.

FINLAND
The pioneer for the breed in Finland was Brita Donner, MONKANS, who took the first Border to Finland in 1950, from Sweden. Her Monkans line was the foundation of many leading Swedish kennels. Aune Luoso imported a very famous dog in 1979, Int. Ch. Farmway Southern Hawk, who had an outstanding show career and, with his daughter, Int. Ch. Rabalder Milda Makter, drew attention to the breed as a serious show dog. They won many Groups.

The breed is now very popular. The breed club has 550 members and was formed in 1982 as a sub-club of the Finnish Terrier Club. It became an independent Breed Club in 1994. It runs a Championship and an Open Show, a Working Test and an Agility Test. Finland comes under FCI regulations. No working qualification is needed to become a Champion.

Those Borders which are used as working terriers encounter fox, badger and racoon dog, which is slightly smaller than the fox, plentiful and more urbanised. All dogs and cats are vaccinated against rabies. Working terriers play an important role in the control of the fox, badger and racoon dog population and thus in the prevention of rabies in Finland. Most working Border owners confine their activities to organised Working Terrier Trials. These are always to fox, in an artificial wooden tunnel, which is very narrow in parts, so that the terrier has to squeeze in on one side. The fox is behind a grill but, once the terrier has decided, after baying it for five to fifteen minutes, to go in closer to try to bolt the fox, the grill is removed. The fox can go further back into a narrower place. Once the terrier tries to attack the fox, the dog is immediately removed but should the dog continue to stand back and bark, the trial will continue for up to twenty minutes.

To get a working CC the dog must work strongly and try to get up to the fox, to try to bolt it. To become a working Champion, the dog needs two CCs at this level and one at an advanced level, when bigger, tougher foxes are encountered and the entrance of the artificial earth is filled with sand, through which the dog has to dig to locate the fox. There are between 20 and 30 Working Champions. The most famous Show and Working Champions are Kelgram The Minstrel, Double Scotch, Ashbrae Dexter, Brackenhills Flagman, Foxforest Devil Herself, Foxforest Clear To Fly and Brackenhills Samaraij. Once a Working Championship has been obtained, the dog cannot take part in further Tests. Borders are starting to compete in blood tracking trials which is something Working Trials Champions can go on to do. This is something people not interested in fox trials can do. The dog can continue to compete in this event after becoming a Champion.

Many young people own Borders in Finland, enjoying their companionship in outdoor life such as skiing and sailing. They also have fun competing with their Borders in Agility at various levels, with success too. Over ten Borders have cleared their way up to the top class. Rated Number Two in the National Top 100 competition, 1995, Foxforest Hurricane was second in the Finnish Championships, 1994. Owned by Maarit Simstedt, this remarkable dog is also the only Obedience Champion Border in Finland, an extremely hard title to achieve, and is also on his way to the blood tracking Championship.

LEADING KENNELS

FOXFOREST: TUIJA AND SEPPO SAARI

This kennel made a remarkably successful start. Tuija and Seppo's first Border came in 1986, and the first litter in 1990. Since then they have bred five International and twelve Finnish Champions and six working certificate holders. The Saaris compete quite successfully in Agility with their dogs, which they find fun for themselves and the dogs. Int. Ch. Digbrack Candy Tuft was the foundation bitch. She only produced six puppies before having to be spayed. However, she did more than her bit for the kennel as four of these are International Champions, three of whom won BIS at all-breed Championship Shows.

In 1992 Int. Ch. Fin. Working Ch. Double Scotch, litter brother to Ch. Another Scot, was purchased, He 'clicked' with Candy's lines and was also widely used by breeders as far apart as France and Sweden. After retiring from the show ring, Double Scotch competed with success in both Obedience and Agility. Two years later, Int. Ch. Ashbrae Archie joined the kennel. His puppies made a flying start to their careers. Archie proved to be one of Finland's fastest small dogs in Agility. The litter sisters, Int. Ch. Fin. Working Ch. Foxforest Devil Herself and Int. Ch. Foxforest Saint Herself, born 1991, were out of Candy Tuft sired by Fin. Ch. Kletters Mac William. Devil Herself won five Groups and one BIS. Her son by Double Scotch, Foxforest Devilsson, won BIS at the Swedish Border of the Year Show, 1995, also a Group and Reserve BIS All Breeds in Finland. His litter sister, Red Demon, won several Group placings before joining Anne Tove Strande in Norway. Int. Ch. Saint Herself has numerous Group placings. By Double Scotch she produced Fin. Sw., Dk. Ch. Fin. Working Ch. Foxforest Scotch Himself, who was exported to Denmark, Fin. Dk. Ch. Fin. Working Ch. Foxforest Scotch Herself and Fin. Est. Ch. Foxforest Make It Double. The litter mates, Int. Ch. Foxforest Light The Sky and Int.

Int. Ch. Foxforest Light The Sky: Winner of four BISs at All Breed Ch. Shows, and Finland's Third Top Dog All Breeds, 1995.

Ch. Fin. Working Ch. Foxforest Clear To Fly, born 1992, by Double Scotch out of Candy Tuft, won titles in many countries. The blue and tan dog, Light The Sky, won fifteen Groups and four BIS at all-breed Championship Shows and BIS at both the Finnish and Danish Terrier Club Shows. He also holds a Working CC. His remarkable succession of Group wins in 1995, eight at eight consecutive Shows, helped to make him Top Terrier and finish third Top Dog all-breeds in 1995.

Clear To Fly won three Groups and one BIS all-breeds. A great win was third in the Group at the World Show in Bern, 1994. Her blue and tan daughter by Archie, Foxforest Flying Finn, at one year old, won one all-breed BIS and was BIS at the Finnish Terrier Club Show. She is doing well in Agility and Obedience and is co-owned with Hurricane's owner.

KLETTERS: AUNE LUOSO
Aune is largely responsible for the breed being known in Finland. She started breeding Borders in 1972 and has bred some thirty Finnish and two International Champions to date, and owned some very influential Borders as well as top show winners. Her original foundation bitch, Sw. Ch. Bombax Josephine, the dam of six Champions, came from Sweden, as did Int. Ch. Nord. Ch. Juniper Klettermus. Fin. Ch. Farmway Seagull produced Int. Ch. Kletters Seastar, a good brood, producing many winners for the kennel. Several successful Farmway imports were made. Int. Nord. Ch. Farmway Kestrelstar was owned by Aune's daughter, kennel Klettermus, Sweden.

Int. Nord. Ch. Farmway Southern Hawk, a Snow Kestrel son, was in a league of his own, winning ten Terrier Groups and BOB at the Finnish Winner Show for nine years. He was unbeaten during his long show career and won 70 BOB awards. Being 'king' for so long (he lived to be 15) he is behind many Finnish Borders and was also used by Swedish breeders successfully. He sired 150 puppies.

His most famous daughter, Int. Ch. Rabalder Milda Makter, was bred in Sweden by Anna-Karin Bergh, and owned by Aune. A top winner in the late 1980s and early 1990s, she was a Group and BIS All Breeds Winner, like her father. In 1987, a dog who became Int. Ch. Fin. Working Ch. Brackenhills Flagman joined the kennel from Krister Giselsson, Sweden. Flagman was a popular stud dog and sired several Finnish Champions and Dual Champions. Out of Milda Makter, he sired the Champion brothers, Kletters Mac William and Mac Kenzie, both sires of Champions. Mac William sired the famous Champion sisters, Foxforest Saint Herself and Devil Herself.

TERRAS: LIISI BROTHERUS
Started in 1982 with a Farmway background, this kennel has consistently produced Champions and was awarded the Finnish Kennel Club's breeders honorary prize, 1987. A famous dog from this kennel was Int. Nord. Ch. Fin. Working Ch. Terras Otto, by Int. Nord. Ch. Farmway Kestrelstar out of Sw. Ch. Terras Twinkle. Fin. Ch. Maljan Catsa, out of a Terras bitch, was brought back into the kennel and mated to Dual Ch. Kelgram The Minstrel and later to Farmway Topflight, breeding Champions in both litters. Fin. Est. Ch. Kelgram Owen Tudor is co-owned by Liisi with Eine Tahko.

EIRE
There has been a small loyal band of Border breeders in Eire since Phoebe Bennett, ARDCAIRN, tried to get the breed going in the 1960s. Her Irish Ch. Dandyhow Becky Sharp of Ardcairn was the first Border to win BIS at an all-breeds Championship Show in Eire. Denis Murphy, RATHVARRAIG, made five Irish Champions between 1976 and 1991, one of which, Hawkesburn John, sired two Irish Champions.

Sue Milne, ROSSTURC, bred her first Irish Champion, Rossturc Ivy, out of Dandyhow Emily, who was also the dam of Ir. Am. Ch. Rossturc Oonah. Ir. Ch. Opinan Draco at Rossturc won her title in 1992. Draco was bred by Arthur Sneeden in Scotland, whose Ir. Ch. Astra of Opinan was the first Irish Champion Border who was not a resident of the Emerald Isle. Jean and John Taylor's Ch. Ir. Ch. Fairfoot Mrs. Charity Barnum was another invader from across the water and the first Border to win titles both sides of the Irish Sea. She won the Group at Killarney, 1991.

Betty and Brian Dickinson and Tracey James, all from Yorkshire, enjoyed several holidays 'doing the circuit' and regularly attending shows in Eire with a team of Borders. They were successful with Ir. Ch. Borterra Fire Fly at Badgerholme and his daughter, Ir. Ch. Badgerholme Ascot Lady, both CC winners in England. Ascot Lady had a super win of BIS at The All Terriers Association Group Championship Show, 1994. Tracey made up Ir. Ch. Blackmine Gold Footprint, co-owned by herself and Beryl Graham. George O'Sullivan from Co. Cork, in 1995, made up Ir. Ch. Nettleby English Rose, co-owned by his daughter, Linda, and Alan and Gwen Small.

Ir. Ch. Antrim Maid of Glenamairgie was the first Champion for Desmond McLernon from Northern Ireland, GLENAMAIRGIE. Next was Ir. Ch. Glenamairgie Foxtrot. Morag Hay's Ir. Ch. Glenamairgie Moonlighter of Huntley, son of Antrim Maid, won his crown in 1995. The principal breeders in Eire are Susan Milne, Frances Brennan of the OTTERFLOW affix, George O'Sullivan and Morag Hay, HUNTLEY.

HOLLAND

For many years Holland has been the European country with the greatest number of Borders after the UK and Sweden. Recently there has been a marked increase in interest in the breed due, in some part, to H.K.H. Princess Margriet owning two Borders. Somewhere over 70 litters were bred in Holland in the past two years. De Nederlandse Border Terrier Club, founded in 1971, currently has around 800 members. Borders cannot work in Holland, by law, but they take part in other activities such as the endurance test undertaken by 20 of them, as reported earlier in this book. The first imports were made in the late 1920s but were not bred from. A period of 25 years elapsed between the first Champion being made in 1933, Ch. Southboro Stanzo, and the second, Ch. Int. Ch. Golden Imperialist, whom Ploon Wetzel-de Raad imported from Phyllis Leatt.

After the Second World War there were no Borders left in Holland. Coby Langhout Stein started the renaissance with the import of a dog from John Renton in 1951, followed by four more. Ploon de Raad also brought in Ch. Int. Ch. Braw Boy and Int. Ch. Winstonhall Dunkie. Then Marius and Erica Bons imported Int. Ch. Deerstone Destina in 1968, and two years later, the first blue and tan in Holland, Int. Ch. Wharfholm Wickersworld. The breed then started to get going and it was several years before more imports were made, although dogs such as Germ. Chs. Tedhars Traveller, Deerstone Decisive and Ch. Int. Ch. Deerstone Dugmore, who were in neighbouring countries, were used.

Mrs De Raad bred 50 litters in her TASSEL'S kennel, of which 49 were sired by her own dogs. She owned or bred eleven Dutch Champions and imported Dutch Champions Garw Thistle and Llanishen Argosy and Dutch Am. Ch. Woodsmoke's Douglas. Mrs Langhout Stein, URTICA'S, bred 26 litters, all by her own dogs. Her imports, Raisgill Rego and Glenluffin Puffin, mated together, produced three Champions. She bred or owned six Champions, including Dutch Chs. His Honour and Sprig of Jasmine which she imported from Willie Veitch.

LEADING KENNELS
OF BRIDDY'S HOME: BEKE ROELOFS BROUWERS

Int. Ch. Day Dream Deidre of Briddy's Home, the first Champion bred here, was born in 1983, by

Pearl-Diver our of a bitch combining Knight Errant with the Roughdunes line. She was owned by Marijke de Jong. Her brother, Diver's Diamond of Briddy's Home, sired two Champions out of Dame Audrey of The Whiskered Gentry. One of these, Dutch Ch. Fearless Faido of Briddy's Home, produced Dutch Ch. Inventive Igor of Briddy's Home. Another in this kennel was Int. Ch. Brompton Bridget of the Half House.

OF THE HALF HOUSE: MINKA CRUCQ
The first Champion bred by Minka was Dutch Ch. Halfpenny of the Half House in 1974. However, her first Champion, completing his title one year before Halfpenny, was the Shady Knight son, Int. Ch. Dandyhow Knight Errant, an important sire with Champion progeny in Holland and Denmark. He sired Dutch Belg. Ch. Honourable Jane of the Half House, out of Halfpenny, and Int. Ch. Miss Muppet of the Half House out of his daughter, Jane. Int. Ch. Dandyhow Fleur de Lis was imported as a mate for Knight Errant. Later, Ch. Int. Ch. Mansergh Pearl-Diver joined the kennel co-owned with Ted Hunt. Diver sired Int. Ch. Lulu The Pearl, out of Jane, and Int. Ch. Brompton Bridget of the Half House out of his daughter, Lulu The Pearl. He, too, sired several Champions in Holland and Denmark.

Hanne Sonne's Ch. Int. Ch. Duttonlea Suntan of Dandyhow spent some time here to be campaigned for his Dutch title and sired Int. Ch. Tinkerbell of the Half House, out of a Fleur de Lis – Knight Errant daughter, and Int. Ch. Uther of the Half House, out of Miss Merel. Int. Ch. Mansergh Tontine to Tinkerbell produced Paul and Yvonne de Vijlder's Int. Ch. Glenmaid of the Half House and, to a niece of Uther sired by Pearl-Diver, Dutch Ch. Jeremy of the Half House. To date Minka has owned or bred 15 Champions.

OF MAC OAKS PRIDE: LOES EIJKELENKAMP-SCHEERS
The foundation, Int. Ch. Roughdunes Tanne Sonne, was a Blue Maestro daughter bred from the Roughdunes lines. To her half-brother, both by Maestro and with a similar background of Roughdunes breeding, she produced Dutch Ch. Antilla My Dear of Mac Oaks Pride. Dutch Ch. Otterkin Valentina and Dutch Ch. Wee Blue Rustler were imported. Rustler, bred by Joy Gordon out of an Otterkin bitch and sired by Ch. Can. Am. Ch. Lynhay Daz, made history by being the first Border to win a Terrier Group in Holland.

VAN DE OSSEKOELE: ELLY WEIJENBORG-WEGGEMANS, HENK & JO WEGGEMANS
From a Roughdunes foundation, incorporating the blood of Dugmore and Knight Errant, Esprit van de Ossekoele was bred. To Blue Maestro, she gave the litter-mates Int. Ch. Frisk and Dutch Ch. Fatal, both van de Ossekoele. Frisk did well in Obedience at all levels. Fatal to Dutch Ch. Handsome Hoagy of Briddy's Home produced Int. Ch. Isha van de Ossekoele Frisk to Hoagy's sister, Dutch Ch. Fearless Faida of Briddy's Home, produced Dutch Ch. Inventive Igor of Briddy's Home.

ROUGHDUNES: ERICA BONS
This kennel lies behind the breed in Holland today. The foundation of the line, Int. Ch. Biddy, made up in 1968, was by Int. Ch. Winstonhall Dunkie out of a daughter of Ch. Deerstone Destiny. Biddy was the dam of four Champions, all by different sires. Her most famous son was Int. Ch. Roughdunes Estate Agent who was sired by Ch. Int. Ch. Deerstone Dugmore. Int. Ch. Deerstone Destina produced three Champions. Her daughter, Int. Ch. Roughdunes Charming Catkin, put to Dugmore, gave Int. Ch. Roughdunes Illustrious Imp, also the dam of three Champions. Int. Ch. Deerstone Dianthus sired four Champions for the kennel.

Int. Ch. Roughdunes Wish Me Luck, daughter of Ch. Int. Ch. Brumberhill Blue Maestro and Dutch Ch. Roughdunes Original Olli.

Estate Agent sired five Dutch Champions including an excellent bitch, Int. Ch. Stepping Stone, who won just about every title possible. Her dam was Cheltor Music. Her breeders, J. and M. Roelofs-Van Embden also bred Biddy, the foundation of the kennel. Ch. Int. Ch. Brumberhill Blue Maestro joined the kennel and sired eight Dutch Champions including Int. Ch. Roughdunes Wish Me Luck out of Dutch Ch. Roughdunes Original Olli, daughter of Stepping Stone and Pearl-Diver. Three Brannigan progeny, Dutch Ch. Villathorn Tiger's Eye at Brumberhill, Ch. Dutch Ch. Brumberhill Bedevilled and Ch. Dutch Ch. Ribbleside Rogue, joined the kennel over a period of time. To date there have been 86 Champions in Holland, 29 of which have been Roughdunes owned or bred. Many of the others stem from Roughdunes ancestry.

OF THE WHISKERED GENTRY: NAN DE BOER-HOUBEN
Bannerdown Lady Abigail, a daughter of Ch. Dandyhow Silver Ring, was the foundation of the line. This small kennel has an excellent breeding record for quality, having bred seven Champion bitches in fourteen litters since 1981. Lady Abigail produced three Champions all by different sires: Int. Ch. Aileen of the Whiskered Gentry by Estate Agent, Int. Ch. Be Fair of the Whiskered Gentry by Knight Errant, and Int. Ch. Lollipop whose sire, By Jove, was a Fancy Fair son.

Int. Ch. Fancy Fair, by Aileen's brother out of Be Fair, to Blue Maestro gave Dutch Ch. Katrin of the Whiskered Gentry who, in turn, produced Dutch Ch. Nosegay of the Whiskered Gentry, who was sired by Dutch Ch. Wee Blue Rustler. Dame Audrey of the Whiskered Gentry, sister to Aileen, produced two Champions for the Briddy's Home kennel. The first Champion bred by Marian Van der Horst-Siraal, Int. Ch. Dinghy of the Windy Spot, was from Iris Cygna of the Whiskered Gentry, a Be Fair daughter.

GERMANY
Maybe because Germany developed its own breed of working terrier, the Border has been slow to become known, although there have been a few there since 1950. The breed pioneer has been Wiebke Steen, who imported her first Border from Phyllis Mulcaster in 1965 and has the oldest kennel of Borders in the country. The breed is now growing numerically, with 53 litters bred in 1994 as compared with nine in 1984. These were bred by 30 breeders. It is hoped that there will be a breed club within the next year or two.

At the moment in Germany a terrier may be tested once only in an artificial earth, to fox. This is a preparation for terriers which will be worked and is only available to people with a hunting licence for their own dog. There are several show titles to be won in Germany, which is an FCI country. The Junior Champion needs four Junior CCs won under three judges in three countries aged between nine and eighteen months. The German Champion needs five under three judges in three different countries aged from fifteen months upwards, with one year between the first and fifth CC. The VDH Champion needs five CCs as above, but two of them must be won at an International CACIB show.

LEADING KENNELS

CHEEKY CHUMS: JURGEN RÖSNER

The first litter was bred in 1979. The foundations were Workmore stock. Then followed Int. Germ. Ch. Cedarcourt Nettle, a son of Ch. Int. Ch. Bombax Xavier. In more recent times the kennel imported Plushcourt stock. Int. Ch. Plushcourt Echo has sired several Champions, while Germ. Ch. Cheeky Chum's Quicky is by Plushcourt Goodwill.

Ch. Int. Ch. Thoraldby Glenfiddich: The first Border to win the Group at an All Breed International Show in Germany, owned by Wiebke Steen and Christopher Habig.

KIKI'S: WIEBKE STEEN

A very famous dog here was Ch. Int. Ch. Deerstone Dugmore who had a great influence on both the Dutch and German Borders. Miss Steen bred the first German-bred title holders out of her first import, Germ. Ch. Portholme Merrybelle, sired by Germ. Ch. Tedhars Traveller. Today her bitch line goes back seven generations to Merrybelle and is still getting winners down that line.

Other famous Borders were Int. Ch. Bugs Billy, Germ. Ch. Campanologia Snarker Pike, Ch. Int. Ch. Digbrack Barley Sugar, Int. Ch. Thoraldby Another Amber and Ch. Int. Ch. Thoraldby Glenfiddich, the latter co-owned with Christopher Habig. Glenfiddich was the first Border to win the Group at an All Breeds International Show in Germany, and is the sire of eight Champions. Wyehawk is Christopher Habig's affix and in partnership with Wiebke are Rannoch Kiki's Ann of Wyehawk, a Barley Sugar daughter, and Dykeside Lady of Wyehawk. Kiki's Noella, a Barley Sugar daughter going back to both Snarker Pike and Dugmore, produced the winning Optimist, sired by Glenfiddich.

MALEPARTUS: JÖRN AND DIANA TILLNER

Borders are worked here, most of the kennel having working certificates. The kennel was founded in 1986 with a German-bred dog, Int. Ch. Don von Vogthof, and Int. Ch. Plushcourt Extravagance who together gave Int. Ch. Malepartus Anthony, sire of two Champions. Don combined the blood of many of the imports made by Miss Steen with that of the Tinsdal Line and proved an important sire with Champions in several countries.

From Jack Price came Oxcroft Tricky, Ch. Oxcroft Rocker and VDH Ch. Oxcroft Trader. From Leslie Gosling came Germ. Ch. Akenside Freckle, a daughter of Oxcroft Rocky. Freckle produced one German Champion. Rocker sired two litters which included one Champion who gave two Champions. Tricky to Don v. Vogthof produced the kennel's best worker, VDH Ch. Malepartus Edda, the dam of four German Champions. Another leading British stud-dog was imported, Ch. VDH Ch. Thoraldby Tiptoes, the grandsire of Don v. Vogthof. He sired six German Champions. The kennel is now successfully combining the Oxcroft and Thoraldby lines.

Other breeders include Drs Wallenburg, VON DER WALLENBURG, who bred Germ. Ch. First Lady von der Wallenburg out of their home-bred Germ. Ch. Alilly von der Wallenburg and also bred Germ. Ch. Lord von der Wallenburg and imported from Sweden Germ. Ch. Tallarnas Tall-Kotte; Herr W.V. Lowchow, VON DE LOWCHOWBURG, whose foundation was Int. Ch. Saredon Peggy Sue and who bred Int. Ch. Alf von der Lowchowburg.

SWITZERLAND

Progress has been slow for the breed since the first registration there in 1960. From the late 1970s, Frau Feuz, RED HUNTERS, bred several litters from her imported Hanleycastle stock. Some ten years later, Marlis Huoni bred the first of the many COLLINETTA litters, out of Kiki's Turvey. A later addition to this kennel was Int. Ch. Kelgram Signorinetta. The foundation of another prolific line, E. and E. Locher's WANDERGUT, had a Colinetta bitch together with St. Blaise of Kelgram.

Elsbeth Clerc, RANNOCH, a well-known Scottie breeder, became interested in Borders through her friendship with Wiebke Steen and imported a Sundalgo bitch. Elsbeth campaigned Ch. Int. Ch. Digbrack Barley Sugar for Wiebke for some time and also bred a litter for her by him out of Int. Ch. Thoraldby Another Amber which contained Int. Ch. Rannoch Amber and Kiki's Ann of Wyehawk, a well-known winner for the Habigs. Elsbeth's husband owns Kiki's Julia of Wyehawk, another international winner.

Int. Ch. Kelgram Sansovino and Kelgram Mill Reef founded Elsbeth and Eveline Zehnder's WOODBOOMERS line. Other breeders are Agnes Brühlmann, BRIGHT FELLOW, E. and H. Müller, RÖMERHAUS, and Carine Petralia, COCAGNE. With several breeders, and registrations now regularly over 50 a year, the breed looks to have a firm footing in Switzerland.

AUSTRIA

The import of Int. Ch. Rocheby Skipalong, sired by Ch. Savinroyd President and bred by Marion Hopkinson, was the foundation of Margarete Huber's VOM LÄRCHENBRUCH kennel. Although there were a few Borders in Austria previously it is through Mrs Huber that the breed has become established there. Her next import was Int. Ch. Rocheby Sparkling Stone, by Ch. Sundalgo Slate Blue. These two bitches produced several International Champions: Falk, Freddy, Erda-Birdy, Ascot and Dolly-Sweety, all von Lärchenbruch. From Sparkling Stone by Int. Ch. Digbrack Jet Way came Int. Ch. Elfe-Highness vom Lärchenbruch who, to Ch. Int. Ch. Thoraldby Glenfiddich, gave Kathy Chipala vom Lärchenbruch, a promising youngster. A further addition to this kennel was Thoraldby Tallan. There is a small but increasing number of Austrian Borders bred by a few dedicated breeders who are making use of good bloodlines in other countries.

AUSTRALIA

Although there were one or two attempts to establish the breed in Australia from the first known Border there in the 1930s, it was not until the 1970s that the foundation of the breed today was established through stock imported from New Zealand from Rosemary Williamson's Patterdale and Jim Graham's Otterhead kennels. The breed boasts two breed clubs, both the brainchildren of

John Caldwell of Victoria. The inaugural meeting of The Border Terrier Social Club took place following the 1982 Canberra Royal. Under that banner three Annual Parades were held.

The club changed its name to The Border Terrier Club (NSW) following recognition by the Royal Agricultural Society Kennel Club (NSW) since when two annual shows have been held – a Sanction Show for training aspirant judges and a Championship Show. Entries are normally between 40 and 50; club membership is around 75. Border owners in Victoria formed a Social Group with a series of Fun-days for both pet and show dogs from 1984 onwards, which culminated in the formation of The Border Terrier Club of Victoria in 1987. This club holds an Open Show and a Championship Show each year. Entries are normally between 30 and 40; Club membership is around 70. Australia is affiliated to the FCI but does not follow their system of judging. There are no critiques. CCs may be awarded to puppies from six months on. The British Standard is used. To become an Australian Champion, 100 points are needed, won in at least four CCs under different judges. Maximum CC is 25 points. The CC is worked on a basis of 5 points plus 1 for each dog in its sex beaten. The Group carries 25 points. No working qualification is needed to become a Champion. Although a number of Borders were regularly worked to fox in Victoria, there was no organised terrier work until 1994, when organised ground trials based largely on AWTA conditions started in Queensland (organised by Ken Iggleden and Tom Morrow) and in NSW (organised mainly by the local Jack Russell Club). Despite a small band of devoted enthusiasts, Border numbers are still low in Australia with approximately 30 registrations a year in NSW and slightly fewer in Victoria.

LEADING KENNELS

SOUTH AUSTRALIA
Dee Patterson, STORMVALE, bred, in one litter out of her NZ import Aust. Ch. Lester Border Gnome to Aust. NZ Ch. Brigand of Brockhole and Lynsett, her Aust. Champions Stormvale Kiwi Trouble and Kiwi Koala Bear and her and Pamela Guilfoyle's Aust. Ch. Stormvale Kiwi Girl who was my BOB winner at Canberra and District Sporting Terrier Club.

WESTERN AUSTRALIA
There have been few breeders in WA. Sally Beck is the only person breeding them there currently. A number have been shown over the years by Peter and Wilda Tallentire of Cairn fame and Lee Gray of Scottish Terrier fame, but these were not bred from.

QUEENSLAND
Undoubtedly the best-known QLD kennel is that of Ken and Fay Iggleden, FOXFOE, started in the late 1970s. The foundation of the kennel lay in the purchase of a puppy bred by George and Merle Massey, out of Aust. Ch. Patterdale Dione by Aust. Ch. Patterdale Dionysus. Aust. Ch. Foxfoe Firey Knight, by Aust. Ch. Rhozzum Venture, was a regular winner in Group competition and Runner Up BIS at the Club Show, 1984. Recently Tom and Anne Morrow, RULEWATER, moved to Brisbane. Tom was president of the BTC (NSW) for five years. An early dog in this kennel was imported from NZ, Aust. Ch. Andrus of Patterdale. The sisters, Aust. Champions Rulewater Vixen and Rulewater Sapphire, by Aust. Ch. Craigend Cheviot Piper out of Foxfoe Flaunt It, had much influence in both the home kennel and the Foxfoe kennel.

VICTORIA
The affix of John and Joyce Caldwell, to whom the breed owes so much, is BARAMABAH. The

import from NZ, Aust. Ch. Otterhead of Dukesfield, gave the breed a much-needed boost in Victoria, where he had considerable influence. A well-known campaigner from this kennel was Aust. Ch. Baramabah Goliath, by Aust. Ch. Rhozzum Venture out of Aust. Ch. Rulewater Alleisha. ONEDIN, a newer affix in Borders but previously well-known in Irish Setters, is that of Jack and Ena Checkley. Their litter-mates, Aust. Champions Onedin Lochain Ben and Onedin Bonny Bridge, bred in their first Border litter, have done well in the Group in Victoria. Paul and Jenny Aburrow, MAYSLEITH, with their best-known dog, Aust. Ch. Maysleith Major Tom, by Aust. NZ Ch. Brigand of Brockhole and Lynsett out of Craigend Pot Pourri, won BOB at Melbourne Royal and BIS at Victoria BTC Championship Show.

NEW SOUTH WALES
An extremely well-known affix in both Borders and Cairns is CRAIGEND, that of Robert Bartram, who has worked hard for years to promote the breed. His start was a puppy from the Masseys from NZ-imported Patterdale parents. Aust. Ch. Brigit of Patterdale, daughter of NZ Ch. Ribbleside Rigger, was imported from Rosemary Williamson, NZ. In 1981 Robert formed a syndicate to import Aust. Ch. Rhozzum Venture (Ch. Duttonlea Mr Softy – Rhozzum Theme), a dual CC winner in England. Venture sired 20 Champions, including Robert's Aust. Ch. Craigend Cheviot Piper, a winner of BIS at NSW Border Club Shows on five occasions and himself sire of 18 Champions. Piper's dam was Aust. Ch. Brigit of Patterdale. Probably the best known of Piper's progeny is Aust. Ch. Craigend Cheviot Major, twice winner of BIS at BTC (NSW) Shows. The win of BIS there in 1995 by Craigend Chowchilla makes four generations in tail male winning that honour: Venture, Piper, Major, Chowchilla.

Carol Maciver and Robert formed a syndicate to import Aust. Ch. Akenside Domino, in whelp to Ch. Savinroyd President, from England. Six puppies were bred in quarantine, including Aust. Champions Craigend Fair Thyme, Sweet Sorrel and Marjoram. Margaret Burgoine, a well-known breeder of Bull Terriers and Miniature Bull Terriers, started with Aust. NZ Ch. Bracklyn Bijoux, bred out of Aust. Ch. Rhozzum Venture's first litter. Since then, Margaret has bred a continuous string of Champions including Aust. Champions Bodalla Fen Swallow and Fen Windmill. The latter spent some time in NZ with Julie Clarke, Lester Borders, and had considerable influence there.

Carol Maciver breeds both Borders and Irish Wolfhounds under the RAMAREGO affix. Out of

Judge Ian Southgate examining Robert Bartram's Aust. Ch. Craigend Cheviot Piper, the sire of eighteen Australian Champions, three New Zealand and one American Champion.

Julia Guilfoyle with Aust. Ch. Stormvale Kiwi Girl (Aust. NZ Ch. Brigand of Brockhole and Lynsett – Aust. Ch. Lester Border Gnome), co-owned by her breeder Dee Patterson and Pam Guilfoyle.

Aust. Ch. Craigend Fair Thyme, one of the successful litter imported in utero out of Akenside Domino and brought in through the efforts of Carol and others, sired by Aust. NZ Ch. Brigand of Brockhole and Lynsett, she bred Aust. Ch. Ramarego Hunter's Moon, CC winner from Peggy Grayson at the BTC (NSW) in 1993 and BIS there the following year. Carol imported Aust. Ch. Rhozzum Argos in 1994 from Marie Sharp. An import of note, NZ Aust. Ch. Brigand of Brockhole and Lynsett, bred by Ann Deighton, was purchased by Elaine Davies, a noted Boxer breeder, affix TONUP, from Lynn Briggs and David Shields in England. Litter brother to their Ch. Blue Dun of Brockhole and Lynsett, Brigand sired many Australian Champions including Stormvale Kiwi Girl, Melilot Hunter's Fell, Ramarego Hunter's Moon and Craigend Snapdragon. Brigand was used in New Zealand where he spent six months en route to Australia. Elaine bred Mike and Margaret Derbyshire's Aust. Ch. Tonup Mytristania.

Pamela Guilfoyle, GUILCROFT, made several Champions, including Aust. Ch. Guilcroft Bracken Lea, BOB at Sydney Royal, in 1994, and Aust. Ch. Stormvale Kiwi Girl. Delma Nelson, a well-known Boxer breeder, CHELVESTON, is a newer Border breeder. Her Aust. Ch. Chelveston Thistle Doo, BOB at Sydney Royal 1994, is by Aust. Ch. Craigend Cheviot Crofter out of Aust. Ch. Chelveston Solitaire, herself a BOB winner at Sydney Royal, 1993.

NEW ZEALAND

The first recorded import into New Zealand was in 1947. An early breeder was Pat Gilcrest, breeding from Tweedside stock for a few years from 1949. The first NZ Champion, Dee of Avalon, was bred from imports made by Mrs Graham and was owned by Mr and Mrs Cooke who bred a further Champion in the late 1950s by putting her back to her sire, who was a son of Ch. Rising Light. In 1968, Marion Forrester, a well-known Stafford breeder, imported NZ Ch. Hanleycastle Ruthless and NZ Ch. Tippy of Petrina and mated them together. Under her guidance, Terry Innes imported two bitches from Australia, one of whom, mated to a dog from Marion's litter, bred the first Border to gain the title CDX, Sandy of Awa E Toru. Despite the efforts of these pioneers, the breed was struggling. None of these early imports appear in the pedigrees of present-day Borders.

In 1965 George and Rosemary Williamson arrived from England with two Borders. From 1973 they imported a further ten from England. In 1974 Jim and Florrie Graham imported two, followed by another a few years later. The imports made by the Williamsons and Grahams gave the breed a fresh start. As so many of today's Borders, both in New Zealand and Australia, come from this background, details of the Patterdale and Otterhead kennels are included.

The breed seems to have a firm footing in New Zealand now, with more breeders and a steady increase in litters born. At Hamilton Show, 1995, the first meeting was held to discuss the formation of a breed club. There are no foxes in New Zealand but Borders kill opossums, animals weighing about twice as much as a Border and armed with long sharp claws. Others go deer, goat and wild pig hunting and there are rabbits for going to ground after. The NZ Kennel Club is affiliated to the UK Kennel Club and associated with the FCI. To become a Champion, eight CCs under five different judges must be won, one of which must be gained over the age of twelve months.

LEADING KENNELS

BOHUNT: GAELA TOLLEY (SOUTH ISLAND)
Quite a migration arrived from England in 1994 with the Tolley Family, twelve Jack Russells and four Borders, one dog and three bitches: the dog, NZ Ch. Brindleoak Hooligan at Plushcourt (by Ch. Plushcourt Blue Hero), two Plushcourt bitches and a Tutmur bitch. Early in 1995, the CC winner NZ Ch. Baywillow Sun An' Air, by Ch. Baywillow Sundazzler, arrived from England. He won his title in seven weeks, with Group placings. The Tolleys introduced terrier racing to South Island, which proved very popular.

HOLLYSTONE: DIANE SIMISTER-BROWN (SOUTH ISLAND)
This kennel started in 1987 with Bordersweet Legacy (NZ Ch. Rushby of Patterdale – Otterhead of Sweethope) and has been very successful, making eight Champions. In 1993 Diane imported a male, NZ Ch. Plushcourt Distinction.

LADEBRAES: MARY WHITTINGTON (NORTH ISLAND)
Mary was converted to Borders from Westies. Her first Border was an important sire, NZ Ch. Otterhead of Catcleugh. He was bred by the Grahams out of NZ Ch. Chevinor Raransay and sired by NZ Ch. Calypso of Patterdale, who was a son of NZ Ch. Red William and NZ Ch. Foxhill Fenomenal. His daughter, NZ Ch. Ladebraes Laverock, a consistent Group winner as well as a good brood, was out of Otterhead of Ancroft, who was by NZ Ch. Wilderscot Bandsman out of

NZ Ch. Ladebraes Larkspur (Aust. NZ Ch. Brigand of Brockhole and Lynsett – NZ Ch. Ladebraes Laverock), bred by Mary Whittington, owned by Bev Rodgers and Julie Clark.

NZ Ch. Chevinor Raransay. To Aust. NZ Ch. Brigand of Brockhole and Lynsett, Laverock bred three puppies, all of which became NZ Champions. To Lester Border Kactus Jak she produced Aust. Ch. Ladebraes Lucci Locket and NZ Ch. Ladebraes Lace N Lavender, the dam of NZ Ch. Ladebraes Lace N Frills.

LESTER: JULIE CLARKE AND SUE SMITH (NORTH ISLAND)

Julie, a well-known breeder of Bull, Mini Bull and Australian Terriers, and her sister Sue, were won over to the breed by an Australian Border, Aust. NZ Ch. Bracklyn Bijoux (Aust. Ch. Rhozzum Venture – Aust. Ch. Craigend Keilder Kate) which Julie showed for Margaret Burgoine of New South Wales. Before returning to Australia, Bijoux was mated to NZ Ch. Otterhead of Catcleugh. A bitch puppy from that mating, NZ Ch. Bodall Fen Windmill, was the foundation of the Lester Borders. To NZ Ch. Wilderscot Bandsman she produced NZ Ch. Lester Border Gnome. To NZ Ch. Tennille Our Sylvester (son of NZ Ch. Headwaiter at Dormic) she gave NZ Ch. Lester Border Sandman, a Group winner, and Lester Border Kactus Jak who sired NZ Ch. Lester Border Tazzy, also a Group winner.

Border Gnome went to Dee Patterson, South Australia, in whelp to Aust. NZ Ch. Brigand of Brockhole and Lynsett. Some years later, a bitch from that mating, Aust. Ch. Stormvale Koala Blue, came back to Lester kennels in whelp to Aust. Ch. Stormvale Red Raven, a Brigand grandson who was also a son of NZ Aust. Ch. Patterdale Minimax, a Group winner in both countries. A dog from this litter won the Terrier Group at ten months of age.

OTTERHEAD: JIM GRAHAM (NORTH ISLAND)

Jim and Florrie Graham imported their foundation stock from England in 1974, NZ Ch. Wilderscot Bandsman (Ch. Int. Nord. Ch. Clipstone Guardsman – Farmway Blue Dove) and Farmway Swansdown (Deerstone Despot Duty – Farmway Red Puffin) followed by Chevinor Raransay (Ch. Ribbleside Ridgeman – Chevinor Rosa) three years later. Raransay to NZ Ch. Calypso of Patterdale produced Mary Whittington's NZ Ch. Otterhead of Catcleugh. Raransay to Bandsman gave three notable brood bitches – Ethelfrith, NZ Ch. Blink Bonny and Ancroft. Catcleugh to Ancroft produced NZ Ch. Ladebraes Laverock and Aust. Ch. Otterhead of Dukesfield, a most successful show dog and sire for the Caldwells in Australia. A bitch, Ch. Otterhead of Liburn was another successful export there. Apart from the good strain of Borders which he established, the breed in New Zealand owes much to the PR work done on its behalf by Jim through talks and articles, as well as keeping it to the fore in the show ring.

PATTERDALE: ROSEMARY AND GEORGE WILLIAMSON (NORTH ISLAND)

It is through the efforts of Rosemary and George, untiring workers for the breed who campaigned their dogs hard so that people would know the breed, that the Border became established as a serious show dog. NZ Ch. Red William, by Ch. Leatty Plough Boy out of a daughter of Plough Boy, accompanied them to New Zealand. It was in 1973 that the Williamsons started showing and breeding. Red William started his show career at the age of ten and quickly became a Champion.

In 1973 the Williamsons imported from England NZ Ch. Farmway Swinging Chick (Farmway Black Hawk – Hobbykirk Barsac) who had a litter to Red William, as did NZ Ch. Foxhill Fenomenal (Ch. Foxhill Fusilier – Ch. Foxhill Foenix) who was imported the following year, as was NZ Ch. Ribbleside Rigger (Ch. Ribbleside Ridgeman – Ribbleside Brockanburr Mandy). Rigger did a great deal of winning, including Reserve BIS at an all breeds Championship Show. The following year, Ribbleside Lady Love arrived and then, in 1977, NZ Ch. Chevinor Ronoch, a male (Ch. Ribbleside Ridgeman – Chevinor Rosa).

NZ Ch. Farmway Red Raven (Ch. Farmway Fine Feathers – Hanleycastle Sally) arrived in 1980. His great win for the breed was at Kumea All Breeds Championship Show where he won BIS. The last imports were made in 1983: NZ Ch. Head Waiter at Dormic (Dormic MacAndrew – Bush Bracken) and Dormic Mood Indigo (Mr Chips of Thoraldby – Ch. Grenze Galanthus at Dormic). Together they produced NZ Ch. Rushby of Patterdale. Head Waiter was a consistent Group winner and also won Reserve BIS All Breeds.

TENNILLE: GAIL O'KEEFE (SOUTH ISLAND)

NZ Ch. Teca of Patterdale was Gail's foundation, purchased in 1985. Teca produced NZ Ch. Howzatt Hadlee and, sired by Aust. NZ Ch. Brigand of Brockhole and Lynsett, NZ Ch. Tennille My Sweet Dove who went to Australia to be mated to Robert Bartram's Aust. Ch. Craigend Cheviot Piper. Three of the resultant litter are NZ Champions. From Australia, NZ Ch. Tonup Shadow Gum was imported.

TAMALEIGH: PAT AND DAVID HERD (NORTH ISLAND)

Pat and David's interest in Borders started in 1990, when their daughter, Andrea, got NZ Ch. Lester Border Return which she showed in partnership with Julie Clarke. At Crufts 1991, they bought NZ Ch. Firgate Robert at Tamaleigh (by Plushcourt Run The Gauntlet). NZ Ch. Plushcourt Dewdrop, a later import owned by Pat and David, was mated to him, a puppy from which litter was sent to Canada.

Other enthusiasts include: Cheryl Smith, North Island, with NZ Ch. Patterdale Danby and Ladebraes Lazy Dazy; Pamela Hall-Jones, BEN BHRAGGIE, South Island, breeder and owner of NZ Ch. Ben Bhraggie Torrdarroch and owner of the import NZ Ch. Plushcourt Scarlet Ribbons, by Ch. Mansergh Doublet at Plushcourt; Murray MacKenzie, BALLACH Kennels, who started with a Brigand pup, NZ Ch. Patterdale Harelyn, and then added NZ Ch. Patterdale Kettlesing to his kennel; Bruce and Wendy Johnstone, TREGONEY kennel, North Island, with NZ Ch. Ladebraes Lace N Frills, winner of BOB in the largest entry to date; Bev Rodgers, KIRKCALDY Borders, North Island, who started in 1989 with Lester Border Kactus Jak and then in partnership with Julie Clarke owned NZ Ch. Ladebraes Larkspur, winner of BIS at Canterbury Combined Terrier Club Championship Show.

En route to Australia from England in 1990, Aust. NZ Ch. Brigand of Brockhole and Lynsett (Ch. Lynsett Trouble Shooter – Careless Wispa of Brumberhill) spent six months with Jan Mace, South Island. Seven bitches were mated to him during this time. 25 puppies were registered by him, of which ten have become NZ Champions.